PRIMATE FIELD STUDIES

PRIMATE FIELD STUDIES

Many of us who conduct field studies on wild primates have witnessed a decline in the venues available to publish monographic treatments of our work. As researchers, we have few choices other than to publish short technical articles on discrete aspects of our work in professional journals. Also in vogue are popular expositions, often written by nonscientists. To counter this trend, we have begun this series. **Primate Field Studies** is a venue both for publishing the full complement of findings of long-term studies and for making our work accessible to a wider readership. Interested readers need not wait for atomized parts of long-term studies to be published in widely scattered journals; students need not navigate the technical literature to bring together a body of scholarship better served by being offered as a cohesive whole. We are interested in developing monographs based on single- or multi-species studies. If you wish to develop a monograph, we encourage you to contact one of the series editors.

About the Editors:

Robert W. Sussman (Ph.D. Duke University) is currently Professor of Anthropology and Environmental Science at Washington University, St. Louis, Missouri, and past Editor-in-Chief of *American Anthropologist*, the flagship journal of the American Anthropological Association. His research focuses on the ecology, behavior, evolution, and conservation of nonhuman and human primates, and he has worked in Costa Rica, Guyana, Panama, Madagascar, and Mauritius. He is the author of numerous scientific publications, including *Biological Basis of Human Behavior*, Prentice Hall (1999), *Primate Ecology and Social Structure* (two volumes), Pearson Custom Publishing (2003), and *The Origin and Nature of Sociality*, Aldine de Gruyter (2004).

Natalie Vasey (Ph.D. Washington University) is currently Assistant Professor of Anthropology at Portland State University in Portland, Oregon. Her work explores the behavioral ecology, life history adaptations, and evolution of primates, with a focus on the endangered and recently extinct primates of Madagascar. She has presented her research at international venues and published in leading scientific journals. She is dedicated to educating students and the public-at-large about the lifestyles and conservation status of our closest relatives in the Animal Kingdom.

The Gibbons
of Khao Yai

The Gibbons of Khao Yai

Seasonal Variation in Behavior and Ecology

Thad Q. Bartlett
The University of Texas at San Antonio

PEARSON
Prentice
Hall

Upper Saddle River, New Jersey 07458

Library of Congress Cataloging-in-Publication Data
Bartlett, Thad Q.
   The gibbons of Khao Yai : seasonal variation in behavior and
ecology / Thad Q. Bartlett.
         p. cm. — (Primate field studies)
   Includes bibliographical references and index.
   ISBN 0-13-191504-5
   1. Gibbons—Behavior—Thailand—'Utthayan hfng Chat Khao Yai.   2. Gibbons—
Ecology—Thailand—'Utthayan hfng Chat Khao Yai.   I. Title.
QL737.P96B355   2009
599.88'209593—dc22   2008025788

Publisher: Nancy Roberts
Editorial Assistant: Nart Varoqua
Marketing Manager: Lindsey Prudhomme
Operations Specialist: Benjamin Smith
Cover Art Director: Jayne Conte
Cover Design: Margaret Kenselaar
Cover Photo: G.A. Bartlett
Manager, Rights and Permissions: Zina Arabia
Manager, Visual Research: Beth Brenzel
Image Permission Coordinator: Frances Toepfer
Full-Service Project Management: Bharath Parthasarathy
Composition: TexTech International
Printer/Binder: RR Donnelley & Sons Company

This book was set in 10/12 Palatino.

Pearson Education Ltd., London
Pearson Education Singapore, Pte. Ltd
Pearson Education, Canada, Inc.
Pearson Education–Japan
Pearson Education Australia PTY,
   Limited

Pearson Education North Asia, Ltd.,
   Hong Kong
Pearson Educación de Mexico, S.A. de C.V.
Pearson Education Malaysia, Pte. Ltd.
Pearson Education Upper Saddle River,
   New Jersey

                                        10 9 8 7 6 5 4 3 2 1
                              ISBN 13: 978-0-13-191504-6
                              ISBN 10:   0-13-191504-5

Dedicated to my mother, Bertrice Bartlett

Contents

List of Figures

List of Tables

Preface

It has now been many years since I first visited Khao Yai National Park to begin my dissertation research, nevertheless, I can still remember the moment when I saw wild gibbons in person for the first time. I had come to the park with Warren Brockelman, who by that time had been working in Khao Yai, off and on, for well over a decade. I was following Warren through the forest as he oriented me to the trail system and topography of the study area. We had been walking for a few hours without a glimpse of gibbons, long enough that I had already started to wonder if I would have to wait another day, or longer, to finally see the animals I proposed to study for the coming year. My anxiety was temporarily eased as we crossed over a small ravine, and Warren pointed up into the crown of an unimaginably large tree. It was a sprawling *Ficus* that soared over a hundred feet in the air, and high overhead was a family of gibbons moving through the distant branches. Certainly it was a climactic moment, but even though I felt a burst of exhilaration, it was quickly followed by a sense of alarm. I was shocked by how hard it was to see the animals, which compared to their surroundings looked more like squirrels than apes, and I began to wonder how I was ever going to follow them for a full day, let alone simultaneously collect behavioral data. An even bigger surprise, as I later wrote in my diary, was how difficult it was to see the fruit the gibbons had apparently come to the tree to eat. I suppose I had expected fruit the size of supermarket produce dangling from every branch. Instead I could barely distinguish the nickel and dime-sized fruit from the branches themselves. This predicament was no small matter because the topic I had come to Khao Yai to study was the feeding behavior of these highly frugivorous primates.

A long-held hypothesis in primatology ties territoriality and monogamy in gibbons to their use of small fruiting trees. But in reviewing the gibbon literature I had noticed that in addition to their reported preference for small feeding patches, gibbons were also described as fig specialists, even though fig trees (like the large specimen described earlier) are often among the largest trees in the forest. One of the goals of my project was to investigate this apparent contradiction, with the hope that the gibbon's true dietary niche would reveal itself during periods of fruit scarcity. Fortunately, in time I grew accustomed both to tracking the gibbons as they foraged and to the cyclical changes in the availability of their foods. This volume examines the relationship between these two phenomena and explores how an understanding of the impact of seasonal scarcity on gibbon foraging behavior may help us to better understand the evolution of gibbon social structure.

Questions about the evolution of gibbon social systems have a long history in primatology, so to place contemporary debates in appropriate context, I begin, in Chapter 1, with a brief overview of the history of gibbon field research. I pay particular attention to the groundbreaking work of Clarence Ray Carpenter, whose brief, but intensive, study of white-handed gibbons in Northern Thailand led to many lasting insights into the behavior and ecology of this primate family. In addition to the description of Carpenter's work in Chapter 1, each of the remaining chapters begins with an epigraph drawn from Carpenter's 1940 monograph, *A Field Study in Siam of the Behavior and Social Relations of the Gibbon (Hylobates lar)*, which I hope will serve as testament to his keen powers of observations.

The physical setting of my research is the focus of Chapter 2, including a description of the flora and fauna of Khao Yai National Park and specifically the Mo Singto study area. Because so much of gibbon behavior depends on the availability of high-quality foods, I also fully describe the phenology (cyclical changes in resource availability) of the site, which shows peak fruit abundance in the hot season, March to May, and greatest scarcity in the dry season, November to February.

In Chapter 3, I describe the impact of resource fluctuations on gibbon activity budgets. On the whole, gibbons show a pattern of energy economy, limiting activity rates (e.g., activity time, travel time, and time spent in encounters) when ripe fruit is scarce. One finding that I did not expect was how sociable gibbons can be, especially during the hot season when fruit is plentiful. Consequently I devote extra attention in this chapter to a discussion of grooming and play.

In Chapters 4 through 6, I take a closer look at the relationship between fruit abundance and diet, range use, and intergroup interactions. As described in Chapter 4, the idea that gibbons select small feeding trees is not supported by my research. On the contrary, Khao Yai gibbons appear to prefer large feeding trees throughout the year. Another key finding is that fig feeding is mostly confined to the cool season, and, thus, figs are best viewed as fallback foods rather than as preferred foods, as other investigators have suggested. In general, figs are thought to be lower-quality food items compared with other fruits. Consequently, as I document in Chapter 5, their shift to a lower-quality resource coincides with a reduction in the distance groups traveled each day. Furthermore, as illustrated in Chapter 6, the cool season is also marked by reduced rates of singing and intergroup encounters. The exception to this pattern concerns conflicts over specific fruit trees (especially figs), which are prevalent during both fruit-rich and fruit-poor periods. I interpret this finding as evidence in support of the view that territoriality in gibbons evolved as a means of defending feeding resources.

In Chapter 7, I take up the issue of primate socioecology. In the period since the inception of this project, it has become fashionable to question some of the core tenets of gibbon socioecology by suggesting, for example, that the appearance of territoriality in gibbons is largely an artifact of intrasexual competition (e.g., mate guarding or infanticide defense). In marked contrast to this approach, I refocus attention on the adaptive significance of reliable resource access to committed frugivores. I argue that social monogamy in gibbons is the outcome of male resource defense territoriality, which improves foraging efficiency by guaranteeing the availability of known feeding patches. Unlike models based on sexual selection, the male resource defense model is consistent with the fact that gibbons defend stable territories. Furthermore, I argue that the marked changes in gibbon foraging that occur during fruit-poor months, as documented in the previous chapters, testify to the importance of resource availability to fitness in gibbons.

Finally, in Chapter 8 I suggest potential areas for future research, such as more-focused analyses on nutritional ecology, which would allow more fine-grained studies of gibbon foraging decisions. I also briefly consider the threats to gibbons in Thailand. I was lucky to work in an area where direct human impact was limited; nevertheless, we must acknowledge the enduring conflict between conservation and economic development if we hope to establish sustainable strategies to protect these amazing primates. If this volume encourages, in some small way, the protection of gibbons and their habitat, then it will have been a success.

ACKNOWLEDGMENTS

It is fair to say that the research that led to this book would never have happened without the assistance of three people: Bob Sussman, Duane Quiatt, and Warren Brockelman. Throughout my graduate career Bob gave me the latitude to work at my own pace and direction. He has shown similar patience as an editor, and I am grateful.

As an undergraduate studying anthropology at Grinnell College I had already settled on gibbons as the animals I hoped to work with for my dissertation research. The semester before I entered graduate school, I went to the physical anthropology meetings in Kansas City, where I became reacquainted with Duane Quiatt. Duane had lived in my neighborhood when I was growing up, and I had gone to the meetings to drive him back to our home in Columbia for a visit. As we talked during that drive, Duane told me about the work he had done in Thailand conducting observations on the social behavior of a single gibbon family group in Khao Yai National Park. During this conversation Duane told me "If after you've been in graduate school a few years you are still interested in studying gibbons, contact me and I'll put you in touch with someone in Thailand."

As it happens, a few years later I was still interested and I reminded Duane of our conversation. He then put me in touch with Warren Brockelman of Mahidol University, Bangkok. Identifying an appropriate research site can be a daunting task. I was fortunate to have had Duane's guidance. From the date of my first contact with Warren he has always been helpful and encouraging. He facilitated every aspect of my dissertation field research and was a welcoming host during my subsequent visits to Khao Yai; I cannot overstate how much he has meant to the success of this project.

I enjoyed the friendship and support of many people in Thailand. In Bangkok the officers and staff at the Thailand–United States Educational Foundation (TUSEF) provided extensive logistical support throughout my stay. Foundation activities eased my transition into Thai society and helped me stay connected to home. I am also fortunate to know and to have worked with Gonthong Lourdesamy. Gonthong taught me much about Bangkok and about Khao Yai and frequently shuttled me between the two. She and Sompong Yousuk, Khao Yai's unofficial goodwill ambassador, helped make the cultural (and gastronomic) experiences I had in Thailand as valuable as the academic ones. Over the years many students and researchers shared their knowledge of both the gibbons and the forest. I am particularly indebted to Saiwaroon Chongko (Awn), Amnart Boonkongchart (Nart), and Chanpen Wongsriphuek (Uey), who to my good fortune were as skilled in the kitchen as they were in the forest. J. F. Maxwell helped identify plant species and helped me see the forest in a different way. Back home in St. Louis I was especially lucky to have enjoyed the hospitality and friendship of Tom and Bettye Dew, who made my periodic returns to campus effortless.

My ideas about the behavior and ecology of gibbons have been shaped by conversations with many people over the years, including Samantha Bricknell, Karen Chambers, Fan Pengfei, Agustin Fuentes, Susan Lappan, Kim McConkey, Tommaso Savini, and Volker Sommer. I would also like to thank the many people who commented on various drafts of this volume, including Claud Bramblett, James M. Cheverud, David Chivers, Charles F. Hildebolt, Jane E. Phillips-Conroy, D. Tab Rasmussen, and Owen J. Sexton. I thank Nancy Roberts for the opportunity to contribute to the Primate Field Studies series, and series editors Bob Sussman and Natalie Vasey whose thoughtful criticisms greatly improved the final product.

My greatest debt of gratitude is owed to my wife Jennifer, who contributed to every phase of this project, from mapping trails to copyediting. I could not have completed this project without her support. In the time between the proposal and final draft of this volume, Jennifer and I have had two children, Quincy and Silas. I ask their forgiveness for the many nights and weekends I had to go back to the office. Finally I would like to thank all of my family members, including my extended family from Wilson Avenue. Each of them has helped to shape me as a scholar, an anthropologist, and a person, no one of them more than my mother, Bertrice Bartlett.

This work was supported with funding from Fulbright, The National Science Foundation, Boise Fund, Sigma Xi, The American Society of Primatologists, Washington University, Dickinson College, and The University of Texas at San Antonio. I am grateful to the Royal Thai Forest Department, National Park Division, and the National Research Council of Thailand for permitting me to work in Khao Yai National Park.

1

History of Gibbon Field Studies

Monogamy, Frugivory, and Territoriality

According to most authorities the gibbon can properly be regarded as one of the anthropoid apes, though in many respects the least advanced one, and is thus included in that small and select group, the so-called higher primates, consisting of man, the great apes and the gibbons.

—*Carpenter (1940:146)*

I first developed an interest in gibbons during childhood visits to the St. Louis Zoo. At the time a pair of siamangs (*Symphalangus syndactylus*) occupied the central display in the zoo's primate house. The cage was a stark enclosure, but a series of bars, shelves, and ropes allowed the occupants to showcase their speed and gymnastic abilities. When they were swinging around the cage, the siamangs captured the attention of almost all the visitors in the building, but during the remainder of the time, they were passed over for more visually conspicuous species such as prehensile-tailed spider monkeys, mohawked tamarins, or estrous baboons. But I was drawn to the siamangs over even the great apes, which were housed in a separate building. In the siamang's upright posture, round face, and pensive expression, I saw clear evidence of evolutionary continuity. It was then that I first began to dream of studying gibbons in the wild. But beyond the information printed on the zoo's plaque, I knew nothing of gibbon behavior or ecology or even to what extent they had been studied in their natural habitat.

In time, after I had returned to St. Louis to attend graduate school at Washington University, I came to appreciate the wealth of data that has been collected on this group of primates. Clarence Ray Carpenter's study of the siamang's smaller cousin, the white-handed gibbon (*Hylobates lar*), in Thailand was one of the first scientific field studies ever conducted on primates. In the intervening years gibbons have been studied in every country in which they are found (Chivers 2001; Bartlett 2007a). As a result the basic behavioral ecology of this primate family, and white-handed gibbons in particular, is well established. But it is the nature of scientific inquiry that each study raises many more questions than it answers. One question that has emerged from the rich history of gibbon research is how gibbons, which are highly dependent on ripe fruit, cope with seasonal shortages of preferred foods (Chivers 1984). To date, the majority of gibbon field studies have been conducted in environments characterized by wet forest with considerable floristic diversity. I set out to study gibbons in a more distinctly seasonal environment to document the impact of seasonality on the lives of these small apes. The data presented in the following chapters represent the results of a yearlong field study of the feeding and ranging behavior of the white-handed gibbon in Khao Yai National Park, Thailand. The forest of Khao Yai offers two specific advantages over sites where gibbons have been studied in the past. First, Khao Yai experiences a marked dry season, with a concomitant drop in the availability of ripe fruit. Second, before my research, the gibbon population in the park had been studied for over two decades (for details, see Brockelman et al. 1998, 2001). These qualities not only made Khao Yai an ideal site for my research, but also mean that Khao Yai will be an important source of information on the behavioral ecology of gibbons for decades to come.

THE GIBBON PATTERN

The 12 species of gibbon—family Hylobatidae—are often referred to collectively as the *lesser* apes. But as those of us who study these acrobatic primates are quick to point out, this label best describes their body size and not their importance in understanding the diversity of nonhuman primates. In fact gibbons differ from great apes (i.e., orangutans, gorillas, and chimpanzees) in many ways other than body size. Unlike their larger relatives, for example, gibbons are strictly arboreal. Accordingly they have traits specifically adapted to life in the trees, including extremely long upper arms with flexible wrist and shoulder joints and long hook-like hands (Groves 1984). When traveling from branch to branch, they exhibit a form of locomotion known as *brachiation,* which involves a rapid hand-over-hand motion that is akin to a child swinging on the monkey bars. Strictly speaking, all apes can brachiate, but unlike human children or any of the great apes, gibbons seamlessly cover long gaps between handholds. Ironically brachiation in gibbons also differs from most species of monkey, which typically travel above branches rather than below. ("Monkey bars," in other words, is a misnomer). Similar to monkeys, on the other hand, gibbons retain *ischial callosities*, or sitting pads, which the great apes typically lack.

Gibbons are behaviorally distinct as well. In most species, both males and females make structurally complex vocalizations, which primatologists call "songs." These vocalizations are often synchronized and take the form of harmonious duets sung by males and females and can be heard from hundreds of meters away or more (Marshall and Marshall 1976). But even more than these songs, the characteristic of gibbons that generates the most interest is their social system. From an evolutionary standpoint

Gibbons travel primarily through brachiation, a mode of locomotion where animals swing below branches, often covering long gaps between handholds.

Gibbons typically live in pair-bonded social groups, including a single adult male, a single adult female, and the dependent offspring of one or both of the partners.

one of the most fundamental questions you can ask about primates as a mammalian order is why they live in social groups at all. For example in most species of mammals, such as bears or deer, males and females come together during certain times of the year to mate but at most other times either are solitary or maintain single-sex groups. Most primates, on the other hand, live in stable heterosexual groups year-round. There is also an amazing variety in the structure of the groups primates live in. For their part gibbons typically live in groups comprised of a mated adult pair and up to four offspring. This form of social structure—generally referred to as *monogamy*—is rare among primates and unique among apes. In contrast terrestrial primates, such as macaques, may live in groups of over 100 animals. In other words gibbons occupy one end of a continuum of group size in the order Primates. Historically evolutionary explanations for small group size in gibbons have invoked specific features of their ecology such as diet and range use. Gibbons as a rule are *frugivorous,* that is, they spend most of their feeding time consuming ripe fruit. Whereas this fact alone does not make gibbons particularly unusual among primates, they are also more *territorial* than most other primate species. This combination of traits—monogamy, frugivory, and territoriality—describes few other primates.

HISTORICAL BACKGROUND

A Study of Anthropoid Life

Today the characterization of gibbons as monogamous, frugivorous, and territorial is taken for granted (Leighton 1987; Bartlett 2007a). But long after these primates were first described by science, details of the daily lives of wild gibbons remained a mystery. Interest in studying primates in their natural habitats did not develop until the mid-1900s; so, early accounts of gibbon behavior were based on brief contact in the wild or, more often, anecdotal observations of captive animals or pets. One of the earliest investigators to recognize the need for detailed studies of wild primates was Robert Yerkes (1876–1956). Yerkes was a psychologist who was interested in using primates, especially great apes, as models of human behavior (Haraway 1989; Strum and Fedigan 2000). His work with captive chimpanzees at the Yale University Primate Laboratory made him acutely aware of the paucity of reliable data on the social lives of the apes in the wild. Moreover he was convinced that observations of naturalistic behavior were essential to interpreting captive data. So along with his wife Ada, he comprehensively cataloged then current knowledge on the morphology and behavior of the anthropoid apes. The result, *The Great Apes: A Study of Anthropoid Life,* was published in 1929. Despite what its title suggests, the volume also included extensive coverage of the Hylobatidae, a decision the authors would later question.

Based on their research, the Yerkes date the earliest scientific account of the gibbons to 1766 with the publication of the 14th edition of the Comte de Buffon's *Natural History.* But over 150 years later detailed knowledge of the behavior and ecology of hylobatids was almost wholly lacking. Particulars as fundamental as the social structure of gibbon groups were the subject of inconsistent reports, and there were believed to be considerable differences between the various species of gibbon. Although some accounts suggested that gibbons lived in couples or small family groups, others reported much larger aggregations. The following passage from *The Great Apes* (Yerkes and Yerkes 1929) demonstrates the perceived variability:

> *The Ungkaputi (agile gibbon) is said to live in isolated couples. This is confirmed by Forbes who says it is found generally in small troops or in pairs. According to Tickell, the white-handed gibbon lives in bands of eight to twenty individuals, although occasionally a solitary male is met with. The largest assemblages are those of the hoolock, which are described by Blanford as found associating in flocks of fifty to one hundred individuals, or even more (p. 70–71).*

This inconsistency was troublesome to the Yerkes, and they were adamant about the need for additional data on all the apes. As I have said, gibbons were not their highest priority. In fact the authors had reservations about their decision to include the gibbons in *The Great Apes*:

> *Included among anthropoid apes in this volume are the Hylobatidae (gibbons and siamang). If we were beginning anew, we should consider only the three types of great apes: orang-outan, chimpanzee, and gorilla, for whereas they are strikingly alike structurally and psychobiologically, the Hylobatidae differ conspicuously from them. Moreover, all things considered, the great apes stand nearer to man, and the gibbons and siamangs nearer to monkey (p. ix).*

Consequently the Yerkes felt the gibbons had less to offer in terms of comparative value. One wonders if they would have held this opinion had their knowledge of hominoid social lives been more complete. For example the Yerkes' particular interest in chimpanzees stemmed in part from their belief that chimpanzees, rather than gibbons, were the most monogamous of the apes (Haraway 1989). Based on their review of the existing literature, they determined that across species, primates exhibit a phylogenetic trend toward family life. Whereas each species might exhibit monogamous and polygamous tendencies to a greater or lesser extent, they conclude, "in any event the family as a social unit seems to become more prevalent and also more stable as we progress from lemur to man" (Yerkes and Yerkes 1929:567).

The Yerkes' ambivalence toward the gibbon notwithstanding, their review of the literature convinced them that field observations of all the apes were necessary to supplement what was known from captive animals, and to this end Robert Yerkes recruited a series of students to go into the field to conduct what he characterized as "naturalistic" observations. The first two students, H. C. Bingham and N. W. Nissen, went to study gorillas and chimpanzees in central and western Africa. For his part Nissen (1931) had a measure of success, encountering chimpanzee on 49 of 64 days in the field and publishing a monograph based on his observations that remained a core reference for decades. In comparison Bingham's expedition was a disaster. Fearing the reported ferocity of gorillas (and other wildlife), he traveled with a large party of porters, guides, and armed guards. During a surprise encounter with a gorilla group, Bingham's party was charged by a large male, which Bingham reportedly shot. Consequently Bingham's (1932) published report contributed little to the understanding of the behavior of gorillas in their natural environment (Montgomery 2005; Sussman 2007). The same could never be said of Clarence Ray Carpenter, who Yerkes recruited to study the Asian apes.

The Asiatic Primate Expedition

Even today much of what we know of gibbon behavior and ecology was first described by Carpenter (1905–1975), who was among the pioneers of field primatology. Carpenter, who like Yerkes was trained as a psychologist, had earned his Ph.D. from Stanford University for his research on the sexual behavior of pigeons. He shifted his focus to primate research when he went to work with Robert Yerkes at the Yale Laboratories of Comparative Psychobiology. Mindful of the mixed success of Yerkes' other students, Carpenter was committed to establishing reliable methods for studying the behavioral characteristics of wild primates (Montgomery 2005). Carpenter's first field study was not on apes, but on mantled

Clarence Ray Carpenter at Tikal, Guatemala, in 1973, which he visited with his wife to observe howler and spider monkeys. Left to right: C. R. Carpenter, Ruth Carpenter, Sr. Jose M. Marquez, an amateur botanist, and Charles Darby. Photo © Claud Bramblett.

howler monkeys (*Alouatta palliata*) on Barro Colorado, an island of tropical forest that was created because of the flooding of the Panama Canal Zone. Carpenter spent approximately eight months between 1931 and 1933 conducting detailed observations on howler monkey's ecology and social behavior. The methods and themes described in his 1934 monograph set the course for subsequent field studies (including his own work on gibbons) and continue to be recognized for bringing scientific legitimacy to primate field research (Montgomery 2005). Carpenter (1935) also published a report on the behavior of spider monkeys (*Ateles geoffroyi*) based on observations he made in western Panama.

In 1937 Carpenter turned his attention to the Asian apes, which until then were even less well known than their African cousins. Along with Harold J. Coolidge Jr. and Adolph H. Schultz, Carpenter became a charter member of what was known as the Asiatic Primate Expedition, or A.P.E. According to Schultz (1938) members of the expedition were quickly labeled the "ape men." The expedition had the dual mission of general zoological collecting and behavioral observation. Before the A.P.E., wildlife expeditions were devoted almost exclusively to collecting (Wallis 1997). During such expeditions animals were trapped live, or more commonly shot, skinned, and sent back to museums in the United States and Europe. In fact Schultz (1938) describes one of his team members as a "big game hunter." What was innovative about the A.P.E. was the inclusion of long-term observations of living primates in their natural habitat. The research team was divided into two units—a collecting unit and a behavioral observation unit. The latter was comprised of Carpenter alone. The focus of the expedition was to be gibbons and orangutans, but whereas Carpenter subsequently conducted a month-long survey of primates, including orangutans, on Sumatra (Carpenter 1938), detailed behavioral observations were achieved only with the white-handed gibbon in Northern Thailand. To this end, in March 1937 Carpenter established a base camp on the slope of Mt. Doi Dao in Northern Thailand, and from March 27 to June 18 he made "intensive daily and almost continuous" observations of 20 gibbon social groups (Carpenter 1940).

Carpenter's observations provided a framework for virtually all subsequent studies of small apes and established methods that still form the basis of primate observational techniques. Over a period of approximately 100 days Carpenter conducted population surveys, intensive observations of group behavior from behind a blind, and when possible, conducted full day follows of individual gibbon groups. He also pioneered the use of sound recordings of primate vocalizations. Carpenter presented his observations in *A Field Study in Siam of the Behavior and Social Relations of the Gibbon* (Hylobates lar), originally published in 1940. Topics covered in the now-classic monograph include, aggression, grooming, group formation, locomotion, vocalization, emotional gestures, predation, object manipulation, and dominance. These topics remain central to primatology today. Carpenter's main conclusions may be summarized as follows:

- Unlike the great apes, gibbons do not build nests. Instead they rotate between "lodge trees" distributed throughout the group's range.
- Gibbons live in monogamous family groups of two to six. Within the family, affiliative bonds are maintained through social grooming.
- The gibbon diet is composed predominantly of fruit and leaves along with limited amounts of insects and animal matter such as birds and bird eggs.
- Group movement is restricted to a confined area of the forest that is defended against encroachment by animals of other social groups both through actual fighting and through vocal displays.
- Among adult gibbons there is an "equivalence of dominance."

Over 60 years later Carpenter's conclusions remain, in large measure, unassailable. Where Carpenter's work diverges most obviously from contemporary primatology is in its theoretical approach, or perhaps, its lack of one. In his final report, he insisted on presenting his findings free of theoretical interpretation. Given the paucity of comparative data, Carpenter (1940) felt that theoretical conclusions would be premature.

> The results of field studies at present need not be heavily weighted with theoretical considerations. It is sufficient to assume that just as there are structural relationships which place man in the same categories with the more complexly developed primates, so there are basic human needs, drives and types of behavior which have elements in common with similar functions of the non-human primate level (p. 160).

Nevertheless his observations are clearly embedded in the theoretical climate of his time. Haraway (1989:90) observes, for example, that Carpenter was preoccupied from the beginning with "sexuality and its relation to group coordination." Furthermore his training in psychology meant he was interested in proximate mechanisms of territorial maintenance and the formation of new groups. He believed that gibbons became conditioned to the location of territorial boundaries (Carpenter 1940:239–240) and hypothesized that new groups might be formed through a process known as *apoblastosis* by which maturing subadults rupture their bond with their parents either through increasing agonism or through increased motivation to form bonds with other animals, such as a new mate. It is also clear that Carpenter's writing predates sociobiology's preoccupation with incest avoidance (Wilson 1975), and in many places he speculated that if openings arise, offspring might supplant their same-sex parents as mates.

Finally Carpenter's research was done in a time when concern for animal welfare and conservation was undeveloped. Thus some of the methods employed by his team—standard practice at the time—would be unthinkable today. The following investigation into the gibbon's swimming abilities is a case in point.

> Taking the ape by hand, I gently threw her about six feet from the bank into water several feet deep. The responses of the animal consisted of throwing back and raising its head, general struggling movements, threshing about and uncoordinated movements of legs and arms. The thick wool rapidly became water soaked and in less than a minute, on three successive trials, she began to sink (Carpenter 1940:188).

Even though the passage above is somewhat comical, the manner by which gibbons were "collected" can only be described as chilling. For example, to confirm field observations he made on group composition, many full groups, including some of those that were under study, were shot. Even in these instances Carpenter's penchant for careful observation is apparent:

> May 19, 1937, Group 19, Doi Dao: Today my hunters and I shot the remaining female and infant of Group 19. When they both had been wounded, the female forced the infant away from her and onto a limb in a dense tree top. She left it there and moved into another adjacent tree. This reaction of gibbon mothers has been observed a number of times during collection trips (Carpenter 1940:231).

In total the expeditioners collected 100 gibbons in Thailand alone. Yet despite their objectionable techniques, the collection of specimens offered many valuable insights into the behavior of gibbons that would not have been uncovered by observation alone. For example, on return to the United States, Schultz (1939) examined the skeletons of collected gibbon specimens for healed fractures, which he found to be astonishingly high. Of 118 wild adult gibbons, 36% had healed fractures and some 14% had multiple fractures. Fractures of the humerus and femur were most common (23 of 65 factures), suggesting the majority of breaks were because of falls. No matter how nimble gibbons may appear from the ground, Schultz's data are a reminder of the costs of life in the trees. Nevertheless the seemingly high survival rate in gibbons suggests that most individuals recover from their injuries.

Carpenter (1940) also found soft-tissue injuries, including split lips and torn ears, which he attributed to fighting. Torn ears were more common in males ($N = 7$) than in females ($N = 1$), leading Carpenter to conclude that males fight more often than females. But ultimately he rejected the conclusion that this was a reflection of male dominance or increased male aggressiveness. His own observations of gibbons in captivity convinced him that male and female gibbons were equally capable of aggressive conflict. Collected specimens also yielded data on gibbon diet. Examination of the stomach contents of one gibbon specimen revealed the crushed skull of a bird. Although Carpenter never witnessed meat eating, the analysis of stomach contents showed meat to be an occasional supplement to their diet.

It is a testament to Carpenter's thoroughness that his research has stood up over so many years. But whereas the amount of data he collected clearly demonstrated the value of long-term observations, subsequent field research on wild primates was slow to materialize. For his part Carpenter continued to publish on primate behavior, but implementation of further primate research on either wild or captive primates was impeded by the onset of World War II (Strum and Fedigan 2000).

The Postwar Period

During the postwar period many factors converged to set the stage for a resurgence of field primatology. Part of this impetus was the publication of an influential article entitled "The New Physical Anthropology" by Sherwood Washburn (1951). In addition to his other impressive credentials, for example a Ph.D. from Harvard University, Washburn had been an ape-man. He had joined the A.P.E. while still a graduate student and had worked alongside Carpenter and Schultz collecting specimens (Marks 2000). Washburn had subsequently traveled to South Africa and met with Raymond Dart and Robert Broom, who were responsible for some of the most remarkable fossil hominin discoveries of their day. Washburn envisioned a holistic study of human evolution that emphasized an adaptive approach that incorporated the study of primate behavior. Washburn himself initiated a study of baboons in 1955, and in 1962 he organized, along with David A. Hamburg, a primate conference at the Center for Advanced Study at Stanford University (DeVore 1965). Among the conference attendees were both Carpenter and J. O. Ellefson, a young graduate student of Washburn's. Two years later, Ellefson would initiate the second major study of gibbons in the wild. The objectives of Washburn's *New Physical Anthropology* were clearly evident in Ellefson's (1974) motivation:

> *Man will not understand himself until he gains a knowledge of his gradual emergence from a nonhuman primate stock because his basic traditions contain nonhuman primate roots. One task physical anthropology has set for itself is to uncover such origins through the comparative study of the behavior of nonhuman primates under natural conditions, i.e., conditions that approximate as nearly as possible those in which the organism presumably evolved its taxonomically diagnostic adaptations. That broad aim underlies the gibbon field study comprising this report (p. 2–3).*

From March 1964 to November 1965 Ellefson conducted over 2000 hours of direct observation on white-handed gibbons at the site of Tanjong Triang, Johore State, Peninsular Malaysia. The first five months were spent conducting surveys to find a suitable site for long-term observations. Ellefson wrote that the survey was not as rewarding as it might have been because of difficulty determining the makeup of the gibbon groups under study.

Although he heard gibbons singing, he was initially unable to identify the sex of the animals he was hearing or if he had located pairs or lone animals.

Given what is now known about gibbon calls, Ellefson's problems identifying coherent groups are somewhat amusing. Adult white-handed gibbons sing duets with sex-specific contributions that can be heard from hundreds of meters away. Therefore even in the absence of visual contact, minimum numbers of adults can be identified based on vocalizations alone (Brockelman and Srikosamatara 1993). But gibbon duets had yet to be described by science. In fact this was among the few fundamental aspects of gibbon behavior that Carpenter had failed to pin down during his groundbreaking research. Ellefson's frustration must have been intense: "Had I been sure of this single simple fact the five-month survey period would have been more rewarding, both from the point of view of obtaining more accurate data and from the personal sense that I was accomplishing something" (1974:4). Nevertheless Ellefson enjoyed considerable success watching gibbons and confirmed much of what Carpenter had described years earlier.

Two aspects of Ellefson's work distinguish it from that of Carpenter. The first relates to a major methodological advance. Whereas Carpenter's primary mode of reporting his data was through detailed behavioral descriptions, Ellefson sought to quantify the activity budget of gibbons through continuously timed records of activity. His methods predated the systematic sampling regimes routinely used today; nevertheless his quantitative approach set the stage for within- and between-species comparisons that have become the foundation of contemporary primatology.

The other major difference was Ellefson's attempt to reconstruct the evolution of gibbon social organization. It was clear to Ellefson that the pattern of monogamy and territoriality—as seen in gibbons—was intimately related to their feeding adaptation. He believed that the key to understanding gibbon social organization was male defense of resources. He reasoned that the small size of gibbon social groups was the product of the amount of territory (resources) a single male could defend. It, however, was apparent to Ellefson that many polygynous primates are also territorial; thus he concluded that small group size in gibbons was imposed by the constraints of a "radically new feeding niche," namely, "terminal branch feeding on many, irregularly dispersed plant species" (1974:122–123). Gibbons, he reasoned, are able to successfully harvest such resources because of anatomical specializations involving small body size and suspensory feeding and locomotion. Monogamous social organization, he concluded, is ultimately the product of (1) food supply, which limits the number of females a territory can support, and (2) same-sex intolerance, especially among males, which promotes "pair-mateship." The evolution of gibbon social systems would dominate gibbon research for the next 20 years (e.g., van Schaik and Dunbar 1990).

Small body size, long arms, and hooklike hands make gibbons well suited to feeding and traveling in small terminal branches.

The Siamang in Malaya

The first long-term field study of a gibbon species other than *H. lar* was that by David J. Chivers on the siamang, also in the Malayan peninsula (Chivers 1974). Chivers studied siamangs at two sites—Ulu Sempam and Kuala Lompat—from January 1969 to May 1970. The morphological differences between siamangs and the smaller gibbons were well established long before field studies on small apes were begun. Brief observations of siamangs both by Carpenter (1938, 1940) and by Ellefson (1974) had demonstrated that siamangs share many aspects of their behavior and ecology, including a monogamous social structure and territorial defense. Nevertheless as Chivers (1974) observed, before his own research "it was not known whether siamang and gibbons have a similar diet and social organization within the family group, or whether they use and maintain territories in the same way" (p. 3).

Like Carpenter and Ellefson, Chivers (1974) believed that behavioral similarities between humans and gibbons—"such as monogamy and habitual orthogradism"—warranted special attention. Yet Chivers was also specifically interested in cross-species comparisons and whether a generic-level distinction between siamangs (then, as now, included in a separate genus) and other gibbons was justifiable on behavioral as well as morphological grounds. As a result he emphasized quantitative descriptions of behavior. Chivers combined both focal-animal scans (more or less continuous observations on a single animal) and group scans: "As the study developed it became possible to sample the major activity and location of each member of the group at 10-min intervals" (p. 23).

Chivers' findings are far too numerous to summarize here, but his conclusions about the ecological differences between gibbons and siamangs warrant attention. While confirming the overall similarity of siamangs and white-handed gibbons in terms of monogamy and territoriality, he notes that siamangs "differ from gibbons in most other respects." First, siamangs have a less-specialized diet than gibbons. They are largely folivorous—young leaves accounted for 58% of feeding time—and when feeding on fruit, favor figs more than gibbons or any other sympatric primate species do. Second, siamang groups are more cohesive than gibbon groups, and their daily activity is more closely synchronized. All group members were engaged in the same activity 75% of the time and in the same tree 50% of the time. Finally, siamangs are less territorial than gibbons in that they occupied smaller territories, defended them less intensely, and sang less often for shorter durations.

Like his predecessors Chivers devoted much of his analysis to a description of siamang diet and activity pattern, but he was also concerned with the future prospect for gibbons and siamangs in the face of deforestation. He stressed that strictly arboreal species face different problems than terrestrial ones. His survey data suggested that siamangs responded well to selective logging, but clear cutting resulted in isolated arboreal islands with little opportunity for dispersal. Today Chivers (2001) continues to be a leader in the conservation of the small apes and of primates in general.

The Proliferation of Small Ape Research

The decade following Chivers' study was an active period for gibbon field research, including both surveys and long-term ecological studies of many of the remaining gibbon species. One source of inspiration was Harold J. Coolidge Jr., one of the original ape-men. With Coolidge's encouragement, W. J. Hamilton and Richard Tenaza, both of the University of California at Davis, initiated a preliminary study of Kloss's gibbon (*H. klossii*) on the Mentawai Islands off the southwest coast of Sumatra (Tenaza and Hamilton III 1971). Field primatology is a small world, and this was especially true in the early decades of the discipline. In that light it is interesting to note that Hamilton and Tenaza visited Chivers in the field before heading to the Mentawai Islands. Furthermore Hamilton and Tenaza subsequently inspired Ron Tilson's (1979) brief study of the hoolock gibbon (*Hoolock hoolock*) in Assam, India (July 1971 and February 1973). Tilson and Tenaza later collaborated on a study of Kloss's gibbons on the Mentawai Island of Siberut (Tilson and Tenaza 1982; Tenaza and

Tilson 1985). There they encountered obstacles absent at other sites because of the heavy hunting pressure on gibbons by local populations. It is, in part, through their efforts that the Teitei Batti Nature Reserve was established on the island (Whitten 1982b).

Chivers' work also inspired a generation of students—many of them his own—to further explore the diversity of the small apes. Many of these studies were modeled on Chivers' research on siamangs and similarly focused on aspects of diet and range use. Included among the studies that followed were those of Jeremy Raemaekers (1979), who continued research at Kuala Lompat focusing on the ecological differences between white-handed gibbons and siamangs; S. P. Gittins (1982), who completed the first study of agile gibbons (*Hylobates agilis*) at Sungai Dal, West Malaysia; A. J. Whitten (1982a), who completed a study of Kloss gibbons at Paitan, Siberut, Indonesia; D. R. Leighton (1987; Leighton and Leighton 1983), who conducted observations on Bornean Gibbons (*H. muelleri*) at Kutai, East Kalimantan, Indonesia; and S. Srikosamatara (1984), who completed a yearlong study of the pileated gibbon (*H. pileatus*) at Khao Soi Dao, Thailand. In addition M. Kappeler (1984) conducted an extensive survey of the wary and highly endangered silvery gibbon (*H. moloch*) at Ujong Kulan, Java, Indonesia. The results of much of this research were presented at a conference held in 1980 at Schloss Reisenbeurg near Ulm in southern Germany. The resulting volume, *The Lesser Apes* (Preuschoft et al. 1984), remains the single most important reference on the gibbon family.

A second research focus to emerge during this period was the relationship between vocal behavior and social organization in gibbons. Jeremy and Patricia Raemaekers (1985; Raemaekers et al. 1984) followed work on the ecology of white-handed gibbons and siamangs in Malaysia with a 20-month study of white-handed gibbon vocalizations in Khao Yai National Park, Thailand. Through the innovative use of field playbacks of gibbon calls, they documented the response of male–female pairs to simulated intrusions by strange gibbons. John Mitani (1984, 1985) employed similar methods with Bornean gibbons at the Kutai Game Reserve, Kalimantan, Indonesia. Such playback experiments confirmed Ellefson's supposition that same-sex intolerance is instrumental in maintaining monogamy among gibbons.

Sexual Behavior and Social Bonds

During the 1970s and 1980s field research on gibbons was very much concerned with documenting the ecological diversity within the family Hylobatidae and with building models of gibbon monogamy. But other than limited reports of emigrating subadults (Aldrich-Blake and Chivers 1973; Tilson 1981), few studies had focused on social dynamics within and between social groups. Those that did largely considered the significance of intrasexual aggression to group formation and territoriality. Considerations of affiliative social behavior were largely lacking. The 1990s witnessed a change in focus that brought the social lives of gibbons into sharper focus. In particular, two studies initiated during this period would radically alter the common perception of gibbon social organization.

The first of these was that of Ryne Palombit, who spent six years studying the social behavior of white-handed gibbons and siamangs at Ketambe, Sumatra. Among the findings of his important study were a documented case of lethal territorial aggression between two neighboring white-handed gibbon males (Palombit 1993); several occurrences of extra-pair copulations (EPCs) (Palombit 1994b); and a series of episodes involving siamangs in which pair-bonds were terminated because of abandonment by one of the partners (Palombit 1994a). Palombit also challenged the view that gibbon monogamy is monotypic. Based on observations made over a 2.5-year period, Palombit demonstrated a qualitative difference between white-handed gibbon and siamang *pair-bonds* [i.e., "partner specific behaviors" (see Anzenberger 1992:205)]. Siamangs, for example, were found to exhibit higher levels of affiliative social contact relative to white-handed gibbons, suggesting to Palombit that female siamangs contribute more to maintaining the pair-bond than do female white-handed gibbons. Palombit concluded that the term "monogamy" masks important distinctions in the pair-bonds exhibited by different gibbon species (Palombit 1996).

Concurrent research on white-handed gibbons at Khao Yai National Park added to the growing view that gibbon social lives were more complex than previously appreciated. Brockelman and co-workers (1998) assembled observations collected over 18 years, including six dispersals by maturing subadults. As Palombit had described in siamangs Brockelman and co-workers reported that two of the six dispersals involved males who replaced resident males in neighboring groups. In one case the resulting family group was composed of the adult female (Andromeda), her offspring, the usurping male (Fearless), and two immature males that moved over with the new male, which were presumably his brothers. Brockelman and co-workers (1998) report that "Social relations within this heterogeneous group remained harmonious: the adults groomed all the young and play occurred between all preadult members" (p. 329). Also of surprise was the finding that the average dispersal distance by emigrating subadults was just 710 m, in other words, one or two territories away. Subsequent research by Reichard (1995) on the same population documented the occurrence of EPCs among white-handed gibbons as well; 8 of 67 observed copulations by the adult female Andromeda over a 10-month period occurred with a male other than her pair mate. Affiliative, although not sexual, encounters by immature members of neighboring groups were also reported—including frequent play bouts between neighboring juveniles (Treesucon 1984; Reichard and Sommer 1997).

The consequence of the findings from Ketambe and Khao Yai was nothing less than a wholesale reconsideration of the cause and function of territoriality and monogamy in gibbons, including an assault on the use of the term "monogamy" to describe the social system of gibbons or any other primate. As many authors have observed one of the problems with the term "monogamy" as applied to primate social systems is that its meaning is imprecise (Wickler and Seibt 1983). It is used to describe both a mating system (i.e., fidelity) and a grouping pattern (i.e., one-male/one-female groups). Furthermore monogamous social groups are often assumed to represent nuclear families, in which all offspring are related to both parents. The work at Khao Yai and Ketambe forced a reconsideration of this view. Indeed when the complex social histories of gibbon groups at Khao Yai were first described (see Raemaekers and Raemaekers 1984; Treesucon and Raemaekers 1984), Quiatt (1985, 1987) proposed that the term "household" (a group that "travels and exploits territorial resources as a single unit") replace "family group" in discussions of gibbon social structure. Elsewhere Quiatt has argued that the advantage of the term "household" is that "membership is less likely to imply either a mating relationship or genes in common with some other members" (Quiatt and Kelso 1987:429). These considerations are even more important in light of recent observations at Khao Yai and Ketambe.

Further criticism of the nuclear-family model grew out of the observation that 10% or more of gibbon groups may contain extra adult members (Fuentes 1998, 2000; Sommer and Reichard 2000). As a result Fuentes (1998, 2000) argues that the term "monogamy" should be dropped as a description of a grouping pattern, proposing instead the label "two-adult group" to describe primates formerly referred to as "monogamous." According to this schema gibbons are further distinguished as exhibiting "pair-bonded groups" because of the mutual attraction between pair mates. Others have addressed the ambiguity more simply, by drawing a distinction between *social* (or sociogenic) monogamy (which subsumes both two-adult and pair-bonded groups) and *mating* (or genetic) monogamy (e.g., Wickler and Seibt 1983; Anzenberger 1992; Gowaty 1996a). Because the descriptions "pair-bonded" and "socially monogamous" are widely used in the primate literature, I will use the two terms interchangeably when describing gibbon social groups.

Unanswered Questions

Almost lost in the remarkable developments in the study of gibbon social systems are still-unanswered questions about the ecological behavior of the small apes. Although the last three decades provided for the first time a basis for cross-species comparison within the Hylobatidae, many details of the feeding behavior and adaptations of gibbons are still being described. In many ways the situation is little changed from that described by Chivers (1984) over 24 years ago.

> Despite the numerous field studies, we still do not understand the relationship between food supply and gibbon densities, or foraging strategies in the face of fluctuating food supplies. The evergreen rain forests are unparalleled in their complexity, in their high diversity and abundance of plant and animal species. A study in marginal habitat (drier, more seasonal, less diverse) could help to remedy these deficiencies (p. 274).

FORAGING ADAPTATIONS IN PRIMATES

All animals divide their active period between feeding, traveling between feeding sites, periods of inactivity, and time spent engaged in social interactions. How an animal balances time spent in these different activities has important consequences for dietary intake, survival, and reproduction (Cant and Temerin 1984; Janson 1992). From the standpoint of foraging theory the nutritional value of a given food is a product of its nutrient content and the time it takes to acquire, process, and digest. Fruit and animal matter tend to be high-value foods (i.e., high in readily available calories), but because they are patchily distributed (in separate fruiting trees, for example), they take more time to acquire. Leaves and the vegetative parts of plants, on the other hand, are more evenly distributed in time and space and are therefore easier to find (Milton 1980; Lambert 2007). Nevertheless the nutritional value of leaves is much lower, and because of the high cellulose content, they can take more time to digest (further discounting their overall value). When nutritious foods are abundant, individuals have little trouble meeting their basic metabolic needs and many animals may store surplus energy as fat (e.g., Leighton 1993; Knott 1998). But in markedly seasonal environments, animals will not be able to rely solely on high-quality foods. They may experience food scarcity for weeks or months. How animals adjust to periods of resource scarcity is important from an evolutionary standpoint, because adequate nutrition is essential to growth and reproduction and thus may represent an important selective pressure (Gaulin and Konner 1977; Oates 1987). Undernourished males will have a hard time acquiring mates, and undernourished females will not be able to nourish fetuses or neonates. Furthermore nutritional stress can also limit parental investment (Lee 1987). Consequently effective mechanisms for dealing with seasonal food shortages are likely to represent evolved adaptive patterns. It should not be surprising then that one of the central questions in the study of primate behavioral ecology concerns the way in which different species respond to seasonal variations in the availability of preferred foods (Oates 1987; Garber 1993; Brockman and van Schaik 2005).

Another reason for this preoccupation is that competition between sympatric species is likely to be greatest during periods when resources are least abundant. Among closely related species foraging patterns tend to diverge during such times (Terborgh 1986; Marshall and Wrangham 2007). As a result the unique aspects of a given species' foraging behavior should be more easily discerned when resources are scarce and when competition within a community is at its peak. Descriptions of gibbon foraging patterns have focused on a limited number of reportedly distinct features of their diet and range use. In particular gibbons have been described as highly selective feeders that are largely dependent on small, scattered fruit patches (Raemaekers and Chivers 1980; Leighton 1987; Chivers 2001). According to some investigators the combination of these features predicts that gibbons should be restricted to relatively aseasonal forests throughout their range (Gittins and Raemaekers 1980). Yet all tropical forests, to a greater or lesser extent, exhibit seasonally recurrent periods of fruit scarcity (Whitmore 1984), and more recent field research has documented gibbon populations in highly seasonal environments (Haimoff et al. 1987; Lan et al. 1990). Thus in addition to documenting how gibbons respond to seasonal changes in fruit supply, a second goal of this study is to evaluate the assertion put forth by many observers that gibbons are uniquely adapted to exploit resources that are rare, scattered, and small. Finally, because some of my findings are at odds with the work of previous investigators, I will also consider the implication of my research to our understanding of the evolution of gibbon social structure.

2

Study Animals, Study Site, and Methods

To describe accurately an individual free ranging gibbon implies a description which includes all of its relations to its natural grouping, its neighbors and its faunal and floral community.

—Carpenter (1940:165)

It might be argued that the behavioral and ecological diversity exhibited by the Hylobatidae is less than that exhibited by other primate families. For the most part all gibbon species share similarities of diet, range use, and social structure. In contrast, great apes, which most taxonomists place in a single taxonomic family, often with humans as well (i.e., Hominidae), differ markedly along these same axes. An explanation for the relative homogeneity in gibbon behavioral ecology can perhaps be found in the "radically new feeding niche" gibbons evolved to exploit. According to Ellefson (1974) the elements of the adaptive complex that define the gibbon pattern—terminal branch feeding (with brachiation), territoriality, and pair living—are mutually interdependent and, therefore, highly resistant to change. Whether or not this scenario is accurate, the existing field data do suggest that gibbon species (at least at the generic level) share many aspects of their behavior and feeding ecology (Chivers 2001; Bartlett 2007a). For this reason I will begin this chapter with an overview of hylobatid evolution and taxonomy. Once I have situated white-handed gibbons within their broader taxonomic unit, I turn to a description of the study area where I worked, including the trail system, fauna, and forest phenology. I close the chapter with a description of the study animals and an overview of behavioral observation methods used during my research.

OVERVIEW OF THE HYLOBATIDAE

Gibbon Evolution and Taxonomy

The 12 species of gibbon belong to the family Hylobatidae, which along with the Hominidae make up the primate superfamily Hominoidea. Among the hominoids gibbons are the most distantly related to humans. Comparative molecular analysis suggests that hylobatids diverged from the hominids at least 16 mya (Goodman et al. 1998; Raaum et al. 2005). At the molecular level four distinct genera are readily distinguished based on chromosome number—*Hoolock* ($2N = 38$), *Hylobates* ($2N = 44$), *Nomascus* ($2N = 52$), and *Symphalangus* ($2N = 50$) (Prouty et al. 1983a,b; Mootnick and Groves 2005). Given the overall ecological similarity among gibbon species, these four groups have typically been distinguished at the subgenus level (Marshall and Sugardjito 1986; Groves 2001). Recent molecular data, however, suggest that the temporal split between the four traditional gibbon subgenera is at least as deep as that between chimpanzees (*Pan* spp.) and humans. Hayashi and co-workers (1995), for example, estimate that *Hylobates* diverged from the other gibbon subgenera at about 6 mya. In light of these findings there is a growing movement to promote the four recognized subgenera to genera (Roos and Geissmann 2001).

Despite the apparent agreement at the generic level, investigators continue to differ on how many gibbon species should be recognized. Given the presumed role of vocal behavior in attracting mates and maintaining the pairbond, many investigators have used the presence of distinct vocalizations to delineate different species (Marshall and Sugardjito 1986; Geissmann 1995, 2002). Using this criterion Geissmann (1995, 2002) recognizes 12 species (Table 2–1), and his taxonomy will be followed here, but it should be noted that other investigators consider distinct songs neither necessary nor sufficient to distinguish gibbon species (Groves 2001; Mather 1992).

Little is known about the evolutionary origins of the family Hylobatidae, which according to Begun (2002:222) "remains shrouded in mystery." Lacking relevant fossil material, investigators have attempted to reconstruct gibbon evolution through morphological, vocal, and/or molecular comparisons, but these attempts have yielded almost as many phylogenies as inquiries (e.g., Groves 1972; Haimoff et al. 1982; Garza and Woodruff 1992; Roos and Geissmann 2001). Whereas most phylogenetic reconstructions have identified either *Nomascus* or *Symphalangus* as the most basal group, a recent analysis of gibbon chromosome rearrangements by Müller and others (2003) determined that *Hoolock* (formerly *Bunopithecus*), which does not share a single chromosomal rearrangement with any of the other genera, was likely the first of the gibbon genera to diverge. The difficulty in

Table 2–1 Species of the Family Hylobatidae

Genus	Species	Common Name(s)	Weight (kg)[1]	Coat Coloration	Duet
Hoolock (diploid number = 38)	H. hoolock	Hoolock or white-browed gibbon	6.1–6.9	Males black, females buff	Yes
Hylobates (diploid number = 44)	H. agilis	Dark-handed or agile gibbon	5.5–6.4	Varied, males have white cheeks	Yes
	H. klossii	Kloss's gibbon or biloh	5.8	Both sexes black	No
	H. lar	White-handed or lar gibbon	4.4–7.6	Both sexes black or buff	Yes
	H. moloch	Silvery or Javan gibbon	5.7	Both sexes silver gray	No
	H. muelleri	Mueller's or Bornean gibbon	5.0–6.4	Both sexes brown to gray	Yes
	H. pileatus	Pileated or capped gibbon	6.3–10.4	Males black, females buff	Yes
Nomascus (diploid number = 52)	N. concolor	Western black crested gibbon	4.5–9.0	Males black, females buff	Yes
	N. cf. nasutus	Eastern black crested gibbon	—	Males black, females buff	Yes
	N. gabriellae	Yellow-cheeked crested gibbon	5.8	Males black, females buff	Yes
	N. leucogenys	White-cheeked crested gibbon	5.6–5.8	Males black, females buff	Yes
Symphalangus (diploid number = 50)	S. syndactylus	Siamang	10.0–14.7	Both sexes black	Yes

[1] See references in Rowe (1996)

From Thad Bartlett, "The Hylobatidae: Small Apes of Asia," in *Primates in Perspective* (Oxford: Oxford University Press, 2007), tab. 16.1, p. 275. Reproduced by permission of Oxford University Press, Inc.

resolving the evolutionary relationships between gibbon genera may be a result of all gibbons diverging from one another in a relatively short period of time (Hall et al. 1998; Müller et al. 2003). If the present distribution of gibbons is any guide (Figure 2–1), major rivers must have served as an isolating mechanism during the initial diversification of the Hylobatidae (Meijaard and Groves 2006). Subsequent speciation of the genus *Hylobates*, beginning about 3 mya, was further influenced by changes in sea level during the Pliocene (Harrison et al. 2006).

Appearance

Most gibbon species are very similar in skeletal anatomy and are more readily differentiated based on pelage (coat color) and characteristics of

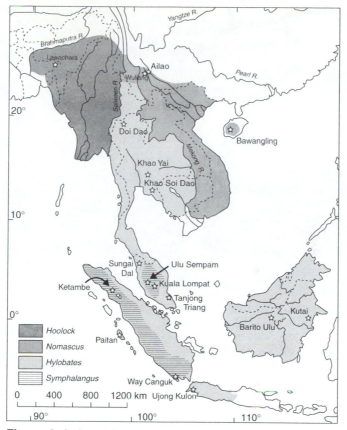

Figure 2–1 Approximate historical distribution of four gibbon genera (following Chivers 1977 and Geissmann 2004). The locations of study sites described in the text, including Khao Yai National Park, are indicated.

From Thad Bartlett, "The Hylobatidae: Small Apes of Asia," in *Primates in Perspective* (Oxford: Oxford University Press, 2007), fig. 16.1, p. 276. Reproduced by permission of Oxford University Press, Inc.

their vocal repertoire (Fooden 1971; Marshall and Sugardjito 1986; Chivers 2001). Hoolock, pileated, and crested gibbons are all sexually dichromatic, whereby males and females have different coat coloration. The predominant color of males is black, whereas females are primarily buff colored. In these species, sexes also differ in the markings of the crown, face, and chest. White-handed gibbons, on the other hand, are asexually dichromatic; males and females are either black or buff, with the exception of a white face ring and white hands and feet. Extensive data on group composition in wild white-handed gibbons suggest that coat color in this species is a Mendelian autosomal trait with black dominant to buff (Fooden 1971; Brockelman 2004). Marshall and Sugardjito (1986) rejected the conclusion

White-handed gibbons in Khao Yai National Park exhibit different color phases irrespective of sex, a phenomenon known as "asexual dichromatism." In this group the adult male and juvenile female are buff, whereas the adult female and her infant are black.

that coat color among white-handed gibbon is a simple Mendelian trait, based on their observation of two family groups in Khao Yai that consisted of two buff-phase parents with a black infant. Recent field studies, including those at Khao Yai, however, have determined that nonnuclear family groups are not uncommon, which may account for their discordant observations.

Vocalizations

Gibbons produce a variety of loud calls that are structurally complex and can be heard over long distances. According to Raemaekers and others (1984:148) many gibbon calls "are grouped into bouts given without obvious external referents and having a structure above the level of the note; they, therefore, deserve the label 'song.'" The characteristics cited are not true of all gibbon calls, thus the authors caution against using "song" as a generic term for all calls. I use the word *song* here to draw a distinction between the complex uninterrupted vocalizations of gibbons and the loud, but less elaborate, calls given by other primates, including great apes (Geissmann 2000). As indicated above, studies of hybrid gibbons demonstrate that there is a significant genetic component to gibbon songs (Brockelman and Schilling 1984; Geissmann 1984, 1993). Gibbon songs also differ from the loud calls of other primates in that males and females produce sex-specific songs; for example, loud calls in Old World monkeys and apes tend to be given mostly by males (Geissmann 2000).

The kinds of songs produced by gibbons can be divided minimally into solos and duets. Among *Hylobates* spp. mated males sing solos frequently, although not exclusively, at or before dawn (Geissmann 2002). In the remaining genera male solos are absent. Females sing solos in just two species, Kloss and silvery gibbons. These two species also lack the highly coordinated duets seen in other taxa. The composition of duet songs differs between species, but they share many elements of their structure, which typically includes an introductory sequence, a female great call, and the male's reply or coda (Marshall and Marshall 1976; Raemaekers et al. 1984). Male and female contributions differ but often blend together or overlap so that different parts of the song are not obvious to the novice listener. Observers speculate that gibbon songs serve both to cement the bond between pair mates and to advertise the location of the gibbon territory (Wickler 1980; Raemaekers et al. 1984). As I detail in the next section the first long-term study of gibbons at Khao Yai National Park focused on aspects of gibbon vocal behavior.

DESCRIPTION OF THE STUDY AREA

Thai Forests

Thailand has a land area of 513,115 km^2, an area just under the size of Texas. It is estimated that as recently as 1950, 60% of the country was forested. This figure has shrunk to less than 15% as of writing this book, but most of what remains is now protected. Owing to the efforts of Dr. Boonsong Lekagul, a hunter-turned conservation advocate, the Thai government passed the *Wild Animals Reservation and Protection Act* in 1960 and the *National Parks Act* in 1961. This legislation led to the establishment of Thailand's first wildlife sanctuaries and national parks. As of 2003, the Thai government had established 75 terrestrial national parks, 44 wildlife sanctuaries, and dozens of nonhunting or otherwise-protected areas. Together they account for over 81,000 km^2—approximately 16% of the country (Srikosamatara and Brockelman 2002). Preserved within these areas is a tremendous array of plant and animal species including, over 2000 species of tree (Royal Forest Department, Thailand), 900 species of birds, and 280 species of mammals (107 of which are bats) (Gray et al. 1991; Lekagul and Round 1991). Many large mammalian species persist in the protected areas, including Asian elephant, gaur, banteng, Malayan sun bear, Asiatic black bear, tiger, and clouded leopard. Reliable census data, however, are scarce, and there is disagreement as to whether the population size of many of these species is large enough for them to be viable.

There are 14 primate species that are native to Thailand (Parr 2003): slow loris (*Nycticebus coucang*), five species of macaque (*Macaca* spp.), four species of langur (*Presbytis* spp.), white-handed gibbon, pileated gibbon, agile gibbon, and siamang. In addition to research on white-handed gibbons long-term socioecological studies have been completed on two species: pig-tailed macaques (*Macaca nemestrina*) in Khao Yai National Park (Maruhashi et al. 2002) and pileated gibbons at two sites, Khao Soi Dao Wildlife Sanctuary (Srikosamatara 1984) and Khao Yai National Park (Suwanvecho 2003). In addition Phayre's langur (*P. phayrei*) is the subject of ongoing research at the Pu Khieo Wildlife Sanctuary in Northeast Thailand (Koenig et al. 2004). Although the amount of primate research in Thailand has expanded in recent years, it remains the case that white-handed gibbons are far better studied than any other species, and with the exception of observations of Edwards and Todd (1991) in Huai Kha Khaeng Wildlife Sanctuary and work by Suwannakerd and Aggimarangsee (2001) at the Tham Nam Lod Wildlife Conservation Development and Extension Center, most research has been conducted in Khao Yai National Park.

Khao Yai National Park

Khao Yai National Park is located approximately 150 km northeast of Bangkok. Established in 1962, it is the oldest National Park in Thailand and is the third largest at 2168 km^2. Khao Yai means "big mountain" in English, and the majority of the park consists of a sandstone plateau ranging between 600 and 1000 m above sea level, which is covered by seasonal evergreen forest (Srikosamatara and Hansel 1996). The park is approximately twice as long (east-west) as it is wide (north-south) and is bisected into uneven portions by a two-lane paved road (Figure 2–2). The park headquarters is located in the northwest quadrant of the park. Before Khao Yai was established as a national park, several villages existed within its boundary. These settlements were forcibly evacuated when the park was founded. A large human population, comprised of park employees, their families, and military personnel, however, continues to occupy the park. This population is concentrated largely in the middle of the park near the headquarters and in several border stations around the periphery of the park. An active Royal Thai Air Force installation on one of the park's highest peaks supports a radar station.

Khao Yai, one of Thailand's most popular parks, was temporarily closed to overnight visitors in 1992 in response to excessive development within the park boundaries, which included the construction of a hotel, a restaurant, and a nine-hole golf course near the park headquarters. As a result the level of tourist traffic when I began preliminary observations in October 1993 was relatively low. By late 1994, however, overnight visitors were again being allowed in the park, although I rarely encountered tourists in the forest.

Rainfall and Temperature. Thailand's climate is influenced by two monsoons (or seasonal winds); consequently central Thailand experiences

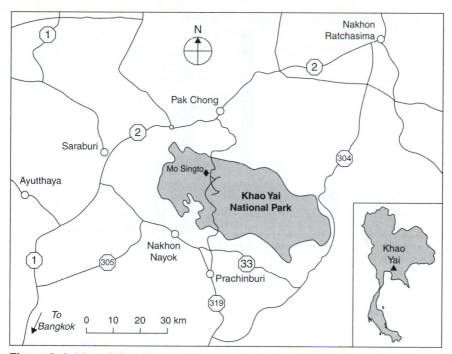

Figure 2–2 Map of Khao Yai National Park, including the approximate location of the Mo Singto study area.

three seasons: (1) the cool season, from November to February, when the northeast monsoon brings cold, dry air in from China; (2) the hot season, from March to May, when temperatures rise as the influence of the northeasterly winds diminish; and (3) the wet season, beginning generally in June and lasting through October, when the southwest monsoon carries moisture in from the Indian Ocean. The onset of the wet season may greatly vary from year to year depending on the arrival of the southwest monsoon. In 1994 rains began in March.

During the study period I received copies of daily weather data from park officials (Figure 2–3). The park weather station is located in an open field approximately 1 km south of the headquarters. During the cool season overnight lows regularly dropped to 7°C (45°F). The average minimum temperature was lowest during January, 10°C (50°F). Daytime temperatures were moderate year-round. The month with the greatest average high temperature was April, 30°C (86°F); temperatures rarely climbed above 32°C (90°F).

Khao Yai National Park receives between 2000 and 3000 mm of rainfall annually (Tangtham 1991). Total rainfall for 1994 was 2695 mm. Typically the vast majority falls in four or five months during the southwest monsoon (June to September). Even during 1994 when the rains came

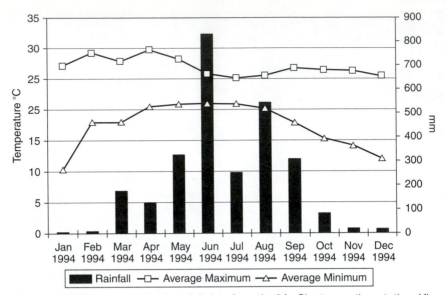

Figure 2–3 Temperature and rainfall data from the Mo Singto weather station, Khao Yai National Park.

early, 75% of total rainfall fell in the wet season, and there was little rain (2% of the annual total) from November through February.

The Mo Singto Study Area

Surveys of gibbon populations in Khao Yai were first initiated by Marshall and co-workers (1972) and Brockelman (1975). During these early visits Brockelman identified the area that is today the Mo Singto study site (Rae-maekers and Raemaekers 1990). The area is distinguished by the density of the gibbon population, the presence of a perennial spring, and its ease of access; the site is located just a 0.5 km east of the park headquarters (101°22′E, 14°26′N). Having learned of the site from Brockelman, Jeremy and Patricia Raemaekers subsequently developed the site for their work on gibbon vocalization in 1981 (Raemaekers and Raemaekers 1985). Various long- and short-term research projects by Thai and Western scientists have continued ever since (Brockelman et al. 1998). The majority of research in the intervening years has focused on social behavior and intergroup inter-actions (e.g., Reichard 1995, 2003). A notable exception is the research of Claudia Whitington, who studied feeding behavior and seed dispersal by white-handed gibbons (Whitington 1990; Whitington and Treesucon 1991). Her identification of many gibbon food species laid the foundation for food species identification in this study. In addition to periodic research projects by degree students, Brockelman (pers. comm.; Brockelman et al. 1998,

2001) has made regular observations on several groups within the study area since 1979. As a result the home ranges and group histories for several social groups were well established before I began my study.

Topography and Trail System.   The topography of the site is dominated by a series of ridges and valleys, and the terrain is rugged and hilly. Elevation ranges between 730 and 860 m above sea level. In 1981 Raemaekers and Raemaekers (1990) began work on an extensive trail system amounting to roughly 15 km of trails marked at 50 m intervals. Many of these trails were originally made by elephants and other animals, and almost all follow physical contours rather than true compass bearings. This trail system has been maintained and augmented by subsequent researchers (e.g., Reichard 1998) and by the time I arrived at the park, it covered the home ranges of three gibbon social groups. To accurately plot range use, I remapped over 8 km of trails using a compass and 30 m tape.

Fauna.   Four species of primates are found within the park: white-handed gibbons, pileated gibbons, pig-tailed macaques, and slow lorises. Except for a small hybrid zone several kilometers east of the study area (see Brockelman and Gittins 1984), the two gibbon species are allopatric. Pig-tailed macaques are regular visitors to the study site and often feed in the same trees as gibbons. Slow lorises are also known to inhabit the study area although I never encountered them. Numerous other fru-givorous species are found throughout the study area including, black giant squirrel, variable squirrel, common palm civet, and binturong (see Srikosamatara and Hansel 1996). Several predator species inhabit the study area. The largest are the tiger and clouded leopard. Reticulated python are not uncommon.

In addition to a rich mammalian fauna, over 300 species of birds have been recorded in Khao Yai; among these are four species of hornbill: brown hornbill (*Ptilolaemus tickelli*), wreathed hornbill (*Rhyticeros undula-tus*), Indian pied hornbill (*Anthracoceros albirostris*), and great hornbill (*Buceros bicornis*). All four species exploit many of the same food species eaten by gibbons (Kitamura et al. 2002). Several species of raptor are also common in the park.

Site Vegetation.   The dominant type of vegetation in Khao Yai, including the forest at Mo Singto, is seasonal evergreen rainforest. Using a range-height finder, I measured the height of 40 gibbon feeding trees, which yielded an average height of 23.7 m (range = 12–37 m, SD = 6.9). The highest emergent, a dipterocarp (*Dipterocarpus gracilis*), was measured to 55 m. Other emergent species in the study area include *Cleistocalyx nervosum, Prunus javanica,* and *Ficus* spp. Two areas of secondary growth occur around the periphery of the study area. They are the result of previous human occupation and are now regenerated to the point that gibbons occasionally enter and feed in some of these areas. In the primary forest rattans and other palms are common in the understory and sometimes make following the gibbons difficult. Strangling, climbing, and free-standing figs (*Ficus* spp.) are abundant at the site. Over 10 species have been collected, the majority of which appear to fruit aseasonally (Brockelman, pers. comm.).

Beginning in early 1994 Brockelman and colleagues began mapping the study area with a theodolite to establish a long-term forest dynamics plot (Brockelman et al. 2001). The corners of 20 m square quadrats were marked with sturdy plastic stakes, and all tress within the quadrat border were marked with a permanent numerical identifier that indicated the location of the tree on the plot. By the completion of my research 4.5 ha had been surveyed and all trees more than 10 cm diameter at breast height (DBH) within 79 quadrats (3.16 ha) had been tagged, measured, and mapped. The sampled area yielded 1640 trees, or 519/ha. The most common tree families are Lauraceae, Elaeocarpaceae, Aquifoliaceae, Meliaceae, and Icacinaceae.

Seasonal Availability of Resources

I employed two methods to document seasonal variation in the availability of potential food items. During December 1993 I established a phenology transect within the known home ranges of the habituated study groups; I marked 252 trees with a DBH of more than 20 cm along 1.5 km of trails. The absolute sample size varied between 249 and 252 trees because of tree falls and subsequent additions to the sample. Trees were selected without knowledge of species. The selection criteria took into account the size of the tree and the visibility of the crown. The average DBH for all trees for which a measurement could be taken was 37.6 cm (SD = 16, range = 15.5–99.29, $N = 231$). Of the 252 trees selected, 191 (76%) were subsequently identified to the genus or species level. The most common species—*Symplocos cochinchinensis* (Symplocaceae)—represents 8% of the sample ($N = 19$); the 10 most common species represent 43% of the sample ($N = 108$). Trees of the genus *Ficus* accounted for 2% ($N = 6$). During two to three days at the end of each month from January 1994 through January 1995, I scored each tree on the phenology transect for the presence or absence of flowers, unripe fruit, ripe fruit, and young leaves. I also noted trees that lost their leaves or were flush with new foliage.

Second, at the same interval I monitored a 3 ha botanical plot for the presence of known gibbon food species used during the previous period. Sixty-six 20 m × 20 m quadrats were selected from the previously surveyed botanical plot (see earlier), and I laid out an additional nine quadrats using a Brunton Pocket Transit and 30 m tape (75 quadrats × 400 m² = 30,000 m², or 3 hectares). Once per month I walked the borders of the 20 m × 20 m quadrats noting the presence and location of all fruit-ing individuals of major food species used during the previous observa-tion period. "Major food species"—including fruiting vines—were defined as those accounting for at least 5% of total gibbon feeding time during the previous month. Thus defined, major food species accounted for between 50% and 90% of total gibbon feeding time each month and for between 80% and 96% of fruit-feeding time.

Food species were identified based on comparison with voucher specimens collected from the botanical plot and stored at the Center for Conservation Biology, Mahidol University, Bangkok. Voucher identifi-cations were made by several individuals, including Warren Brockelman (Mahidol University), James F. Maxwell (Chiang Mai University, Chiang Mai), and Tem Smitinand (Royal Forest Department, Bangkok). Species identification for trees on the botanical plot is ongoing (Brockelman et al. 2001), and therefore the species names provided here should be considered provisional. Species that were not identified were given a unique name or number that was maintained throughout the course of the study.

Results of the Phenological Study.   Phenological data from the 12 consecutive months from February 1994 to January 1995 are reported in this section. Despite the marked dry season, only 10% of the trees in the phenology

Long-term ecological monitoring at Mo Singto is overseen by ecologist Warren Brockelman of Mahidol University, shown here sorting dried botanical samples.

sample were deciduous, losing their leaves in the cool season, November to February. The percentage of bare trees was highest in December (6%) and lowest from May to August when all trees sampled were covered with mature foliage. The peak availability for new foliage was January (5%). Many tropical species produce new leaves throughout the year, and as a result young leaves were available in all months. There, however, was a relative decline in the availability of young leaves during the wet season. The month with the lowest availability was June when only 5% of sample trees had young leaves, as compared with February and November when 31% had young leaves (Table 2–2).

The cool season was also the peak season for flowering. Trees in flower were most abundant from November to February when from 9% to 20% of sample trees were in flower (Table 2–2; Figure 2–4). In contrast the availability of ripe fruit was greatest during the hot and wet seasons. During the 12 months of study fruit abundance showed a bimodal pattern with the first peak in May and second, less pronounced, peak in September. The second peak is greatly influenced by the fruiting of a single highly favored species *Choerospondias axillaris*, which accounted for 47% of the September sample. On a seasonal basis fruit abundance was greatest during the hot season, March to May, whereas fruit abundance was lowest during the cool season, November to February. In 1994 total rainfall during the cool season was below 60 mm per month. At this threshold it is estimated that evaporation exceeds precipitation, leading to water stress, which influences forest

Table 2–2 Monthly Measures of Resource Abundance

Month	Phenology Walk (% of Trees)			Botanical Plot (Trees/ha)
	Fruit	Flowers	Young Leaves	Fruit
February 1994	1.2	9.1	31.0	2.3
March 1994	4.0	6.7	11.9	2.0
April 1994	9.2	2.8	25.5	2.7
May 1994	12.4	3.2	13.1	4.0
June 1994	8.8	2.8	5.2	4.3
July 1994	4.0	3.2	6.8	2.7
August 1994	5.6	2.4	13.1	3.0
September 1994	7.6	4.0	14.7	4.7
October 1994	2.0	4.4	16.3	1.3
November 1994	1.2	12.4	31.3	0.0
December 1994	0.4	9.6	18.5	0.0
January 1995	2.8	19.7	24.9	1.0
Mean	4.9	6.7	17.7	2.3
SD	3.8	5.2	8.7	1.5

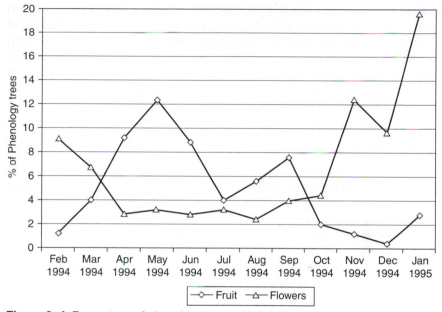

Figure 2–4 Percentage of phenology trees with fruit and flowers each month.

productivity (Whitmore 1984). Compared across months, there was a strong correlation between fruit abundance and rainfall (r_s = 0.78, p = 0.010).

The availability of known gibbon foods followed a pattern of abundance similar to that based on the phenology transect and correlation between the two measures is high (r_s = 0.83, p = 0.006). Between 0 and 5 fruiting individuals of the preferred species were available per hectare over the course of the study. Peak availability occurred in May and June and again in September. During September fruiting *Choerospondias axillaris* trees accounted for 43% of fruiting trees on the plot. The months with lowest availability were October to January when there was one or fewer food patches per hectare (Table 2–2).

OVERVIEW OF BEHAVIORAL DATA COLLECTION

Study Groups

By the time I arrived in Khao Yai, two white-handed gibbon social groups with home ranges in the study area were already habituated to observers (see Reichard and Sommer 1997). These groups were first described by Raemaekers and Raemaekers (1985) and retain their designations: A and C. A third group, B, whose territory neighbors both of the above groups', was partially habituated, and three other groups, K, H, and N, all had habituated members.

Because they were already accustomed to human observers, I selected groups A and C for systematic observation of feeding and ranging behavior. In April 1994 the subadult male, Chet, of group C migrated into neighboring group B, and as a result, I regularly monitored group B for the remainder of the study period. Group composition for all three groups is given in Table 2–3. Age classes follow those of Brockelman and colleagues (1998): *infant* (0–2 yrs.), *juvenile* (2–5 yrs.), *adolescent* (5–8 yrs.), *subadult* (8+ yrs.), and *adult* (mated with territory). After the age of eight, animals that have yet to emigrate are considered subadults regardless of age. The mean dispersal age for the six subadults at Mo Singto is 9.7 years (Brockelman et al. 1998). Gibbons are individually recognizable based on coat color, relative size, and the shape of their face ring. Proper names are given to each animal for comparison between studies. For proper names the initial letter is the same as the letter of the group in which the animal was first observed. For example Fearless, the adult male of group A, migrated from group F in 1983 (see Treesucon and Raemaekers 1984; Brockelman et al. 1998). His mate, Andromeda, was already in group A when that group was first surveyed. Her group of origin is unknown.

Data Collection

From October 1993 through January 1994 I made preliminary observations on the two main study groups, A and C. During the same period I

Table 2–3 Composition of Gibbon Study Groups from 1994 to 1995

	Coat Color	Age Class	Sex	Name	Comment
Group A	Black	Adult	Male	Fearless	
	Buff	Adult	Female	Andromeda	
	Black	Adolescent	Male	Amadeus	
	Buff	Juvenile	Male	Aran	
	Buff	Infant	Female	Akira	b. October 1993
Group B	Black	Adult	Male	Bard	
	Black	Adult	Female	Bridget	
	Buff	Adolescent	Female	Brenda	
	Black	Juvenile	Female	Benedetta	
Group C	Buff	Adult	Male	Cassius	
	Black	Adult	Female	Cassandra	
	Buff	Subadult	Male	Chet	m. April 1994
	Black	Adolescent	Male	Christopher	
	Buff	Juvenile	Female	Caleb(a)	
	Black	Infant	Female	Cyrana	b. November 1993

b. = born; m. = migrated

reopened trails and established the phenology transect. In mid-January 1994 I began systematic observations. Each study group was followed from night tree to night tree, whenever possible, for a period of five consecutive days per month. I began collecting data as soon as it was light enough that the animals could be followed without being lost. This depended in part on the activity level of the animals. The gibbons often left night trees very early and moved quickly to the first feeding tree of the day, which required that I track gibbon silhouettes backlit by the predawn sky. At such times it was impossible to simultaneously collect data and not lose track of the animals. At other times gibbons lingered in the vicinity of night trees until full light, in which case it was possible to begin recording data immediately. Data collection ceased as soon as the focal animal entered its night tree, although I regularly remained at night trees for up to an hour to confirm that the animal did not subsequently relocate. Data collection continued through January 1995.

The combined observation hours for the two groups is 1137.8. I was more successful following group A (697.3 hours) than group C (440.5 hours). The average number of full-day follows per month was 5.4 for group A and 3.7 for group C. I define "full-day follows" as those observation days during which the study group was located within 1 hour of leaving night trees and followed for the remainder of the day; in all but 9 cases, full-day follows were also night-tree-to-night-tree follows.

The author observing gibbons high overhead in a feeding tree.

During each observation day I recorded the behavior of a single focal animal on the instant every 5 minutes—"instantaneous focal animal sample" (per Martin and Bateson 1986; see also J. Altmann 1974)—noting activity, identity of the nearest neighbor, number of group members within the same tree, and location relative to the nearest trail marker. Activity classes are provided in Table 2–4. Food items were classified as nonfig fruit, fig fruit, leaves, young leaves, flowers, vine shoots, and insects. The plant species was recorded when known.

Fig feeding was distinguished from feeding on other fruit species because of the presumed importance of figs to the diet of gibbons. Structurally fig fruit are quite different from true fruit. Unlike true fruit, which develop from flowers and are composed of seeds surrounded by a fleshy pericarp, figs are compound inflorescences that are made up of numerous tiny flowers that extend into the body of a fruitlike mass, or syconium. In a sense figs are inside out because the tiny flowers develop out of view at the core of the fruitlike capsule. Most of the 900 or so species of fig are pollinated by a unique species of wasp, the males of which live out their entire lives in the dark interior of the fig. Only females eventually migrate to other fruit (Dawkins 1996). Fig trees are also phenologically unusual, because individual trees of the same species often fruit asynchronously. Moreover individual trees may have irregular fruiting cycles, and many trees fruit twice a year. As a result fig abundance tends to lack the seasonal peaks and valleys typical of most other fruit species (Janzen 1979; Whitmore 1984).

During behavioral data collection I divided observation days into roughly equal halves and followed different animals in the morning and in the afternoon. I thereby ensured that I collected data on all animals in each group during each monthly sample. Each month focal animals were rotated to ensure equal representation of all group members (excluding dependent infants). In the event that a group broke up during foraging, which was rare, I continued to follow the focal animal. If the focal animal was temporarily out of view, I recorded the behavior of another animal with priority given first to an individual in the same age class and second to an individual of the same coat color. This helped to reduce bias in the selection of any particular animal.

Feeding sources (trees or climbers) that were continually fed in for at least 5 minutes were marked at the time of use with flagging tape. These food sources were later relocated, measured (DBH only), identified to species, and mapped relative to the trail system. Onset and duration of group songs and intergroup encounters were recorded, as they occurred. Observations were generally made during the third and fourth weeks of each month.

Data Analysis

The analysis presented in the following chapters is drawn from 125 full- and half-day follows taken from the 12 consecutive month period of

Table 2–4 Definitions of Gibbon Activity Classes Recorded During the Study

Behavior	Description
Auto-grooming	Grooming one's self, usually during rest. Gibbons often groom themselves after entering night trees; however, night-tree behavior was not included as part of the activity period.
Drinking	Gibbons drink by pushing one hand into naturally occurring cups or basins in trees and either catching the run-off in their mouth or licking the water from the fur on the back of their hand.
Feed	Pulling a food item from a tree or vine, chewing food, or brief pauses during a feeding bout. At times, the animals were out of view in a known food tree and were inferred to be feeding based on fruit fall. When feeding on invertebrates, breaking open nests and foraging through epiphytes were also scored as feeding behavior.
Grooming	Using the fingers or mouth to slowly comb through the fur of another individual. During grooming bouts, the groomer and groomee were indicated.
Individual play	Biting or manipulation of a nonfood item such as a vine or twig or vigorous acrobatic body movement. An uncommon behavior seen almost exclusively in young juveniles and infants.
Intergroup encounter	Any behavior, except vocalization, directed toward or performed with a member of another social group. This includes resting behavior where opposing animals, especially males, are in view of one another (i.e., vigilance). This excludes, however, neutral encounters where different groups shared feeding trees but did not interact.
Interspecies encounter	Any behavior, except vocalization, directed toward or performed with an individual of another species (e.g., macaques, squirrels, and birds).
Move	Within tree movement of at least an arm span. The distinction between travel and move was abandoned during data analysis.
Play	Active but nonaggressive interactions, including body contact, between two individuals. Play behavior was specified as Wrestle, Pull/Slap, or Chase.
Rest	Any period of inactivity lasting at least five seconds.
Social contact	Two or more animals sitting adjacent to one another with body contact. This occurred generally as a prelude to grooming or as an interlude between alternate grooming bouts.
Travel	Sustained movement between trees.
Vocalization	Any vocalization, including Solo calls, Duetting, Alarm Calls, or sustained Contact Calls, such as when a juvenile was separated from the group.

February 1994 through January 1995. In all, this represents 10,907 behavioral observation samples for the two main study groups: A ($N = 6670$, 61%) and C ($N = 4237$, 39%). There was an observational bias toward adult gibbons as they were easier to keep in view. This is more pronounced in group C than in group A. The subadult from group C emigrated during the second month of observation and is not well represented (Table 2–5). Data

Table 2–5 Percentage of Observational Samples by Age-Sex Class for Each Gibbon Study Group

	Group A	*Group C*
Female	24.2	28.1
Male	26.6	29.0
Subadult	—	0.9
Adolescent	26.0	23.2
Juvenile	23.2	18.8

Table 2–6 Comparison of Activity Budgets (%) Calculated by Pooling Data Across Individuals Versus Groups

Activity	*Individual (N = 8)*	*Group (N = 2)*	*Difference*
Feed	32.6	32.6	0.0
Rest	26.2	26.6	0.4
Travel	24.2	23.6	0.6
Social	11.3	11.0	0.3
Vocal	4.0	4.0	0.0
Intergroup encounter	1.9	2.1	0.2

Data for the C subadult are excluded

were pooled each month either by social group or by individual, depending on the analysis. Feeding and ranging are highly coordinated activities among Khao Yai gibbons, so in the analysis of feeding and ranging behavior, data were pooled monthly by group. Where differences in age-sex classes were of interest (e.g., activity budgets), data were pooled monthly by individual, excluding the C subadult. A comparison of annual activity budgets calculated in these two ways shows virtually no difference in the percentage of time devoted to each activity (Table 2–6). Unless indicated otherwise annual means are the average of the 12-monthly means.

Statistical analysis was conducted using Statview (Abacus Concepts, Inc.). Most parametric statistical tests assume that individuals are drawn at random, that samples are independent of one another, and that the underlying population distribution is normal or at least represents a known distribution. Primate field studies often violate one or more of these assumptions. The use of nonparametric, or distribution-free, tests addresses many of these problems without losing much in the way of statistical power (Martin and Bateson 1986; Fowler et al. 1998). A further advantage of using nonparametric tests is that they are widely used in primate research and are therefore familiar to many researchers and provide a basis of comparison between studies. All statistical tests presented in the following chapters are nonparametric.

3

Activity Budgets
and Social Behavior

*Many instances of grooming were observed in the forest. The pattern is similar
to that generally seen in other primates. Grooming not only serves to keep the dense
woolly coats of gibbons free from ecto-parasites but this activity also helps establish
and reinforce affinitive social bonds among animals of the family.*

—Carpenter (1940:266)

Primates spend the majority of their waking hours feeding, resting, and
traveling between feeding sites. Their remaining time each day is devoted
to what can be characterized as nonsubsistence behaviors, including affiliative, or friendly, social interactions, such as grooming and intergroup
encounters. The proportion of the *activity period* (the period of time an animal or group of animals is active each day) devoted to each of these
behaviors is reflected in what is referred to as an *activity budget*. The construction of activity budgets is fundamental to primate field research
because the proportion of time spent by each animal in different activities
can serve as a proxy for energy use (Halle and Stenseth 2000). For the individual, survival, growth, and reproduction are dependent on maintaining
a balance between energy intake and energy expenditure (Pianka 1988).
Thus differences in the average time budgets between populations, within
populations over time, or between different age-sex classes may point to
the presence of some form of ecological pressure (Dunbar 1992).

For example, primate populations in degraded habitat devote more time to foraging at the expense of nonsubsistence activity. Li and Rogers (2004) found that white-headed langurs (*Trachypithecus leucocephalus*) living in high-quality habitat spent less time feeding and more time in play relative to those in low-quality habitat. Within populations seasonal changes in resource abundance have a similar effect on time budgets. Many frugivorous primates increase feeding time and decrease travel time when fruit abundance falls [*Cebus albifrons* (Terborgh 1986); *Eulemur* spp. (Overdorff 1993); *Pan troglodytes* (Doran 1997)]. An alternative response to resource scarcity is to reduce the time devoted to social interactions. Defler (1995) reports that among woolly monkeys (*Lagothrix lagotricha*) rates of feeding and travel did not change significantly over the year, but time devoted to social activity dropped significantly during periods of resource scarcity. Robinson (1986) documented a similar response in wedge-capped capuchin monkeys (*Cebus olivaceus*). He notes that play behavior, in particular, "almost disappeared completely during the dry season" (p. 28).

Intrinsic differences between age-sex classes can also give rise to intragroup differences in activity budgets. In particular the energetic demands of pregnancy and lactation may be reflected in differences in the activity budgets of males and females or of females in different reproductive states (Altmann 1980; Matsumoto-Oda and Oda 1998; Vasey 2005). Although less research has been done on age differences in activity budgets, younger animals typically exhibit higher rates of social activity, especially play (Defler 1995; O'Brien and Kinnaird 1997).

As described in Chapter 1 gibbons are highly frugivorous. Thus in a distinctly seasonal forest such as that of Khao Yai National Park, we should expect gibbons to modify their activity budget in response to fluctuations in the availability of ripe fruit. Assuming that an individual's energetic demands remain relatively constant over time, energy balance can be maintained during periods of fruit scarcity by (1) traveling further to find more food, (2) feeding more heavily on readily accessible, but lower-quality, foods, (3) limiting energetically expensive activities (e.g., travel) and resting more, or (4) some combination of the above (Doran 1997; Di Fiore and Rodman 2001; Vasey 2005). If gibbons match the pattern documented in most other frugivores, we should expect them to increase feeding time, reduce travel time, and/or reduce social activity during months when resources are scarce.

I begin this chapter with a qualitative overview of the gibbon day, describing in general terms the way the gibbon day unfolds. Next I provide a quantitative analysis of the gibbon activity budget, including patterns of variation across the day and year, and describe how activity budgets differ between age-sex classes. The percentage of time devoted to different classes of activity is then compared with the overall abundance of resources in the environment to determine how gibbons cope with fluctuations in preferred foods. Finally I take a closer look at intragroup social interactions, including grooming, play, and intragroup agonism, because these activities are poorly described in the gibbon literature.

OVERVIEW OF THE GIBBON DAY

On the majority of clear mornings, the adult male gibbon, or an older juvenile male, sings a solo call before first light. Males often sing from their night tree, although occasionally they will move to another taller tree before they begin calling. Calls from one or several neighbor males may be heard at the same time. The other animals in the group arise just after first light. They then leave their sleeping position and hang from an exposed branch to urinate and defecate. Occasionally an individual might forage for a few minutes in its sleeping tree but more often exits into a neighboring tree to forage briefly for insects or young leaves. Shortly thereafter all members of the group begin to coalesce near the adult female's sleeping tree. Before full light the full group sets off to the first major feeding tree of the day, where they feed on fruit for 10 to 20 minutes. On cold mornings the group members sometimes sun for several minutes near their night tree before traveling to the first major feeding tree. Generally before midday the adult pair sings a duet.

The remainder of the day consists largely of travel between and visits to major feeding sites. Periods of travel may consist of slow dispersed foraging by all group members or, less often, rapid directional travel to a preferred food source. At least once during the day the group pauses for up to an hour for a prolonged bout of rest, play, or grooming. During social bouts gibbons typically pair off, although pairs will rearrange themselves over time. During this time of day infant gibbons make their first forays away from the mother. Approximately 3 hours before sunset the group rapidly departs its last feeding tree and moves directly toward a preferred sleeping area, where each animal selects a separate night tree. Night trees may be tens of meters apart or more. Less often two or three group members may share a single tree. Once having entered their night trees gibbons typically remain inactive other than scratching or grooming themselves, yet they may remain awake for up to several hours.

METHODS SPECIFIC TO THIS CHAPTER

In mid-January 1994 I began systematic observations on the activity of the gibbons in groups A and C. Chet, the subadult male of group C, emigrated in April 1994, and the small number of activity records for him have been removed from this analysis.

During focal follows 11 behavioral categories were recorded (see Table 2–4). These were pooled for the present analysis as follows: *feed* (feed and drink), *rest* (rest and autogroom), *travel* (travel and move), *social* (groom, play, and social contact), *vocalization* and *intergroup encounters*. Whenever the focal animal was engaged in social activity, I recorded the social partner; during grooming I recorded the direction of grooming as either groom or receive. Two of the behavioral categories listed in Table 2–4, *Interspecies Encounter* and *Individual Play*, together comprised less than 1% of the total activity time and are not included in this analysis.

I defined the *activity period* as the time from which the first animal was detected leaving its night tree until the last animal entered its night tree at the end of the day. When approaching the area of their night trees, group members tend to move apart; therefore, in practice, the activity period lasted until the focal animal entered its night tree because the other animals were generally out of view. On most days all animals appeared to enter their night trees within minutes of one another. The time of sunrise and sunset for Khao Yai National Park for the 12-month period from February 1994 to January 1995 was calculated using a Sunrise/Sunset Computer (Fly-By-Day Consulting, Inc.) and verified against published times periodically obtained from Thai newspapers.

Data Analysis

The results reported below are based on 10,832 behavioral records collected during 125 observation days, including 109 full-day follows, conducted from February 1994 to January 1995. To determine the diurnal activity cycle, focal animal data for each hour of the day were pooled monthly by social group and averaged. Gibbons were only rarely active before 0600 hours or after 1600 hrs and combined behavioral records for the duration before 0600 hrs and after 1600 hours represent less than 1% ($N = 72$) of the overall sample. In fact 7 of the 19 (37%) behavioral records for the hour before 0600 represent dawn calls sung by the A adolescent, Amadeus, during two days in May. Therefore I determined that the sample sizes for these two hourly blocks were too small to be representative of group activity and excluded the records for these hours from the analysis. For all other analyses data for each individual were pooled monthly. For each individual ($N = 8$) the percentage of time devoted to a given behavior, such as feeding, is the number of 5-minute time-point samples for which that behavior was recorded divided by the total number of samples for that animal during the month.

To determine if the gibbon activity budget varied significantly during the year, I used the Kruskal-Wallis test, a nonparametric statistic designed to compare the averages of several samples simultaneously (Fowler et al. 1998). Monthly correlations between groups and between the mean activity budget and habitat characteristics (e.g., fruit abundance) is described using the Spearman rank correlation coefficient (Siegel 1956). The two tests are corrected for ties.

RESULTS

Activity Period

The mean monthly activity period for the two groups was 8.7 hr. (SD = 0.8, $N = 12$). The longest activity period was in May, 10.0 hr., and the shortest was in November, 7.3 hr. Group A (mean = 9.1, SD = 0.8, range = 7.5–10.7, $N = 12$) was active longer than group C (mean = 8.4, SD = 0.7, range = 7.2–9.4, $N = 12$) in all months, but the monthly correlation between the two groups is high ($r_s = 0.85$; $p = 0.005$). There is a significant positive correlation between the mean monthly activity period and day length ($r_s = 0.71$; $p = 0.018$) and between mean monthly activity period and the overall abundance of ripe fruit in the environment ($r_s = 0.72$; $p = 0.017$). Gibbons left their night trees within 15 minutes on either side of sunrise in all months. Relative to the time of sunrise, night-tree departure was delayed during rainy months ($r_s = -0.63$; $p = 0.036$). On average, gibbons entered night trees 3.4 hr. (SD = 0.4, $N = 12$) before sunset. They entered night trees earliest in November, 4.0 hr. before sunset, and latest during May, 2.8 hr. before sunset. Night-tree entry is not related to monthly rainfall ($r_s = -0.27$; $p = 0.375$).

Annual Activity Budget

On an annual basis Khao Yai gibbons divided their activity period as follows: Feed 32.6%, Rest 26.2%, Travel 24.2%, Social Activity 11.3%, Vocalization 4.0%, and Intergroup Encounter 1.9%. The two groups differed slightly in the way they divided their day. Group C fed, traveled, and engaged in social activity somewhat more frequently, whereas group A engaged in higher rates of rest, vocal behavior, and intergroup encounter (Figure 3–1).

Diurnal Activity Cycle

Rates of feeding and of travel were greatest in the morning just after animals had left their night trees and again just before entering night trees at the end of the day (Figure 3–2). Rates of resting behavior were largely consistent over the middle of the day, showing a slight increase during the morning (0700–0900 hours) following the first feeding bout. Social behavior occurred at a low rate until after the first feeding bout of the day then remained at a constant level until 1400 hours when it began to subside. Vocal behavior and intergroup encounters occurred at a low rate at all times but were more prevalent before 1200 hours. Because pooling data over all months can mask changes in the diurnal pattern, I compared diurnal activity cycles also across seasons. In the case of social behavior there

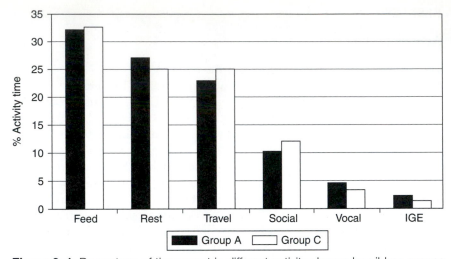

Figure 3–1 Percentage of time spent in different activity classes by gibbon groups A and C. (IGE = Intergroup Encounters.)

was a marked difference in the diurnal activity profile during the hot season, March to May. Although there was a small peak in social activity around midmorning in all three seasons, during the hot season gibbons devoted much of the afternoon hours to social activity (Figure 3–3). During the period from 1100 to 1500 hours gibbons devoted an average of 26% of each hour to grooming and play.

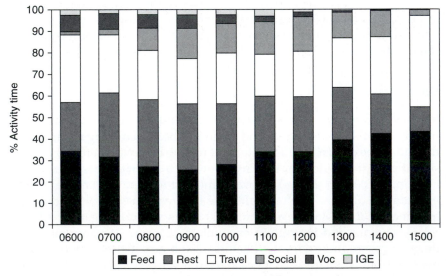

Figure 3–2 Diurnal activity cycle. (IGE = Intergroup Encounters.)

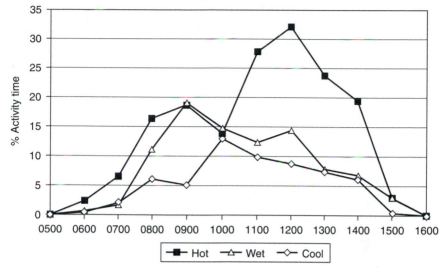

Figure 3–3 Diurnal variation in social activity by season.

Monthly Activity Budget

On average the proportion of the activity period gibbons devoted to feeding, resting, travel, social activity, and intergroup encounters varied significantly over the course of the year (Table 3–1). For example feeding time in November (42.0%) was almost twice that in May (21.8%). Time at rest followed a similar pattern (November, 35.7%; March, 13.7%), whereas the pattern was reversed in the case of travel (November, 18.3%; March, 29.4%), social behavior (November, 2.6%; May, 19.9%), and intergroup encounters (December, 0.2%; April, 4.0%). Vocal activity (November, 1.1%; April, 6.5%) followed a pattern similar to travel, social behavior, and intergroup encounters, but variation across months was not found to be significant.

Activity Budget and Resource Abundance. Over the course of the year there was a negative correlation between the amount of fruit available in the environment and feeding time (Table 3–2). That is, the lower the overall abundance of fruit in the forest, the more of their activity budget gibbons devoted to feeding. The reverse is true with respect to time spent in non-subsistence behaviors, including social and vocal activity and intergroup encounters. On the other hand if we compare the monthly activity budget with the abundance of flowers, we see that the correlations reverse themselves. When flowers were most abundant, gibbons spent a greater proportion of their activity time feeding and a smaller proportion in social and vocal activity. This stands to reason given that fruit and flowers are generally available at different times, with fruiting following flowering

Table 3–1 Average Percentage of Time Spent in Major Activities by Khao Yai Gibbons

	Feed	Rest	Travel	Social	Vocal	Intergroup Encounter
February 1994	33.4	16.4	25.5	17.6	4.5	2.5
March 1994	37.4	13.7	29.4	14.3	2.6	2.6
April 1994	26.6	19.1	24.9	18.9	6.5	4.0
May 1994	21.8	25.4	25.4	19.9	4.8	2.7
June 1994	26.4	22.6	27.0	16.3	4.5	3.1
July 1994	27.1	25.0	26.2	14.8	4.6	2.3
August 1994	34.5	28.8	22.9	8.9	4.4	0.5
September 1994	36.0	26.7	25.9	5.8	4.8	0.9
October 1994	32.3	34.7	20.2	6.2	4.3	2.3
November 1994	42.0	35.7	18.3	2.6	1.1	0.3
December 1994	38.1	33.6	20.2	5.3	2.6	0.2
January 1995	35.2	32.5	24.1	4.6	3.0	0.6
Mean	32.5	26.3	24.1	11.3	4.0	1.8
SD	5.9	7.4	3.3	6.3	1.4	1.4
H[a]	**	**	*	**	NS	*

NS = Not significant
[a] Kruskal-Wallis Test (df = 11)
*$p \leq 0.05$
** $p \leq 0.001$

(see Figure 2–4). There is also a significant negative correlation between travel time and the abundance of young leaves.

Age-Sex Differences in Activity Budget

On an annual basis all age classes devoted the greatest proportion of their activity budget to feeding with the exception of adult males, which rested

Table 3–2 Month-to-Month Correlation Between Mean Activity Time and Resource Abundance

Activity	Fruit	Flowers	Young Leaves
Feed	−0.688*	0.674*	0.406
Rest	−0.435	0.372	0.343
Travel	0.485	−0.341	−0.660*
Social	0.632*	−0.639*	−0.329
Vocal	0.755*	−0.670*	−0.220
Intergroup encounter	0.680*	−0.511	−0.323

Spearman rank correlation coefficient corrected for ties ($N = 12$)
* $p \leq 0.05$

more than they fed (Table 3–3). Juvenile gibbons traveled more and rested less than any other age-sex class. It is important to remember that, as I have defined it, the category travel includes both movement within and locomotion between trees. In fact juvenile gibbons were highly active in both contexts. During bouts of feed, rest, and social activity, juvenile gibbons routinely changed positions within the tree and engaged in brief forays into other trees, even feeding trees, before rejoining the remainder of the group. This is less true of adolescent gibbons, although they too traveled more and rested less than adults.

Rates of social behavior were highest among juveniles (13.7%) and lowest among adult females (9.3%). But it is important to note that during the period of observation the female of each study group had a dependent infant, which was recorded as social partner only during times when it was moving independent of its mother (e.g., during bouts of play with older animals). Thus a certain amount of female social time may have gone unrecorded. As the study progressed, the infants of both social groups gradually increased the amount of time they were free of the female (although both infants continued to be carried by the female during travel until the end of the study at which time they were 14 and 15 months old).

Rates of vocal activity and intergroup encounters also varied as a function of age-sex class. Whereas males and females devoted comparable amounts of time to vocalizing, rates of intergroup encounters among males (3.6%) were over three times that of females (1.1%). Juvenile gibbons spent very little time either singing or participating in agonistic intergroup encounters, although they did participate in bouts of play and grooming with members of neighboring groups. In contrast adolescent gibbons sang regular dawn calls and often participated in agonistic encounters with adult males. Vocal activity and intergroup encounters will be considered in detail in Chapter 6. In the following section I take a closer look at intragroup social activity.

Table 3–3 Average Percentage of Time Spent in Major Activities by Khao Yai Gibbons by Age-Sex Class

Activity	Males	Females	Adolescents	Juveniles
Feed	28.9	33.2	33.5	34.6
Rest	33.1	29.4	23.5	18.7
Travel	18.5	22.7	24.3	31.1
Social	11.3	9.3	10.7	13.7
Vocal	4.6	4.3	5.7	1.2
Intergroup encounter	3.6	1.1	2.2	0.6
Total	100.0	100.0	100.0	100.0

A juvenile gibbon scans the environment, while the adult pair grooms to his right.

Intragroup Social Interactions

Social activity was divided into three subclasses: *groom, play,* and *social contact*. The majority of gibbon social time was comprised of grooming, which made up 6.2% of total activity time, and play, which accounted for 4.1%. The remainder of social activity was made up of social contact, 0.6%, and otherwise-unspecified social activity, 0.3%. Social activity varied considerably based on age (Table 3–4). Adults groomed far more than they played. Adolescent gibbons balanced their time between the two activities, whereas among juveniles the rate of play far exceeded that of grooming.

Table 3–4 Average Percentage of Time Spent in Social Activities by Khao Yai Gibbons by Age-Sex Class

Social Behavior	Males	Females	Adolescents	Juveniles
Grooming	9.3	6.5	5.5	3.7
Play	1.1	1.6	4.6	9.1
Contact	0.8	0.7	0.4	0.6

Grooming.   All group members engaged in grooming bouts, which often occurred just after feeding visits and lasted for periods of up to 1 hour. Grooming bouts generally consisted of alternating turns, often of less than a minute in duration, between two individuals. Less often three or more animals would all groom together. This typically occurred when a juvenile interrupted an ongoing bout of grooming between two older animals, one of which would typically turn its attention to the juvenile. On average 37%

An adult female grooms a juvenile.

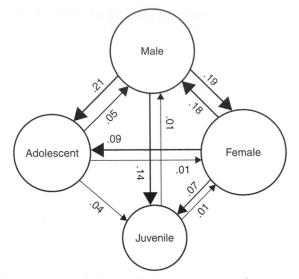

Figure 3–4 Mean grooming frequency between group members as a percentage of all grooming records.

of all grooming records involved mutual grooming between adult pair mates, with females grooming males almost as often as they were groomed by them (Figure 3–4). The pattern, however, differs slightly between the two pairs. In group A the female groomed the male more often than the male groomed the female, whereas the reverse is true in group C (Table 3–5). In both groups males spent more time grooming adolescents and juveniles combined than they spent grooming their mates. In fact the A male, Fearless, groomed the adolescent Amadeus at twice the rate that he groomed his pair mate, Andromeda.

Play.   Play behavior, which includes chasing, wrestling, slapping, and biting, was primarily exhibited by adolescents and juveniles. Adults of both sexes were occasionally drawn into play bouts by younger gibbons, but more often the adults would groom as the adolescent and juvenile played together. As the infants became more independent of their mothers, they increasingly became the focus of the juvenile gibbons' attention. The most common form of play between adolescent and juvenile gibbons was wrestle play, which involved each participant hanging from one arm and grappling, pulling, and hitting with their free hand and feet. Wrestle play also included mock bites and nearly constant but quiet squeals and growls. Bouts of wrestling were typically offset by rapid back-and-forth chases. Although these chases might continue from one tree to another, more often they were confined to a single tree crown with gibbons chasing

Table 3–5 Individual Grooming Time as a Percentage of All Grooming Records

	Receive				
	Group A				
	Male	*Female*	*Adolescent*	*Juveniles*	*Total*
Male		16	32	14	62
Female	18		6	6	31
Adolescent	4	0		2	6
Juvenile	1	0	0		1
	Group C				
	Male	*Female*	*Adolescent*	*Juvenile*	*Total*
Male		22	10	15	48
Female	17		12	8	37
Adolescent	6	2		6	14
Juvenile	1	1	0		2

each other around the trunk of the tree. During this study play between juveniles and infants always took the form of wrestling. Their limited mobility meant that infants were unable to retreat and rough play bouts were often interrupted by the adult female. Rates of both grooming and play dropped with the onset of the cool season, but rates of play seem to have been most affected; play behavior accounted for less than 1% of activity time from October to January (Figure 3–5).

Social Contact. Social contact is defined as actual physical contact between one or more individuals. This typically occurred as a prelude to grooming or as an interlude between direction changes during grooming bouts. I did not record "close proximity" or "sitting together" (cf. Palombit 1996) as a subclass of social activity. Had I, the overall rate of social behavior would have been higher.

Intragroup Agonism. In contrast to affiliative social interactions, agonistic (or aggressive) interactions within gibbon social groups were extremely rare and never recorded during time samples. I recorded only 10 instances (over 12 months) in which animals were actively chased, slapped, or grabbed by one of the other members of their social group (Table 3–6). Such cases were typically accompanied also by squeals or screams from the targeted animal. In one case the target was not identified. In all other cases the principal target of the attack was an adolescent male, and all but two attacks occurred in the context of feeding bouts. In 5 of the 10 cases

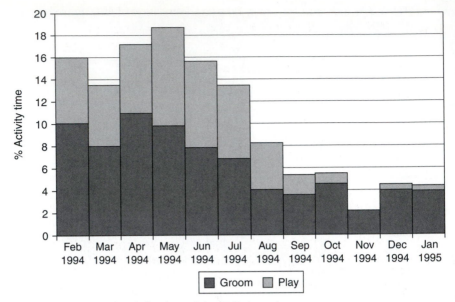

Figure 3–5 Annual variation in social activity by category.

From Thad Bartlett, "Intragroup and Intergroup Social Interactions in White-Handed Gibbons," *International Journal of Primatology* 24, no. 2 (2003): 239–259. Reproduced with kind permission of Springer Science and Business Media.

Table 3–6 Intragroup Agonistic Encounters by Gibbons of Groups A and C

Group	Month	Target	Context
A	March	Adolescent	Adult female slaps at adolescent while feeding on column of termites.
A	April	Adolescent	Adult male chases adolescent from drinking hole.
C	July	Adolescent	Adolescent squeals and retreats from adult male during travel.
C	August	Adolescent	Adult male attacks and grapples with adolescent in feeding tree.
C	August	Adolescent	Adult male chases adolescent from feeding tree.
A	August	Adolescent	Adult female chases adolescent from feeding tree.
C	December	Adolescent/ Juvenile	Adolescent and juvenile fight in feeding tree; adolescent exits tree when male approaches.
A	December	Adolescent	Adolescent squeals and retreats from unidentified adult while singing solo.
A	January	Adolescent/ Juvenile	Both immatures chased by adult female in feeding tree.
A	January	Unknown	Squeals and chasing out of view.

the aggressor was an adult male; in 3 cases, an adult female; and in one case the adolescent, Christopher, and juvenile, Caleb, of group C fought over a location within a feeding tree. While they grappled, the C male, Cassius, approached the immatures, and Christopher dropped from the crown and did not reenter the tree. In one case the adolescent Amadeus was chased by an A adult after singing a dawn call, although the aggressor was not clearly seen. Finally in three cases in addition to the aggressive encounters described, adolescents were excluded from the crowns of small feeding trees, although other group members fed. In each case the adolescent moved to edge of the crown from an adjacent tree but did not enter the tree until the other group members had finished feeding.

Avoidance Behavior and Emigration by the Subadult Chet.   Although none of the agonistic encounters I witnessed involved the subadult male Chet, Chet was displaced from grooming dyads on four occasions by Cassius before emigrating from group C in April 1994—twice while grooming with the adult female and twice while grooming with Christopher. There was no chasing or contact aggression in any of these cases, but Chet appeared weary of Cassius on each occasion.

DISCUSSION

Activity Budgets and Resource Availability

As expected, the study animals altered their activity patterns in accordance with annual changes in the availability of ripe fruit. When fruit was abundant, the animals spent more time engaged in nonsubsistence-related behaviors, such as grooming, playing, singing, and encounters with neighboring groups. Alternatively when fruit was scarce, they spent more of their activity time feeding. As described earlier a similar pattern of energy conservation during periods of food shortage has been identified in an array of species (Robinson 1986; Terborgh 1986; Overdorff 1993; Defler 1995; Doran 1997). Unlike many primates, however, gibbons sharply curtailed activity time too. The mean activity period ranged from 10.0 hr. in May, when fruit was plentiful, to 7.3 hr. in November, when fruit was scarce. One of the assumptions of traditional models in optimal foraging theory is that animals have a fixed amount of time each day to eat as much as they can (Schoener 1971; Richard 1985). Although gibbons did have more time for nonsubsistence activities, such as grooming and play, during the periods when ripe fruit was plentiful, they never fully maximized energy intake. For example even in months when ripe fruit was abundant, Khao Yai gibbons entered night trees nearly 3 hours before sunset. In this regard gibbons may be viewed not as energy maximizers, but as time minimizers. That is, they balance their energy budget by limiting energy expenditure rather than spending as much time as possible acquiring food.

The fact that gibbons enter night trees early compared with sympatric primates is well described (Gittins and Raemaekers 1980), but the reasons for this pattern remain unclear. One possibility is that a short activity period is necessitated by constraints imposed by territoriality (Raemaekers 1979). Gibbon territories are small relative to frugivorous primates of similar body size, and gibbons travel back and forth across their entire range at regular intervals (see Chapter 5). During periods of fruit abundance such intensive use of their range is easily accommodated because there is more food available than gibbons could possibly exploit. On the other hand during periods of low fruit abundance when food patches are more sparsely distributed, increased foraging time would translate into much more intensive use of the available resources. Perhaps gibbons are only able to ensure continued access to favored resources by exploiting their ranges less intensively during these periods. Whether a short activity period characterizes all territorial and monogamous species is unknown, but Pollock (1977) reports that the activity period of indri (*Indri indri*), a pair-living prosimian, ranges between 5 and 11 hr.

Activity Period and Predator Pressure

An alternative explanation for the short activity period exhibited by gibbons involves predation pressure (Richard 1985; Reichard 1998). According to Richard (1985) primates might minimize feeding time if "they must expose themselves to predators in order to acquire food; under such conditions, they should try to meet their needs as quickly as possible to retreat to a safer area" (p. 204). Khao Yai gibbons are certainly wary of predators (Reichard 1998; Uhde and Sommer 2002). During my study animals regularly gave mild alarms (one or a short series of hoots) when raptors flew overhead. Yet no predatory attack was ever made on a gibbon during my observations, and most of the raptors observed would have been too small to represent a threat to any but the smallest infant. Gibbons respond more strongly to arboreal snakes, occasionally alarming for periods of 1 hour or more (C. Lourdesamy pers. comm.). Large pythons, such as those found in Khao Yai, could easily take an infant, and Schneider's (1906 cited in Uhde and Sommer 2002) discovery of a fully grown siamang in the belly of a python indicates that even adults are vulnerable. In addition gibbons frequently responded to the alarm calls of other species, both arboreal (e.g., squirrels) and terrestrial (e.g., barking deer).

The potential threat of terrestrial predators is further supported by the hesitance of gibbons to come to the ground. During the period of my study I saw a gibbon on the forest floor on two occasions. In one case the A male, Fearless, was forced to the ground during a territorial encounter. Despite my proximity, he did not respond with alarm, although he quickly climbed back into the canopy. In the second instance the group C infant, Cyrana, who was approximately 14 months old at the time, fell from a height of over 20 m during a bout of social activity. The infant hit several branches on the way to the ground and lay motionless for a few moments once she had landed. The initial response of the other group members was to sing an alarm call. Subsequently as they continued to sing, all group members, including the infant's mother, Cassandra, moved low in the canopy. During the observation I backed away to a distance of approximately 20 m. Despite my moving away (perhaps because I was still too close), Cassandra was completely unwilling to move to the ground to recover her infant, even after Cyrana had regained consciousness and started squealing. Cassandra grabbed Cyrana only after the infant had crawled on all fours to a nearby sapling and climbed a couple of meters off the ground. In my experience the only other time gibbons regularly came close to the ground was when immatures from neighboring groups joined in play bouts (see Bartlett 2000; Chapter 6). Adults typically do not participate in these encounters. The willingness of young gibbons to engage in this high-risk behavior may be because of the added vigilance of the extra adults.

The two study groups divided their activity budgets in much the same way, yet they systematically differed in the length of their activity periods. On average group A was active 39.4 min. (or 8%) longer each day than group C. This is comparable with the difference reported by Reichard (1998) for the same two study groups two years earlier. The reason for this difference is unclear, although a difference in the degree of habituation between the two groups is one possibility. If I were seen as a threat, group C may have acted to minimize its activity period. In fact, group C was more easily lost and, especially at the beginning of my study, often engaged in long hurried travel bouts just before entering night trees. Group A, on the other hand, has been the subject of multiple long-term studies (see Brockelman et al. 1998) and as a result was completely accustomed to the presence of human observers. Thus differences in activity patterns between groups may further support the role of predator pressure in determining activity period in gibbons.

Additional evidence that gibbons are vulnerable to predators comes from research by Reichard (1998), who observed the sleeping habits of Khao Yai gibbons from 1992 to 1993. According to Reichard two aspects of gibbon sleep habits demonstrate the importance of predator pressure in shaping gibbon activity patterns. First, gibbon sleeping trees, particularly those used by females with infants, are among the tallest trees in the forest (see also Ahsan 2001). Tall trees often extend above the canopy limiting avenues of approach. Second, despite long hours of inactivity, gibbons are remarkably still (or at least inactive) when confined to their night trees. Reichard interprets these aspects as cryptic antipredator behavior. Taken together, the observations from Khao Yai stand in stark contrast to the often-held view that gibbons are largely free of predator pressure (Carpenter 1940; Ellefson

1974; van Schaik and van Hooff 1983; Leighton 1987). If predator pressure is sufficiently high, it may well be that gibbons minimize activity time to limit risk. In fact, they may specifically retire 2–3 hours before sunset year round to ensure that they are in night trees before nocturnal predators become active (Caine 1987; Reichard 1998).

Nevertheless predation pressure alone cannot explain why gibbon activity periods vary according to fruit availability. One question that remains is whether gibbons store calories in the form of fat during periods of fruit abundance as, for example, orangutans do (Leighton 1993; Knott 1998), which might account, in part, for longer activity periods when abundance is high.

Age-Sex Differences in Activity Budgets

Sex differences in activity budgets were slight, but in the expected direction. Among mammals, including primates, males and females have different energetic demands. Males in most ape species are larger than females and spend a greater period of time feeding as a result [e.g., *Pongo pygmaeus* (Rodman 1977); *Pan troglodytes* (Ghiglieri 1984)]. But in most of the smaller primates even among sexually dimorphic species, males generally feed less and rest more than females (Clutton-Brock 1977). One likely explanation is that the energetic demands of pregnancy and lactation mean that females must spend a greater proportion of their activity

A female gibbon carries her infant during travel.

period feeding (Altmann 1980; Strier 1987a). Just before the onset of this study the adult females of both groups gave birth to an infant and were lactating and carrying infants during the full period of data collection. On an annual basis both of the adult females fed for a greater percentage of their activity budget than they rested, whereas the reverse was true of the adult males. The high rates of resting behavior by males might also indicate a higher rate of vigilance—although vigilance per se was not measured in this study. Females may further compensate for high energy demands through priority of access to feeding sites (see Chapter 5).

Gibbon Social Behavior

As I have described elsewhere (Bartlett 2003) Khao Yai gibbons engage in relatively high rates of affiliative intragroup social behavior compared with other gibbon populations. On an annual basis Khao Yai gibbons devoted 11% of their activity period to social behavior. Although hylobatids have often been characterized as engaging in especially low levels of sociality (Leighton 1987; Chivers 2001), a recent review of 60 diurnal group-living primate species determined that most primates "devote less than 10% of their activity budget to active social interactions" (Sussman et al. 2005: 84). Only spider monkeys, macaques, leaf monkeys, and chimpanzees devoted appreciably more time (>15%) to social activity than Khao Yai gibbons. Moreover, in some months rates of sociality among gibbons reached as high as 20%. A seasonal comparison indicates that the high rates of social activity during the hot season were a result of long bouts of play and grooming during the afternoon hours. In contrast, rates of both play and grooming fell off during the cool season. For example social behavior accounted for only 3% of activity time in November. Play behavior, which is comprised of high-energy bouts of wrestling and chasing, appears to have been especially limited when ripe fruit was scarce, which is consistent with research on other primates (Robinson 1986; Defler 1995). Rates of sociality also varied as a function of age and sex. Adolescent and juvenile gibbons engaged in high rates of play behavior, whereas adults devoted much more of their social time to grooming.

Grooming. Reichard and Sommer (1994) have argued that grooming serves a hygienic rather than a social function in gibbons. They report that gibbons groomed areas that recipients could not see, such as the upper arms and face, disproportionately. Based on similar observations Carpenter (1940) commented, "It is interesting to note that precisely these areas are most difficult for an animal to reach during self-grooming" (p. 261). Although it seems likely that social grooming in gibbons serves a hygienic function, the disparity in grooming effort among age-sex classes suggests that social relationships play an important role in determining the direction and frequency of grooming, if not vise versa. In particular the adult males of both groups (a) overall spent more time grooming than other animals and (b) devoted more time grooming immatures (adolescents and juveniles combined) than they devoted to their pair-mate. Even if the only function of social grooming in gibbons is hygiene, it is significant that much of the responsibility for this care falls to the resident male.

According to Kleiman (1977) who was among the first to consider the role of fathers in the evolution of monogamy in mammals, not all forms of paternal care are equal. Specifically she distinguished between two forms of parental investment, indirect and direct. "Indirect paternal investment includes nest-building and defense of home range or nest, whereas direct interactions involve both proximity and responsiveness to young" (p. 54). White-handed gibbon males never carry infants during travel as is common in siamangs (Chivers 1974; Dielentheis et al. 1991) and pair-bonded New World monkeys (Wright 1986). For this reason most investigators have concluded that gibbons lack direct parental care. They therefore dismiss the role of paternal care in the evolution of gibbon social systems (e.g., van Schaik and Dunbar 1990). The grooming effort by male gibbons at Khao Yai suggests that parental investment by male gibbons has been underestimated.

A second putative social function of grooming in gibbons is that it contributes to pair-bond formation and maintenance (Geissmann and Orgeldinger 2000). On average, grooming between adults accounted for

A juvenile gibbon looks away as the adult male presents for grooming.

37% of total grooming time in this study, more than grooming between any other dyad. In group A, however, grooming between Fearless and Amadeus actually exceeded that between Fearless and his mate, Andromeda. These two relationships also differed in terms of reciprocity. Whereas grooming effort by the A adults was equal, the relationship between Fearless and Amadeus was decidedly one sided. If we assume that reciprocal grooming is an important element of pair-bond formation, these findings are not surprising. But reciprocal grooming between gibbon pairs is not reported universally among gibbons. In fact, Palombit (1996) determined, in two white-handed gibbon groups at Ketambe, Sumatra, that male pair mates groomed females far more than the reverse. Among sympatric siamangs, on the other hand, the time devoted to the grooming relationship was more equal (see also Gittins and Raemaekers 1980). Palombit (1996) argues that differences in grooming effort indicate that white-handed gibbon males contribute more to the maintenance of the pair bond than females do, whereas in siamangs the effort is more equal. He suggests that higher rates of intragroup feeding competition may indicate a higher cost for bonding in the smaller-bodied white-handed gibbons. "Thus," he concludes, "the pair bond of the white-handed gibbon seems less an arrangement in which a female benefits substantially from associating with a male than one in which she tolerates his presence." It is important to note that the time-sample method I employed is less appropriate for studies of social interaction. For example I have no information on approach or initiation of grooming bouts. Nevertheless time samples are appropriate for comparing rates of behavior, and it is clear that the disparity in grooming reciprocity reported by Palombit was not found in the two groups described here. It may be relevant that both of the males in this study spent more time overall grooming immatures than they did grooming their pair mates; they may have groomed immatures at the expense of grooming the female. It is also possible that reciprocity varies over the life of the pair-bond, which may account for variation between study sites.

Play. On an annual basis juvenile gibbons spent over 9% of their time at play. This is twice the rate of adolescents on average and nearly six times as much as adults. Why juveniles devote so much time to play is a question that has generated a considerable amount of interest within behavioral ecology (Byers and Walker 1995; Spinka et al. 2001). Play behavior is costly both in terms of energy expenditure and because it entails certain risks, such as increased vulnerability to predation and injury (Fagen 1993). The potential costs of play suggest that the rewards are high. According to Fagen (1993:185) "Since animals readily stop playing for extended periods, it seems likely that any form of play lacking direct benefits would be eliminated by natural selection over evolutionary time." Play is generally interpreted as practice for the physical challenges (Byers and Walker 1995;

Thompson 1998) and/or social challenges (Spinka et al. 2001; Sharpe 2005) encountered later in life. Arboreal locomotion is inherently dangerous and probably particularly so for gibbons, which routinely lose contact with supports during travel (Schultz 1939; Treesucon 1984). I did not see the events that led up to Cyrana's fall (described earlier in this chapter), but Treesucon (1984) twice saw an infant gibbon fall to the ground while traveling. In each case the infant was unsuccessful in crossing a gap previously crossed by its mother. One role of play may be to improve locomotor skills for brachiation. Practice may be essential for proper cognitive and muscular development (Byers and Walker 1995). Furthermore locomotor agility may be particularly important during conflicts between neighbors, which are rare compared with routine travel but are assumed to have important consequences for fitness. Conflict also involves unexpected events that can be simulated only during social play (Spinka et al. 2001). Given the proposed benefits of play, future studies would benefit by focusing on age and sex differences in the frequency and styles of play seen in gibbons.

Intragroup Aggression.   Although agonistic interactions between primates have received considerable attention in discussions of the evolution of primate behavior, rates of agonism are generally quite low relative to rates of affiliation (Sussman et al. 2005). Even gibbon males, which take the lead in range defense, spend far more time in affiliative interactions than in agonistic ones. Rates of intragroup agonism are low by any standard. When they do occur, my observations suggest that they occur over food access and that adolescent gibbons are disproportionately targeted. Of course the absence of a subadult in either group during most of the study means there was inadequate opportunity to observe adult–subadult interactions. The few occasions when the C subadult, Chet, was displaced by the C male Cassius before the time when Chet emigrated did not occur in the context of feeding. It has been argued that dispersal by maturing subadults is hastened by aggression from the same-sex parent. Chet's weariness of Cassius is consistent with this finding and hints at prior agonism that was not witnessed. On the other hand the adolescent male in group A was displaced by the adult female on three occasions, all during feeding bouts. Given that a juvenile gibbon was targeted just once, it seems likely that the peripheralization of subadult group members is a gradual process that starts with intolerance at shared feeding sites and escalates to the point where they are excluded even from affiliative interactions.

CHAPTER SUMMARY AND CONCLUSIONS

Like many other frugivorous primates, Khao Yai gibbons responded to seasonal fluctuations in the abundance of ripe fruit. When ripe fruit was abundant, gibbons were more active. During the hot season (March–May) in particular, Khao Yai gibbons engaged in long bouts of grooming and play. When resources were scarce, Khao Yai gibbons spent more of their activity time feeding and less time engaged in nonsubsistence behaviors. Unlike many other primates, gibbons also sharply curtailed activity time when fruit was scarce. Gibbons retired to night trees well before sunset even when ripe fruit was abundant. This may represent a response to predation pressure or a result of limits imposed on foraging by territoriality. Social activity varied as a function of age-sex class. Males spent more time grooming than other group members and spent more time grooming younger gibbons than they did females. These findings suggest that the role of direct male parental care in the evolution of gibbon social organization has been underestimated.

4

Diet and Feeding Behavior

In summary, observations and examinations of stomach contents show
that gibbons are principally frugiverous but that a considerable amount of leafy
mash is also eaten.

—Carpenter (1940:195)

The feeding behavior of gibbons has been studied more than any other aspect of their behavior. Broadly speaking, gibbons are best described as *frugivore-folivores*. In all species of gibbons, except for crested gibbons and Malayan siamang, ripe fruit accounts for over half of the gibbon diet, whereas the remainder is comprised mostly of young leaves (Leighton 1987; Palombit 1992). But although the basic composition of the gibbon diet has long been known, the way gibbons respond to seasonal fluctuations in fruit availability has not been well documented. According to Chivers (1984) one reason for this omission is that the majority of gibbon field studies have been conducted in optimal environments characterized by relatively wet forest and high floristic diversity. In contrast Khao Yai National Park experiences a distinct period of low rainfall and reduced fruit abundance. As I described in Chapter 3 the fluctuations in fruit availability at Khao Yai correspond to clear changes in the activity profile of white-handed gibbons. Most notably Khao Yai gibbons reduced the time devoted to nonsubsistence behaviors when fruit abundance was lowest. In this chapter I focus on changes in diet and foraging behavior in the face of fluctuating food supplies.

Many primates sustain moderate drops in food availability by increasing day range (Marsh 1981; Robinson 1986; Boinski 1987), increasing foraging time, (Terborgh 1983; Overdorff 1993; Doran 1997), or increasing home-range size (Clutton-Brock 1977). As preferred resources become increasingly scarce, most primates are forced to alter their diet by including greater amounts of lower-quality items, often labeled *fallback foods* (van Schaik and Brockman 2005; Hanya et al. 2006). For frugivores this might entail feeding more heavily on nonreproductive plant parts, such as leaves, bark, pith, or sap. Alternatively some species are able to maintain high rates of fruit in the diet by making increased use of *keystone foods* (Gilbert 1980). Keystone plant resources represent a special class of fallback food that Terborgh (1986) defines as any reliable food item that plays a prominent role "in sustaining frugivores through periods of general food scarcity" (p. 339). Among primates palm nuts and figs are the foods most often identified as keystone resources (Terborgh 1983; Hemingway and Bynum 2005). For example Terborgh (1986) found that two frugivorous primates at Cocha Cashu, Peru, coped with seasonal food shortages differently. Whereas capuchins exploited palm nuts during lean periods, squirrel monkeys, which are too small to break into the hard outer husk of palm nuts, fed heavily from large fig trees.

Most studies of gibbon diet have determined that gibbons also rely heavily on figs, so much so, in fact, that some investigators argue that gibbons display a dietary preference for figs (MacKinnon and MacKinnon 1980; Chivers and Raemaekers 1986; Palombit 1997). This finding suggests that compared with squirrel monkeys (and many other frugivorous primates) gibbons seek out figs whenever they are available. If so, given the asynchronous fruiting pattern exhibited by figs, we might expect the diet and feeding behavior of gibbons to be relatively unaffected by overall fluctuations in fruit abundance.

Another perceived aspect of the gibbon feeding niche is their selection of small inconspicuous food sources, which is thought to allow them to avoid competition with sympatric primates (Leighton 1987; Chivers 2001). The fig trees typically exploited by gibbons, however, are very large (Gittins and Raemaekers 1980). Thus the suggestion that gibbons are both fig specialists and small-patch specialists is hard to reconcile (Bartlett 2007a). The primary goal of this chapter is to explore this seeming contradiction in the feeding behavior of white-handed gibbons. In so doing I will also describe the way gibbons cope with seasonal changes in food abundance.

OVERVIEW OF GIBBON FEEDING BEHAVIOR

In describing the foraging behavior of the agile gibbon, Gittins (1982) observes that "while foraging the gibbons may take food from almost every tree passed through" (p. 60). This is also true of the animals I studied;

Gibbons frequently feed while suspended below the fruit-bearing branches of a tree.

nevertheless the majority of feeding by Khao Yai gibbons occurs in discrete food patches, usually individual trees distributed throughout the home range. On entering a feeding tree, group members spread out to the peripheral branches, each selecting a separate part of the crown. Even as they move around the crown of the tree searching for food, each individual maintains several meters of distance from other animals. Gibbons generally feed from a suspensory position, rapidly placing individual fruit or handfuls of young leaves in their mouths with their free hand. When processing larger fruit or fruit with a thick rind, gibbons may occasionally move to a larger branch, where they sit while they eat the fruit with both hands. It is extremely rare for a gibbon to leave a feeding tree with unprocessed food in its hands or mouth. Feeding bouts last approximately 15 minutes before the full group leaves the tree, usually within minutes of one another. In larger trees the group often breaks into play or grooming dyads for a period of a few minutes. After a bout of social interaction the full group resumes feeding for a short period before exiting the tree. In smaller trees the full group may exit into an adjacent tree to rest, groom, or play and then return briefly to feeding before leaving the area. Between major feeding bouts, gibbons forage for young leaves, vine shoots, and insects. Among the insects eaten by gibbons are termites, which they eat by dipping the backs of their hands in marching columns and then licking the insects from their fur. Grubs, caterpillars, and other insects are extracted from rolled-up leaves or clumps of dead vegetation. Before entering night

Gibbons supplement their frugivorous diet with young leaves from trees and vines.

trees at the end of the day, gibbons sometimes visit two or more fruit trees in quick succession.

METHODS SPECIFIC TO THIS CHAPTER

Feeding data were collected using 5-minute instantaneous time-point sampling on focal animals. For each feeding record I identified the food class consumed by the focal animal, the total number of group members in the same tree (excluding infants), and the food species when known. Six food classes were recognized: *nonfig fruit, fig fruit, leaves, flowers, vine shoots,* and *insects*. Initially I distinguished between mature leaves and young leaves, but because mature leaves were rarely eaten by gibbons, I dropped this distinction in this analysis. Fig fruit were considered separately because of their putative importance to gibbons (Vellayan 1981; Chivers and Raemaekers 1986). I also noted whether a feeding site was a tree or woody climber. Gibbons were observed to feed on epiphytes, but this food class represented a negligible percentage of the total feeding time and, thus, is not considered here.

Because gibbons may feed from virtually any tree or climber they enter, I distinguished between major and minor feeding visits. *Major feeding visits* are visits to food patches during which the focal animal fed continuously for five or more minutes. Such patches are subsequently referred to as *major feeding sites*. Major feeding sites were marked at the time of use with flagging tape and later relocated, measured for diameter at breast height (DBH), identified to species when possible, and mapped relative to the trail system. DBH was used as an indicator of general patch size. For the purpose of this analysis a food patch is defined as the crown of a single tree, unless the crown is continuous with that of another individual of the same species. Various studies have shown that DBH is positively correlated with both crown volume (Leighton and Leighton 1983; Symington 1988; Chapman et al. 1992; but see Stashko and Dinerstein 1988) and fruit crop mass (Leighton 1993) in a variety of tropical tree species. In addition Chapman and co-workers (1992) conclude that measurement of tree diameter is the most consistent and time-efficient means of estimating food abundance in tropical forests. I made no attempt to measure patch size of woody climbers. In previous studies investigators have summed the DBHs of all supporting trees (e.g., Strier 1989), but this method was deemed unreliable for climber species in Khao Yai. Encounters with other social groups and other species during feeding were noted ad libitum.

Data Analysis

The following results are based on 3365 individual feeding records for groups A and C obtained during 125 observation days, including 109 full-day follows. Feeding data were pooled monthly by group. Khao Yai gibbons feed in cohesive parties and correlation between the two main study groups is high. Thus, reported values represent the mean of the two groups unless otherwise noted. Annual means represent the average of monthly means. The Spearman rank correlation coefficient (r_s) is used to evaluate the degree of monthly correspondence between seasonal trends in forest phenology and gibbon feeding behavior. All statistical values are corrected for ties.

RESULTS

Annual Diet

Over the course of the year Khao Yai gibbons fed on 101 different plant species; 29 of these species each accounted for at least 1% of the mean annual diet and 3 species each accounted for over 5%. Of the three most common plants in the diet the first was *Choerospondias axillaries*, or hog plum, which alone accounted for 9.2% of the annual diet. Fruit of *C. axillaris* were consumed over a three-month period, August to October. The second most common species, *Gironniera nervosa*, accounted for 9.0% of the annual diet and was exploited almost exclusively for young leaves, although small amounts of fruit and flowers were consumed. *G. nervosa* leaves were eaten in every month but one, and this species accounts for the majority of leafy matter in the gibbon diet at Khao Yai. The third most common species in the diet was *Prunus javanica,* which accounted for 6.1% of the annual diet. Trees of this species are generally very large with abundant fruit crops. All three species are common forest trees (Brockelman et al. 2001). Five different fig species (*Ficus* spp.) accounted for at least 1% of the annual diet, but this figure does not include several unidentified species. In all I estimate that gibbons fed from at least 13 different fig species. All identified plant species consumed during the study period are provided in Table 4–1.

Table 4–1 Tree and Woody Climber (W.C.) Species Fed In by Khao Yai Gibbons During the Study Period

Family/Species	Author(s)	Type	Part and Month Available
Anacardiaceae			
Choerospondias axillaris	Burtt and Hill	Tree	*Fruit:* August–October
Annonaceae			
Alphonsea boniana	Finet and Gagnep.	Tree	*Fruit:* June–August
			Flower: February–March
Desmos dumosus	(Roxb.) Saff. Var. glabrior Craib.	W.C.	*Fruit:* December–March
Miliusa lineate	(Craib) Ast.		*Fruit:* June–July
Platymitra macrocarpa	Boerl.	Tree	*Fruit:* July–August
Polyalthia simiarum	Benth. and Hook. f.	Tree	*Fruit:* May
			Leaf: January–February
Uvaria cordata	(Dun.) Alst.	W.C.	*Fruit:* June–July
Apocynaceae			
Melodinus cambodiensis	Pierre ex Spire.	W.C.	*Fruit:* February
Aquifoliaceae			
Ilex chevalieri	Tard.	Tree	*Fruit:* August
			Leaf: November
Celastraceae			
Salacia chinensis	Linn.	W.C.	*Leaf:* March–April, September
Dipterocarpaceae			
Dipterocarpus gracilis	Blume	Tree	*Flower:* January
			Leaf: November–December
Ebenaceae			
Diospyros glandulosa	Lace	Tree	*Fruit:* October–November
Elaeagnaceae			
Elaeagnus conferta	Roxb.	W.C.	*Fruit:* December–February
Elaeocarpaceae			
Sloanea sigun	(Bl.) K. Schum.	Tree	*Flower:* November

(Continued)

Table 4–1 Continued

Family/Species	Author(s)	Type	Part and Month Available
Euphorbiaceae			
Baccaurea ramiflora	Lour.	Tree	*Fruit:* April
Balakata baccata	(Roxb.) Esser	Tree	*Fruit:* May–July
Fagaceae			
Castanopsis acuminatissima	(Bl.) A. DC.	Tree	*Flower:* January
Flacourtiaceae			
Scolopia sp.		W.C.	*Fruit:* May
Guttiferae			
Calophyllum pisiferum	Planch. and Triana	Tree	*Fruit:* March
Garcinia benthamii	Pierre	Tree	*Fruit:* August–September
Leguminosae, Mimosoidae			
Acacia megaladena	Desv. var. indo-chinensis Niels.	W.C.	*Leaf:* February–March, June–August
Leguminosae, Papilionoideae			
Erythrina subumbrans	(Hassk.) Merr.	Tree	*Leaf:* June
Mucuna macrocarpa	Wall.	W.C.	*Flower:* February
Malvaceae			
Hibiscus macrophyllus	Roxb. ex Hornem.	Tree	*Fruit:* July–September
Meliaceae			
Sandoricum koetjape	(Burm. f.) Merr.	Tree	*Fruit:* June–July
Walsura robusta	Roxb.	Tree	*Leaf:* October–January
Moraceae			
Ficus altissima	Bl.	Tree	*Fruit:* April, November–December
Ficus annulata	Bl.	Tree	*Fruit:* March, August–September *Leaf:* February, April, November–December
Ficus kurzii	King	Tree	*Fruit:* February, September
Ficus nervosa	Hey. Ex Roth	Tree	*Leaf:* April
Ficus pumila	Linn.	W.C.	*Fruit:* December–February
Ficus tinctoria	Bl.	Tree	*Fruit:* November–January
Ficus vasculosa	Wall.	Tree	*Fruit:* March–April, October–November *Leaf:* November
Myristicaceae			
Knema elegans	Warb.	Tree	*Fruit:* April
Myrtaceae			
Cleistocalyx nervosum	(DC.) AJDH Kostermans	Tree	*Fruit:* June–July

(Continued)

Table 4–1 Continued

Family/Species	Author(s)	Type	Part and Month Available
Oleaceae			
Chionanthus ramiflorus	Roxb.	Tree	*Fruit:* December–January
Podocarpaceae			
Podocarpus neriifolius	D. Don	Tree	*Fruit:* May–June
Rhizophoraceae			
Carallia brachiate	(Lour.) Merr.	Tree	*Fruit:* January
Rosaceae			
Prunus arborea	(Bl.) Kalkm.	Tree	*Fruit:* February–March
Prunus javanica	(T. and B.) Miq.	Tree	*Fruit:* February–April
Rubiaceae			
Aidia densiflora	(Wall.) Masam.	Tree	*Fruit:* August–November
Anthocephalus chinensis	(Lam.) Rich. ex Walp.	Tree	*Fruit:* August–November
Sapindaceae			
Nephelium melliferum	Gagnep.	Tree	*Fruit:* April–May
Sarcospermataceae			
Sarcosperma arboretum	Benth.	Tree	*Fruit:* February–March
Symplocaceae			
Symplocos cochinchinensis	(Lour.) S. Moore	Tree	*Leaf:* November–December
Thymelaeaceae			
Aquilaria crassna	Pierre ex H. Lec.	Tree	*Fruit:* May–June
Ulmaceae			
Aphananthe cuspidate	(Bl.) Planch.	Tree	*Fruit:* August–September
Gironniera nervosa	Planch.	Tree	*Fruit:* January, July, October *Flower:* January *Leaf:* All Months
Vitaceae			
Tetrastigma laoticum	Gagnep.	W.C.	*Fruit:* October–December

On an annual basis the gibbon diet was divided as follows: nonfig fruit, 46.7%; fig fruit, 18.8%; leaves, 22.3%; insects, 8.7%; vine shoots, 2.2%; and flowers, 1.3%. Group C fed somewhat more heavily on figs and leaves, whereas group A spent almost twice as much time feeding on insects (Figure 4–1). Virtually all fruits eaten by gibbons were ripe, although gibbons did occasionally feed on unripe figs, most notably of the species *Ficus tinctoria*, the syconia of which were eaten unripe in November and ripe during December and January. During November a single *F. tinctoria* patch accounted for 54% of group A's feeding time, including two visits of over 2 hours each. While they fed heavily and consistently during the visit, the gibbons appeared to reject many or most of the unripe figs they tested. Besides bite marks, fallen fig fruit appeared ruptured. Although I

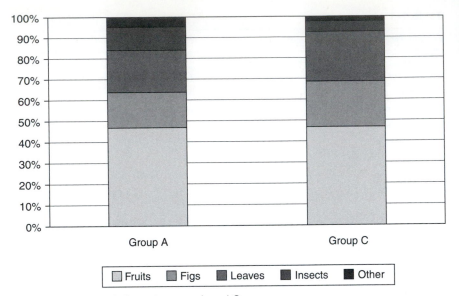

Figure 4–1 Annual diets of groups A and C.

cannot be sure, it seems as though these figs were being exploited for some other purpose, perhaps as a source of wasp larvae (see Redford et al. 1984). Because I could never verify the source of the gibbon's intense interest in these figs, these feeding observations were recorded as fig feeding; however, I removed this tree from subsequent analyses of patch use.

Major Feeding Visits. Major feeding visits accounted for 71% of total feeding time and just over 89% of fruit feeding time. Averaged across months, gibbons made 6.9 major feeding visits per day (SD = 0.95, range = 5.0−8.8), or 0.79 per hour (SD = 0.12, range = 0.63−1.02). The lowest number of patch visits per hour occurred during April when gibbons devoted most of their feeding time to *P. javanica* fruit. In contrast gibbons made the most patch visits per hour during August, when gibbons divided their feeding time between four highly favored fruit species, *Alphonsea boniana*, *Aphananthe cuspidata*, *Garcinia benthamii*, and *Choerospondias axillaris*.

To approximate the average patch occupancy time, each month I added the total number of feeding samples per patch visit and multiplied the sum by 5 minutes (the interval between time point samples). Based on this estimate gibbons spent 14.5 min. (SD = 2.7) feeding per patch visit. Compared across months, gibbons spent the least amount of time feeding per patch in May, 9.1 min., which is less than half the value for December, 18.9 min. There is a significant negative correlation between feeding time per visit and fruit abundance ($r_s = -0.80; p = 0.003$). In other words the greater the overall abundance of fruit in the environment, the less time gibbons

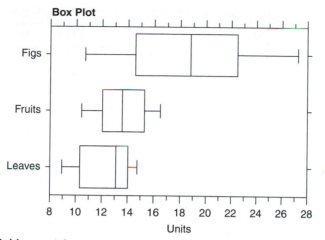

Figure 4–2 Mean patch occupancy time divided by food class.

spent feeding per food patch visit. The length of time gibbons spent feeding also varied as a product of food class. Visits to fig patches (mean = 18.9 min., SD = 6.1, range = 10.0–30.3) were longer than visits to either fruit (mean = 13.6 min., SD = 2.4, range = 8.9–18.1) or leaf patches (mean = 12.2 min., SD = 2.4, range = 7.5–15.0) (Figure 4–2). Most of this difference was the result of long visits to fig patches from September to January. Feeding visits to fig patches were longest in November (24.2 min.) and December (30.3 min.) when fruit abundance was lowest (Figure 4–3).

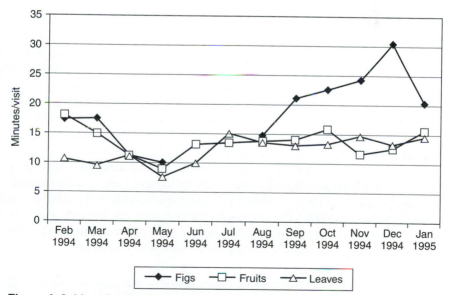

Figure 4–3 Mean feeding time per food patch for three food classes.

Table 4–2 Mean Monthly Diet Based on Percentage of Feeding Records

	Fruit	Fig	Leaf	Insect	Shoot	Flower
February 1994	34.1	30.8	18.6	10.0	1.4	5.1
March 1994	57.8	9.6	17.1	14.2	0.5	0.9
April 1994	39.2	13.9	29.7	15.7	1.2	0.3
May 1994	56.8	13.7	9.1	19.3	1.1	0.0
June 1994	82.0	0.0	5.9	10.0	1.7	0.3
July 1994	78.9	0.8	9.2	10.0	1.1	0.0
August 1994	59.2	11.0	20.3	7.5	1.9	0.0
September 1994	58.0	14.6	20.9	3.6	3.0	0.0
October 1994	48.8	3.3	39.1	4.0	4.3	0.7
November 1994	5.4	52.7	32.9	2.2	3.4	3.5
December 1994	9.4	45.9	36.7	3.3	4.1	0.5
January 1995	30.9	30.0	28.5	4.2	2.2	4.1
Mean	46.7	18.8	22.3	8.7	2.2	1.3
SD	24.0	17.3	11.1	5.5	1.3	1.8

Monthly Variation in Diet

The makeup of the gibbon diet varied considerably over the course of the year (Table 4–2). Nonfig fruit made up the bulk of the diet in most months with the exception of November and December when the percentage of feeding time devoted to this food class fell below 10% (Figure 4–4). November and December were also the only two months when the contribution of fig fruit to the diet exceeded that of nonfig fruit, although gibbons also fed heavily on figs in January and February. Following fruit gibbons devoted the majority of their feeding time to leaves, especially young leaves. Feeding time spent on insects was generally of tertiary importance, but from May through July gibbons spent more time feeding on insects than they did on leaves. In May, for example, gibbons spent 19.3% of their feeding time on insects and just 9.1% on leaves. From August to February, on the other hand, leaves far outweighed insects in terms of their contribution to the diet. Over all months there is a significant negative correlation between time spent feeding on insects versus leaves ($r_s = -0.67$, $p = 0.027$). In other words during months when gibbons fed extensively on insects, they spent little time foraging on leaves. Flowers were eaten almost exclusively in the cool season (November to February). Flower feeding was greatest in January and February when it accounted for approximately 4% of feeding time. Flowers were of negligible importance during the remainder of the year.

Diet and Resource Abundance. Over the course of the year the amount of feeding time devoted to nonfig fruit ($r_s = 0.63$, $p = 0.036$), leaves ($r_s = 0.69$,

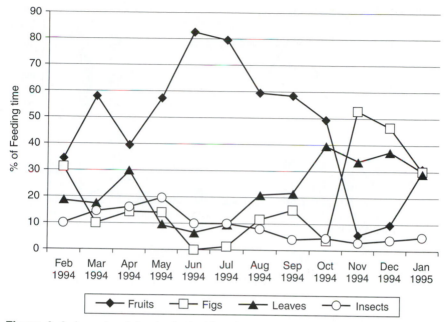

Figure 4–4 Annual variation in diet by Khao Yai gibbons.

$p = 0.021$), and flowers ($r_s = 0.78$, $p = 0.010$) correlates positively with the abundance of these food classes. In contrast the time spent feeding on fig fruit is negatively correlated with overall fruit abundance, although not significantly ($r_s = -0.52$, $p = 0.085$) (Figure 4–5).

Dietary Diversity

On average the single most important food species each month accounted for 37% (SD = 12, range = 22–56) of total gibbon feeding time, the most visited 5 species accounted for 83% (SD = 10, range = 65–96) of feeding time, and the most visited 10 species accounted for 96% (SD = 5, range = 83–100) of feeding time. The month with the highest diversity was December when the most visited species for each group was a *Ficus*. The month of lowest dietary diversity was October when *C. axillaris* fruit alone accounted for 56% of feeding time on average, 61% and 51% of the diet of groups A and C respectively.

Another measure of dietary diversity is the total number of different plant species consumed during each monthly sample. Because the number of observation days varied by month, I divided the total number of plant species eaten during a given monthly sample by the number of observation days for that month—this calculation yields the mean

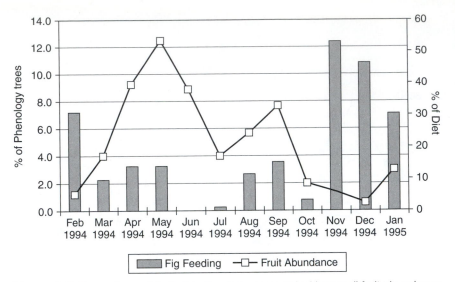

Figure 4–5 Percentage of fig fruit in the diet compared with overall fruit abundance.

number of new plant species eaten per observation day for each group. On an annual basis gibbon groups fed on 2.8 distinct species per day. There is a negative correlation between the number of food species consumed and the abundance of fruit, but this correlation is not significant ($r_s = -0.53$, $p = 0.081$). Nevertheless the four months of the cool season (November to February) represent four of the five highest ranked months in terms of the number of food species consumed per day (Figure 4–6). The lowest ranked month was October, at the end of the wet season, when gibbons fed on only 1.3 species per day. Although October too was a fruit-poor month, gibbons were able to maintain high amounts of fruit in their diet by feeding heavily on *C. axillaris*. This species was also eaten during August and September, but few other fruit species were available during October, which may account for the low dietary diversity in this month.

Dietary Selectivity

Twenty species (excluding figs) accounted for at least 1% of the mean annual diet of the two groups. Individual *Ficus* species are generally rare and occur at a density of much less than one individual per hectare and are not considered here. The average density of fruiting trees for these 20 species was approximately one individual per hectare (mean = 0.94, SD = 0.85, range = 0.0–2.7). The contribution of the same 20 species to the gibbon diet correlates positively with their density ($r_s = 0.51$; $p = 0.025$) (Figure 4–7).

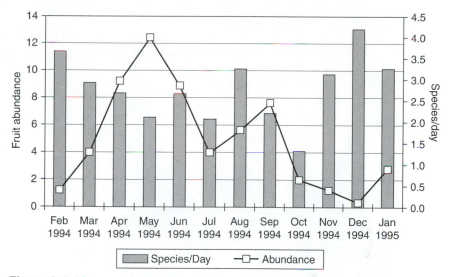

Figure 4–6 Mean number of new species eaten per day compared with overall fruit abundance.

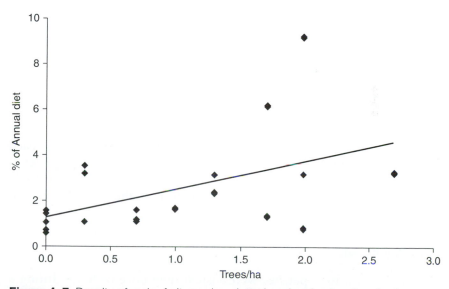

Figure 4–7 Density of major fruit species plotted against feeding time for the same species.

Major fruit species were typically available over a period of two to three months. As an illustration of this, Figure 4–8 is a plot of the percentage of feeding time devoted to the top 10 nonfig fruit species exploited by gibbons. In most months one or two fruit species dominated fruit-feeding time. Over the course of the year gibbons moved systematically from

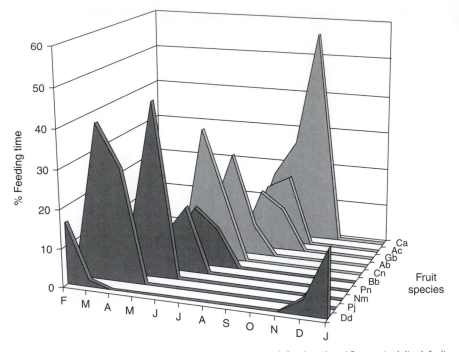

Figure 4–8 Percentage of feeding time accounted for by the 10 most visited fruit species in the diet of Khao Yai gibbons. Dd = *Desmos dumosus*; Pj = *Prunus javanica*; Nm = *Nephelium melliferum*; Pn = *Podocarpus neriifolius*; Bb = *Balakata baccata*; Cn = *Cleistocalyx nervosum*; Ab = *Alphonsea boniana*; Gb = *Garcinia benthamii*; Ac = *Aphananthe cuspidata*; Ca = *Choerospondias axillaris*.

one species to another as they became available. Five species were each eaten over a period of three or more months: *Desmos dumosus, Prunus javanica, Balakata baccata, Alphonsea boniana,* and *Choerospondias axillaris.* During November and December gibbons turned almost exclusively to fig fruit.

Fruit Patch Visits

Most individual food patches were visited only once or twice during a given monthly sample. But each month a particular individual fruit tree or climber was visited recurrently. On average the single most visited fruit patch accounted for 22% of monthly feeding time. Table 4–3 lists those individual fruit patches that accounted for the most feeding time each month for each study group. The frequency of visits to each patch is calculated by dividing the number of days gibbons were recorded within a given patch by the total number of observation days for the given group

Table 4–3 Frequency of Visits to the Most Heavily Exploited Fruit Patch Each Month

Month	Species	Type	Patch ID	Number of Days Visited	Number of Days Observed	Frequency	Feeding Time (%)
			Group A				
February 1994	*F. pumila*	Woody climber	22-113 (14)v	4	6	0.67	10.8
March 1994	*P. javanica*	Tree	03/21/94-02	7	7	1.00	33.1
April 1994	*F. altissima*	Tree	04/21/94-03	4	6	0.67	15.7
May 1994	*P. neriifolius*	Tree	05/19/94-02	5	7	0.71	16.7
June 1994	*C. nervosum*	Tree	PW #111	4	5	0.80	28.6
July 1994	*A. boniana*	Tree	25-086 (13)	5	5	1.00	20.0
August 1994	*A. cuspidata*	Tree	28-321 (08)	5	5	1.00	26.0
September 1994	*A. cuspidata*	Tree	22-113 (14)	6	6	1.00	24.8
October 1994	*C. axillaris*	Tree	RT #61	2	6	0.33	12.3
November 1994	*F. tinctoria*	Tree	11/24/94-03	5	6	0.83	54.3
December 1994	*Ficus* D5	Tree	12/20/94-01	2	6	0.33	12.3
January 1995	*F. pumila*	Woody climber	RT #61v	5	6	0.83	15.4
Mean				4.5	5.9	0.76	22.5
SD				1.4	0.7	0.24	12.3
			Group C				
February 1994	*Ficus* F1	Tree	02/13/94-01	2	6	0.33	30.3
March 1994	*S. arboreum*	Tree	03/07/94-01	3	3	1.00	21.5
April 1994	*P. javanica*	Tree	04/10/94-06	5	6	0.83	15.0
May 1994	*Ficus* M1	Tree	05/15/94-01	3	4	0.75	19.2
June 1994	*M. lineata*	Tree	06/15/94-02	3	3	1.00	26.0
July 1994	*B. baccata*	Tree	07/10/94-06	3	3	1.00	16.9
August 1994	*F. altissima*	Tree	08/18/94-01	3	4	0.75	14.3
September 1994	*F. annulata*	Tree	CR #373	3	5	0.60	15.3
October 1994	*C. axillaris*	Tree	09/20/94-02	3	5	0.60	16.3
November 1994	*Ficus* N1	Tree	11/14/94-03	5	5	1.00	37.9
December 1994	*F. altissima*	Tree	18-078 (08)	4	4	1.00	28.9
January 1995	*D. dumosus*	Woody climber	CR #275v	4	5	0.80	16.5
Mean				3.4	4.4	0.81	21.5
SD				0.9	1.1	0.22	7.6

each month. On average gibbons visited the most visited fruit patch on 79% of observation days. In other words individual fruit patches were regularly revisited on consecutive days each month. This was true of both fig and nonfig fruit patches. Of the 12 most visited patches for the two groups

Table 4–4 Frequency of Visits to the Most Heavily Exploited Patches: Figs Versus Nonfig Fruit

	Group A		Group C	
	Figs	Fruit	Figs	Fruit
Mean	0.67	0.83	0.74	0.87
Range	0.33–0.83	0.33–1.00	0.33–1.00	0.60–1.00
SD	0.20	0.25	0.25	0.16
Count	5	7	6	6

($N = 24$), 11 were *Ficus* species and 13 were nonfig fruit trees and climbers (Table 4–4).

Patch Size

The mean DBH for all feeding trees was 51.7 cm (Table 4–5). This value places the average gibbon feeding tree in the 90th percentile of all trees measured in the botanical plot ($N = 1562$). Trees from which gibbons fed on reproductive plant parts (fruit, figs, and flowers) were much larger than leaf-feeding trees (Figure 4–9).

The average number of animals in the same patch during feeding bouts varied based on food class. Groups were most cohesive when feeding on figs (mean = 3.4, SD = 0.24, $N = 615$) and fruit (mean = 2.8, SD = 0.53, $N = 1230$). Feeding-group size was smaller when feeding on flowers (mean = 2.6, SD = 1.11, $N = 46$) and leaves (mean = 2.2, SD = 1.17, $N = 638$) and smallest when foraging for insects (mean = 1.4, SD = 0.80, $N = 200$).

Encounters Between Species

Encounters with other species in feeding trees were relatively uncommon. The species that were most frequently encountered were black giant squirrels (*Ratufa bicolor*), one of four species of hornbill, and pig-tail macaques. Many encounters occurred in large fruiting fig trees, often on

Table 4–5 Average DBH of Major Feeding Trees Based on Food Class

	Mean (cm)	Range	SD	Count
Feed Trees	51.7	5.7–211.0	28.9	257
Figs	92.7	38.3–211.0	48.1	16
Fruit	54.6	9.6–154.5	21.9	156
Flowers	52.5	13.6–93.2	23.7	12
Leaves	36.2	5.7–211.0	27.1	73
Plot Trees	23.1	10.0–124.7	15.5	1562

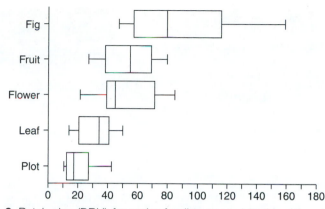

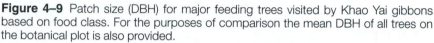

Figure 4–9 Patch size (DBH) for major feeding trees visited by Khao Yai gibbons based on food class. For the purposes of comparison the mean DBH of all trees on the botanical plot is also provided.

subsequent days. Binturongs (*Arctictis binturong*), which are nocturnal, would occasionally remain active past sunrise in highly abundant fig trees. Unlike macaques, black giant squirrels and binturongs were generally tolerated by gibbons, but periodically, gibbons—especially juveniles—did chase the other animals in the tree, probably as a form of play. Macaques typically did not remain in the same feeding tree as gibbons, although on a number of occasions a lone male macaque did feed together with gibbons in large fruit trees. On one occasion the group A juvenile, Aran, entered a wild persimmon tree (*Diospyros glandulosa*) occupied by a pair of Malayan sun bears (*Helarctos malayanus*). The juvenile briefly fed on fruit before exiting the tree. None of the other group members approached the tree or showed any interest in the bears' presence. A similar observation was made by Raemaekers and Raemaekers (1990).

As I alluded to above, gibbons also fed in fruit-bearing feeding trees simultaneously with neighboring social groups several times. Five of these instances occurred during successive days in a single fruiting *Ficus altissima* tree that stands in an area of overlap between the home ranges of groups A, B, and C. In fact on one morning this single tree was simultaneously occupied by all three gibbon groups as well as a binturong, several black giant squirrels, and two species of hornbill.

Drinking Behavior

Gibbons occasionally drank standing water by pushing their cupped hands into tree holes. After allowing their fur to become soaked, they take their hands and let the water drip off their fingers into their mouths. An individual will typically repeat this action with the same hand between 10 and 20 times. Frequently one or more animals will follow the first at the drinking hole. Less often two or even three animals drink together pushing

Gibbons drink by pushing their cupped hands into tree holes and licking water from their fur.

their hands into the hole in turn. Drinking accounted for just 0.1% of total activity time, and over half of all occurrences (8 of 15) took place during six observation days in April. April was not a particularly dry month, with total rainfall of 129.3 mm. Less rainfall was recorded during five other months. April was, on the other hand, the hottest month (average high temperature of 29.7°C) of the study period.

DISCUSSION

Annual Diet

Like other small-bodied gibbons white-handed gibbons in Khao Yai National Park are highly frugivorous. Together figs and nonfig fruit accounted for 66% of the mean annual diet. After fruit the next most common item in the diet was young leaves (22%), especially those of the species *Gironniera nervosa*. Insects, shoots, and flowers made up the remainder of the diet. Carpenter (1940) reported that the skull of a small bird was recovered from the stomach of a shot gibbon, but I never saw gibbons approach or stalk vertebrates of any kind. Although gibbons continually look for food items as they travel, the majority of their feeding took place during distinct visits to trees or climbers. Furthermore in most months gibbons clearly focused their feeding effort on a limited number of species and, within species, on a limited number of individual trees or climbers. As a result individual feeding trees were often visited multiple times during the same monthly sample. Although certain fruit species were regularly eaten in multiple months, no species was the most preferred food item in consecutive months. Ostensibly this pattern appears to be comparable with the *stable* foraging strategy Garber (1993) describes for tamarin monkeys (*Saguinus* spp.), which he says carefully track a series of target species as they become available. Garber concludes, "although the particular set of plant species that is utilized by moustached and saddle-back tamarins changes every few weeks, their overall foraging pattern and feeding ecology remains markedly consistent throughout the year" (p. 160). Interestingly McConkey and co-workers (2003) describe a similarly stable pattern of resource use by hybrid gibbons (*H. muelleri* × *H. agilis*) in Borneo: "close tracking of resources means that they are able to locate preferred and locally abundant fruit crops at all times of the year. Thus during general fruit scarcity in the forest, it is possible that the gibbons may still have a relatively rich fruit supply if favored species are fruiting" (p. 30). This pattern suggests that in at least some environments gibbons are relatively unaffected by changes in resource abundance. Yet McConkey and co-workers acknowledge that longer periods of fruit scarcity might necessitate a shift in diet (see Bricknell 1999). As I will describe in the next section this appears to be the case with Khao Yai gibbons.

Monthly Variation in Diet

When ripe fruit was abundant, gibbons fed most heavily on it. Nonfig fruit was the most exploited food class in 10 of the 12 months sampled, and during six different months ripe fruit (excluding figs) accounted for over 50% of gibbon feeding time. Accordingly when compared across months, high rates of fruit in the diet correspond to lower amounts of other food classes. Alternatively when ripe fruit was scarce, gibbons responded, in part, by increasing the breadth of their diet. According to optimal foraging theory the value of preferred foods decreases as the time it takes to procure them increases; therefore, animals are expected to rely more heavily on lower-value, but less-dispersed, items when preferred foods are scarce (MacArthur and Pianka 1966; Charnov 1976). In the case of Khao Yai gibbons this was apparent in two ways. First, gibbons increased the amount of young leaves and shoots in their diet, and second, they fed from a greater number of plant species each month. This pattern of altering the diet to include lower-quality items is consistent with the energy conservation strategy I described in Chapter 3. Broadly speaking there are two ways for an animal to balance its energy budget: by reducing expenditures and by increasing earnings (i.e., the energy-capture rate). During the cool season low levels of fruit availability appear to have limited the ability of gibbons to find new sources of ripe fruits. By shifting to lower-quality items that were more evenly distributed in the environment, they were able to reduce energy expenditure. Gibbons also fed more heavily on flowers during the cool season. But in contrast to shoots and leaves, flowers are nutritionally rich, and increased feeding time on this food source was almost certainly a response to increased availability (see McConkey et al. 2003).

Insectivory

Some frugivorous primates rely on insects to supplement their diet when ripe fruit is scarce. Robinson (1986), for example, found that insects replaced fruit as the most preferred food class in the diet of wedge-capped capuchins (*Cebus olivaceus*) during fruit-poor months. Given the way gibbons broadened their diet when ripe fruit was scarce, it is perhaps surprising that they did not feed more heavily on insects during fruit-poor months. On the other hand it is a mistake to assume that insects are a ubiquitous resource. In fact insect abundance fluctuates in a manner similar to other rainforest resources. Thus rates of insectivory by Khao Yai gibbons might have been limited by patterns of seasonal abundance. Although I did not measure insect abundance as part of my study, data from seasonal forests where insect phenology has been studied indicate that insect biomass tends to peak following the first rains (Wolda 1978; Tanaka and Tanaka 1982; Boinski and Fowler 1989). During March 1994 significant amounts of rain began to fall in Khao Yai. If insect biomass at Khao Yai follows the pattern seen at other sites, we would guess that the availability of insects would be highest beginning in March or later. Of course gibbons do not feed indiscriminately on insects, and it is likely that different insect families exhibit different patterns of abundance (see Gursky 2000). Thus any estimate of insect availability is highly speculative. Nevertheless it is interesting that insect feeding by Khao Yai gibbons was heaviest in April and May (the two months following the onset of the rains), which were also two of the peak months in terms of fruit availability. It is possible that gibbons follow a strategy similar to that Di Fiore and Rodman (2001) describe for woolly monkeys (*Lagothrix lagotricha poeppigii*) whereby they capitalize on the high abundance of fruit to increase feeding on highly nutritious insects.

Keystone Resources

As outlined earlier one of the ways Khao Yai gibbons coped with periods of fruit scarcity was by feeding more heavily on alternative or fallback foods, but remarkably even when the overall abundance of fruit in the environment fell precipitously, the contribution of fruit and figs never fell below

Strangler figs, which can be among the largest trees in the forest, dominate feeding time during the cool season.

50%. This was accomplished via a marked shift in focus from nonfig fruit to fig fruit during the cool season, November to February. During this period figs never accounted for less than 30% of the diet. During the rest of the year figs never accounted for more than 15% of the gibbon diet, and during three months figs account for less than 5%. Following Terborgh's (1986) definition it is clear that figs represent a keystone resource for Khao Yai gibbons in that they support them through periods of resource scarcity. More recently Shanahan and co-workers (2001) have argued for a more-disciplined application of the keystone resource concept. They assert that "future research must take into account the availability of non-*Ficus* resources, *Ficus* density, fig phenology, and frugivore mobility and confirm that figs are suitable for, available to, and required by the frugivores in question" (pp. 556–557). Here I have demonstrated that gibbons turned to fig feeding when the overall abundance of fruit was low, but the frequency of fig trees in the phenology sample (see Chapter 2) was too low to demonstrate annual fluctuations in the availability of figs as distinct from overall fruit abundance. Thus the possibility that fig feeding correlates with fig availability cannot be dismissed completely. Nevertheless there is good reason to believe that figs represent a year-round resource in Khao Yai. The year before the onset of this study, Poonswad and co-workers (1998) completed a 19-month study of the phenology of *Ficus* species at a site a few kilometers to the north of Mo Singto. There they monitored 30 trees of at least 9 fig species twice per week and found that ripe figs were available in all but four weeks during that period. Peak fig abundance occurred in April 1993 when 12 of 30 fig trees had ripe fruit, whereas fig crops were most scarce in October and November of the same year. It is worth noting that these two periods correspond to the high and low periods of overall fruit abundance I found at Mo Singto the following year, suggesting that fig feeding by gibbons may be negatively correlated to their abundance. In any case Poonswad and co-workers' data clearly demonstrate the asynchronous fruiting pattern of *Ficus* spp. in Khao Yai, which is consistent with abundant data from forests around the world (Leighton and Leighton 1983; Terborgh 1986; Lambert and Marshall 1991; McConkey et al. 2003).

Do Gibbons Prefer Figs over Other Fruit?

Given the importance of figs to the diet of gibbons, a number of authors have argued that hylobatids are specifically adapted to exploit this plant family. MacKinnon and MacKinnon (1980:186), for example, conclude that the "ranging behavior, unique mode of locomotion and social organization [of gibbons] all seem specialized towards life as a *fig exploiter*" (emphasis added). Raemaekers (1977, cited in Chivers and Raemaekers 1986) initially drew a distinction between white-handed gibbons, which he labeled "fruit-pulp seekers," and siamangs, which he labeled "fig seekers." But more recently Chivers and Raemaekers (1986) have argued that this distinction is superfluous: "When opportunities taken are expressed as percentages of those provided, it is clear that both gibbon species selected figs more strongly than other fruit and flowers overall, and these more strongly than young leaves overall" (p. 46). A distinction between siamangs and white-handed gibbons is called into question also by Palombit (1992), who studied both gibbon species at Ketambe, Indonesia. Palombit concludes, "the Ketambe hylobatids both show a clear dietary preference for figs" (p. 204).

There is no question that figs are an important component of the diet of gibbons at Khao Yai and that this is true throughout much of the year. Annually fig feeding accounted for 19% of feeding time, and on a monthly basis fruiting fig trees represented 11 of the 24 most heavily exploited fruit patches (see Table 4–3). Nevertheless a dietary *preference* for figs is not supported by the data from Khao Yai. In fact the opposite is more likely the case: namely figs were consumed most when other (more favored) fruits were unavailable. During dry months fig feeding accounted for 30%–53% of feeding time, but during June and July when fruit feeding was at its highest level, gibbons fed on figs very little, or not at all, despite the fact that figs were known to be available. Tutin and co-workers (1997) report a similar observation in the case of African apes: "It was striking that fig crops available in poor fruit months attracted gorillas and chimpanzees without fail, but figs were often ignored in good fruit months when a variety of succulent fruit was available" (p. 13).

Leighton and Leighton (1983), who studied vertebrate responses to seasonal fruiting in the Kutai Nature Reserve in Borneo, Indonesia, found that visits to fig trees by Mueller's gibbon fell to near zero when the abundance of nonfig fruit was greatest. The same was also true of sympatric orangutans (*Pongo pygmaeus*). More recently McConkey and co-workers (2003) found no relationship between fig abundance and fig feeding by hybrid gibbons (*H. muelleri* × *H. agilis*). In light of this evidence and that outlined earlier, the label "fig-seeker" does not appear to describe gibbons in general any more than it does other frugivorous primates that rely on figs to sustain themselves during periods when the abundance of ripe fruit of other species is rare [e.g., *Saimiri sciureus* (Terborgh 1986); *Gorilla gorilla, Pan troglodytes* (Tutin et al. 1997)]. As for Khao Yai gibbons their preference during most months for succulent fruit invites reconsideration of Raemaekers' classification of white-handed gibbons as "fruit-pulp seekers" (cf. Chivers and Raemaekers 1986; Chivers 2001). Further discussion of the gibbon feeding niche is provided in the next section.

What Is the Gibbon Feeding Niche?

Apart from fig feeding, gibbons have most often been described as having a preference for food distributed in small patches. As described by Gittins and Raemaekers (1980:98) "the gibbons' feeding niche appears to be the succulent fruit occurring in smaller scarcer sources." Despite the persistence of this view (e.g., Leighton 1987; Chivers 2001), the size and dispersion of gibbon-feeding sources has rarely been quantified. Furthermore this characterization is clearly at odds with the heavy reliance by gibbons on large fruiting fig trees (at least during some times of the year). These two views might be reconciled if gibbons selected large feeding trees only during the dry season when figs comprise the majority of their diet, but, in fact, Khao Yai gibbons carefully seek out and exploit the largest fruiting trees available each month. For example during four different monthly samples, group A devoted over 25% of its total feeding time to a single large fruiting tree. In only one of those months was the tree in question a fig (*Ficus tinctoria*) (see Table 4–3). The other three trees were nonfig-fruit species (*Aphananthe cuspidata, Prunus javanica*, and *Cleistocalyx nervosum*) that were visited recurrently during the course of the sample. Although other authors have recognized that gibbons exploit large patches, they have nevertheless downplayed their importance. According to MacKinnon and MacKinnon (1984:293), for example, gibbons "make good use of the large fruiting trees but are unable to take much advantage of superabundances, which are more effectively harvested by orangutans, macaques and birds." Data presented in this chapter suggest the reverse; Khao Yai gibbons do take advantage of superabundances, but in most cases they do so through repeated visits over multiple days as opposed to extended feeding bouts. Energetically they benefit from revisiting known feeding sites, rather than expending time and energy seeking out new sources of food. Furthermore when resources are scarce, gibbons make additional use of exceptionally large patches, namely fig trees, by feeding more cohesively and feeding for longer periods per visit. To the extent that gibbons do exploit small food patches, they principally do so when feeding on young leaves rather than fruit. In sum the evidence from Khao Yai rejects the notion of gibbons as small-patch specialists. Although gibbons do exploit small patches, the bulk of their diet comes from recurrent visits to large fruit patches. Thus the benefit of small group size to gibbons may come not from their ability to feed simultaneously in small feeding trees, but from their ability to exploit large patches over longer periods of time than primates living in larger groups. Nevertheless we need to be cautious about extending these findings to gibbons in other forests. For one thing Khao Yai gibbons lack the large number of primate competitors found at many other sites. It is possible, for example, that gibbons at Khao Yai are able to exploit resources that would otherwise be more quickly depleted were they sympatric with a larger numbers of large-bodied frugivores.

Finally it has also been argued that gibbons are adapted to exploit exceptionally rare resources (Gittins and Raemaekers 1980). Here again the data from Khao Yai differs. Nonfig fruit, leaves, flowers, and probably insects as well, are all fed on in proportion to the availability of these foods in the environment. There is a significant positive correlation between the contribution of a given fruit species to the diet and the density of those species on the plot. Rather than being adapted to exploit rare resources, the pattern at Khao Yai suggests that gibbons, like most primates (Hemingway and Bynum 2005), carefully track resource abundance through the seasonal cycle taking advantage of the best available foods at any given time.

CHAPTER SUMMARY AND CONCLUSIONS

Despite a distinctly seasonal environment, Khao Yai gibbons fed heavily on fruit all year with fruit and figs combined accounting for greater than 50% of the total diet in all months. Most feeding occurred in separate patches, especially large fruiting trees, which groups visited repeatedly over a series of days. When fruit was abundant and energetic demands easily met, gibbons supplemented their diet with insect matter. During the cool season gibbons responded to low fruit abundance, in part, by expanding the diet to include greater amounts of flowers, shoots, and leaves. But the most distinctive aspect of gibbon foraging during the cool season was their long visits (some up to 2 hours) to large fruiting fig trees.

5

Ranging Behavior

*A group of gibbons in its native habitat is, strictly speaking, not free ranging
except within the limits of the territory to which it has become conditioned and
which it defends against the encroachment of other groups of gibbons.*

—Carpenter (1940:239)

All primates confine their travel, feeding, and social activity to a fixed area
of their habitat called a *home range* (Bates 1970), which can vary in size
from a few hectares to many square kilometers. When such an area, or a
portion thereof, is defended against incursion by members of other social
groups, as is the case with gibbons, it is designated a *territory*. Although
the concepts of range use and territoriality are closely linked, it is useful
from a theoretical standpoint to present them separately. In this chapter I
will focus on the way ecological pressures influence gibbon ranging
behavior, relying on the cost-benefit approach described in previous chapters. I will then turn to a discussion of gibbon territoriality in Chapter 6.

With regard to ranging behavior, two patterns of range use are generally
of interest in the study of primate behavioral ecology: first, the overall distance an individual or group of primates travels in a day—its *day range*, or
daily path length; second, the regularity with which animals use all portions of their home range. Although no primates are truly migratory, some
species do respond to changes in resource availability by shifting their
range into areas that are not visited during other times of the year. For

example, Overdorff (1993) reports that two rufous lemur (*Eulemur fulvus rufus*) study groups disappeared from their known range during a period of low fruit availability. Despite attempts to relocate the animals using radiotelemetry, their whereabouts remained unknown for approximately five weeks. Nevertheless major shifts in habitat use, such as the example above, appear to be the exception; instead most primates respond to changes in food abundance by altering travel distance or range use (Hemingway and Bynum 2005).

Given the energetic costs of travel relative to resting or grooming, it stands to reason that seasonal fluctuations in food availability would impact the distance a group travels. Interestingly, however, comparisons across species show no consistent pattern of response (Clutton-Brock 1977; Oates 1987); for example, when resources are scarce, primates are as likely to increase daily movement [e.g., *Procolobus badius* (Marsh 1981); *Cebus olivaceus* (Robinson 1986); *Saimiri oerstedi* (Boinski 1987)] as decrease it [e.g., *Brachyteles arachnoids* (Strier 1987b); *Presbytis pileata* (Stanford 1991); *Pan troglodytes* (Doran 1997)]. Furthermore some species respond very little or not at all to fluctuations in resource abundance [e.g., *Saguinus* spp. (Garber 1993); *Cercopithecus* spp. (Kaplin 2001)]. Chapman (1988), for example, studied range use by three primate species (*Ateles geoffroyi, Alouatta palliate,* and *Cebus capucinus*) in Santa Rosa National Park, Costa Rica, for 24 months. Despite the fact that the study area was located in a highly seasonal forest, he found no significant correlations between seasonal measures of range use (e.g., percentage of time traveling, percentage of home range used, distribution of range use) and seasonal differences in resource availability for any of the three primate species, although changes in diet were considerable.

There are many reasons why gross measures of range use might not vary consistently with changes in resource abundance (Clutton-Brock 1975; Chapman 1988). First, animals are more likely to respond to the fruiting cycles of specific tree species than to community-wide measures of resources abundance (Gautier-Hion et al. 1981; Chapman 1988). Specifically, large, asynchronously fruiting trees may exert strong short-term pressure on range use (McKey and Waterman 1982; Terborgh 1986). Second, movement by primates, even when food is locally abundant, may reflect a need to monitor resources (Di Fiore 2003) or patrol territorial borders (Peres 1989). Third, animals may alter ranging patterns to obtain a varied diet and/or to avoid excessive levels of secondary compounds (see McKey and Waterman 1982; Garber 1987). Finally, group travel may be influenced by other aspects of the environment that do not correlate with food availability, such as the availability of standing water (Altmann and Altmann 1970), weather conditions (Iwamoto and Dunbar 1983), parasite avoidance (Freeland 1976), forest structure (Gautier-Hion et al. 1981), or reproductive timing (Vasey 2006).

If Chapman's (1988) observation that range use in primates is largely "situation dependent" is accurate, then the relationship between food availability and range use in other species, including gibbons, may prove difficult to establish. That said, given the seasonal influence on activity patterns and the diet of white-handed gibbons described in the previous chapters, we should expect Khao Yai gibbons to modify their range use in a way that is consistent with the pattern of energy economy described earlier. In particular we should anticipate that gibbons will limit the total distance traveled when ripe fruit is scarce. Alternatively effective territorial maintenance requires that the animals regularly cover all portions of their range (Mitani and Rodman 1979); therefore, it is expected that the proportion of the home range visited each month will be only partly dependent upon fluctuations in the abundance of fruit.

As in previous chapters I begin here with a general overview of the ranging behavior of white-handed gibbons. I then continue by quantifying ranging behavior, including home-range size and overlap, daily path length, and distance traveled between feeding sites. Next to understand those factors that contribute to seasonal variation in gibbon range use, I compare patterns of range use with environmental factors, such as rainfall and fruit abundance. I also compare ranging behavior with the makeup of the gibbon diet. Finally I consider the question of group leadership by documenting the order of progression within social groups.

OVERVIEW OF GIBBON RANGE USE

Gibbons are well known as quintessential *brachiators,* capable of rapid hand-over-hand movement through the forest canopy. Keeping up with gibbons from the ground, while negotiating often-dense undergrowth, can be amazingly difficult and, at times, impossible. Early in my field study I underestimated the speed with which gibbons could change the pace of travel. As a result there were times when I literally lost the study animals before I was aware of their absence. Because breaks in visual contact during full-day follows were routine, I was often caught waiting for the gibbons to reappear from behind the crown of a tree, when in fact they were already 40–50 m away. Sometimes I was lucky enough to catch a glimpse of them climbing the next ridge, but other times it was as if they simply disappeared. But as difficult as it can be to stay with a fast moving gibbon group, tracking well-habituated gibbons over the course of their daily routine is quite doable. Unbroken bouts of high-speed travel are relatively rare and typically occur only when moving to or from night trees. During most of the day gibbons forage slowly between major feeding trees, stopping often to rest or scan the vegetation.

Where gibbons go is highly dependent on the location of the specific trees in fruit at a given time. Nevertheless certain arboreal pathways were used repeatedly when moving from one part of the range to another, and at times they seemed almost to trace the boundaries of their home range over the course of the day. During any given month gibbons visit most portions of their home range. That said, there were times, even several months into my field study, when the study animals traveled into areas that were unknown to me. The destination in most of these cases was a large tree in peak fruit.

As a rule gibbons continue to forage normally during periods of light or even medium rainfall, but during periods of heavy rain all activity comes to a halt. Heavy downpours are generally of short duration, and during such periods all members of the social group tend to rest some distance apart, with their arms over their knees and heads down. Once the heavy rain subsides, the animals continue to forage. Just before entering night trees gibbons tend to move more quickly, often visiting two or more feeding trees in quick succession. Once they arrive in the area of their sleeping trees the group members fan out into a cluster of nearby, although rarely adjacent, trees. Movement typically ends abruptly as each animal quickly moves to a sleeping spot within its chosen tree.

METHODS SPECIFIC TO THIS CHAPTER

To monitor the range use of the study animals, the location of the focal animal was recorded every half hour. Location samples took the form of an estimated distance and compass bearing from a known trail location or some other landmark. Animals were rarely more than 25 m from a major trail. When animals were far from a trail, the tree occupied by the focal animal during the location sample was marked with flagging tape and subsequently relocated and mapped relative to the trail system using a 30-meter measuring tape and compass. To re-create day ranges with as much accuracy as possible, the 30-minute location samples were combined with the location of known feeding and night trees used during a given day. I also recorded any previously marked tree the focal animal passed through. The average number of follows from night tree to night tree each month was 5.1 for group A and 3.2 for group C.

Data Analysis

All location points, including the location of feeding and night trees, from all full-day follows were entered into *Pathfinder,* a cartographic database manager developed by Michael E. Winslett (Austin, Texas). *Pathfinder* uses entered location points to calculate daily path lengths and home-range areas (see Overdorff 1996; Vasey 2006). Measurement errors between fixed location points (e.g., known trail intercepts) are averaged over the length of the trail. In this way errors of closure are eliminated. As an estimate of the distance traveled between gibbon feeding patches or interpatch distance (IPD), I divided daily path length by the total number of major feeding patches (see Chapter 4) used in a given day. This measure includes movement to and from night trees, but assuming that the distance traveled to and from night trees is relatively stable over the year (which is consistent with my subjective impression), IPD should register changes in the actual distance gibbons traveled between major feeding sites.

Pathfinder calculates home-range size by drawing a minimum convex polygon (MCP) around the cumulative day-range map for a given social group. Using the home-range boundaries produced in *Pathfinder*, I determined the area of home-range overlap between the two study groups in NIH Image (Wayne Rasband, NIMH, Bethesda, Maryland). To better compare range-size estimates with other studies, I also calculated home-range size by digitally superimposing grids of 0.25 and 1.0 ha quadrats on the cumulative day-range maps generated by *Pathfinder*. Because the resultant home-range size may vary depending on the placement of the overlapping grid relative to the cumulative range map, I conducted 10 trials for each grid size.

To determine if there is a difference in the distance traveled during wet days versus dry days, I used the Mann-Whitney U test. Monthly correlation between groups and between the mean measures of home-range use and habitat characteristics (e.g., fruit abundance) are described using the Spearman rank correlation coefficient (r_s). The two tests are corrected for ties.

RESULTS

Daily Path Length

The mean daily path length (DPL) for the two groups was 1245 m per day (Table 5–1). DPL was greatest in April (1791 m) and lowest in November (672 m). Group C (1329 m) traveled farther than group A (1160 m) in all but two months, but the monthly pattern of fluctuations in range use is the same ($r_s = 0.94, p = 0.002$) (Figure 5–1). The sample day ranges for group A depicted in Figure 5–2 illustrate the considerable variation in the distance traveled in a single day between months.

Over all months there is a significant positive correlation between DPL and fruit abundance ($r_s = 0.64, p = 0.033$). The distance gibbons traveled between food patches, the IPD, shows a similar pattern of variation to DPL (see Table 5–1). Annually gibbons traveled 184 m between feeding patches. During April this distance climbed to 292 m, then fell to 113 m in October. Nevertheless the relationship between IPD and fruit abundance is not significant ($r_s = 0.37, p = 0.217$).

Table 5–1 Annual and Monthly Measures of Range Use by Khao Yai Gibbons

	Daily Path Length (m)			Interpatch Distance (m)			Monthly Range
	Group A	Group C	Average	Group A	Group C	Average	Size (ha%)[1]
February 1994	1120	1578	1349	181	210	196	16.25 (56.5)
March 1994	1500	1698	1599	240	212	226	15.25 (53.0)
April 1994	1655	1927	1791	296	289	292	20.25 (70.4)
May 1994	1610	1607	1609	239	230	234	18.00 (62.6)
June 1994	1216	1417	1317	187	202	195	17.00 (59.1)
July 1994	1417	1845	1631	221	264	242	16.00 (55.7)
August 1994	1026	1183	1105	125	127	126	14.00 (48.7)
September 1994	916	1226	1071	117	144	131	14.00 (48.7)
October 1994	764	797	780	116	111	113	13.50 (47.0)
November 1994	724	620	672	172	108	140	10.50 (36.5)
December 1994	909	1017	963	130	191	160	16.75 (58.3)
January 1995	1060	1037	1048	151	154	153	14.25 (49.6)
Mean	1160	1329	1245	181	187	184	15.48 (53.8)
SD	321	416	361	58	59	56	2.50 (8. 7)

[1]Values for group A only; percentage of annual home range given in parentheses

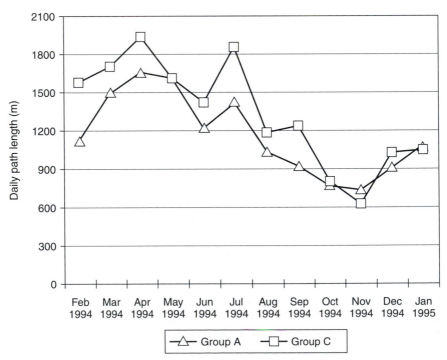

Figure 5–1 Average daily path lengths for gibbon groups A and C.

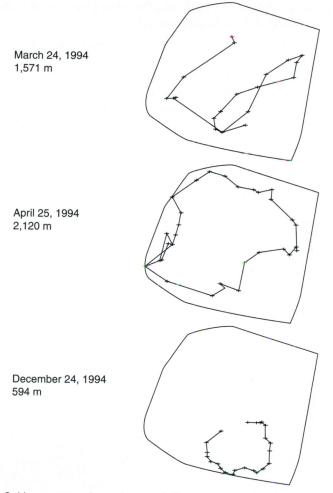

March 24, 1994
1,571 m

April 25, 1994
2,120 m

December 24, 1994
594 m

Figure 5–2 Home-range boundary and three sample day journeys for gibbon group A.

Day Range and Rainfall

Annually there was no difference between the distance traveled on dry days ($N = 71$) versus wet days ($N = 28$) ($U = 970.0$, $Z = -0.186$, $p = 0.852$). Nor is there a significant relationship between average monthly rainfall and the average DPL when compared across months ($r_s = 0.35$, $p = 0.246$). Nevertheless, *heavy* rain, or the prospect of it, may have impacted travel. On several occasions I observed gibbons entering night trees earlier than I had anticipated, apparently in response to darkening skies and heavy thunder. The relatively low DPL during June, which was the wettest month, illustrates this point. Path lengths were much greater in adjacent months when rain totals were much lower.

Home Range

Home-range size for groups A and C was calculated from the cumulative day-range map of each group. Day ranges were drawn from 62 and 38 night-tree-to-night-tree follows for groups A and C, respectively (Figure 5–3). MCPs circumscribing the range maps of each of the two groups yielded annual home-range sizes of 25.4 and 21.4 ha (mean = 23.4). On average, home-range sizes based on the 0.25 and 1.0 ha grids exceeded those based on MCP by 17% and 43%, respectively (Table 5–2). By comparison the variation in estimated range sizes that resulted from differences in how I aligned the overlapping grids was low (5.7%–9.3%).

Home ranges of neighboring groups often overlap one another by a distance of 50–100 m. The area of overlap between the home ranges of groups A and C is 1.6 ha. Assuming an equal degree of overlap by all neighboring groups, it is possible to estimate the total area of overlap for each group.

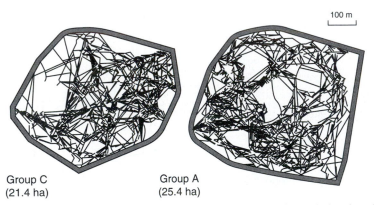

100 m

Group C
(21.4 ha)

Group A
(25.4 ha)

Figure 5–3 Cumulative day-range maps and home-range boundaries for gibbon groups A and C.

Table 5–2 Mean Range Size in Hectares for Gibbon Groups A and C Based on Superimposed Grids of Two Sizes

	Group A		Group C	
	0.25 ha	1.0 ha	0.25 ha	1.0 ha
Mean	28.7	35.3	24.9	32.4
Range	28.00–29.75	35.0–37.0	24.25–25.75	30.0–33.0
SD	0.59	0.67	0.51	1.07

Group A shared areas of overlap with five groups for a total estimated overlap area of 8.0 ha, or 31% of total annual home range. Group C shared parts of its range with four known groups, which together yield a total overlap area of 6.4 ha, or 30% of total annual home range. Stated another way the two study groups maintained estimated nonoverlapping ranges of 69% and 70%. The relationship between these measurements and territoriality will be discussed in Chapter 6.

Monthly Variation in Home-Range Use.   Gibbons regularly used most portions of their range. Figure 5–4 is a plot of the cumulative home-range size for both groups. After the first two months of observation, 10 and 5 full-day follows, home-range size (based on MCP) for social groups A and C had reached, respectively, 73% and 81% of their final values; after four months of observation, 21 and 11 full-day follows, home-range size had reached, respectively, 90% and 89% of their final values; and after nine months home-range size for both groups had reached a plateau.

To evaluate variation in home-range use, I calculated the monthly home-range size. For each month of the year I counted the number of 0.25 ha quadrats gibbons entered and divided the sum by the total number of quadrats entered over the course of the year. For the comparison to be valid, the number of observation days each month should be equal.

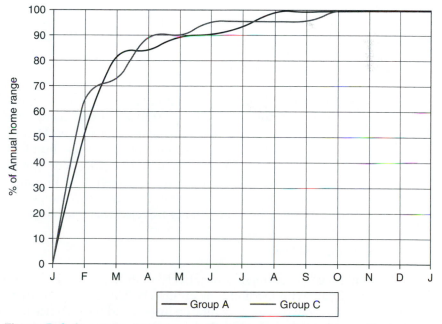

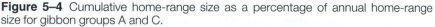

Figure 5–4 Cumulative home-range size as a percentage of annual home-range size for gibbon groups A and C.

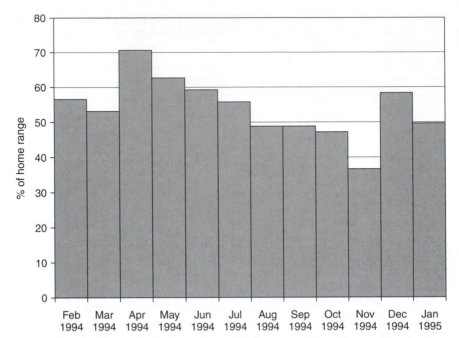

Figure 5–5 Monthly home-range size for study group A based on quarter-hectare quadrats.

Because I was consistently able to follow group A for 5 days per month, I calculated the monthly home-range size for this group only (Figure 5–5). On average group A used 54% of its home range during each monthly sample (see Table 5–1). The percentage of range use was greatest during April (70%) when fruit was abundant and smallest in November (37%) when fruit was scarce; however, the correlation between monthly range size and fruit abundance is not significant ($r_s = 0.50, p = 0.100$). Samples of monthly range use for group A, including April, November, and December, are depicted in Figure 5–6. In April when ripe fruit was abundant, group A ranged widely over their home range. In one fruit-poor month, November, its movement was confined mostly to one-half of its range, whereas in another fruit-poor month, December, group A ranged as widely as in April, although the total distance traveled was much less.

Ranging Behavior and Diet

Over all months DPL is correlated negatively with the feeding time on leaves and positively with feeding time on insects. There is also a strong positive correlation between feeding time on insects and the distance traveled between food patches (Table 5–3). Leaves are low energy resources that require time to digest, so it is not surprising that gibbons should

April 1994

November 1994

December 1994

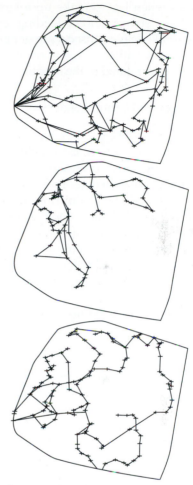

Figure 5–6 Monthly range use by study group A as indicated by five consecutive full-day follows each month.

Table 5–3 Correlation Between Monthly Range Use and Diet

Food Class	Monthly Range Size[a]	Daily Path Length	Patch Distance
Nonfig Fruit	0.31	0.48	0.11
Fig Fruit	−0.17	−0.43	−0.15
Leaves	−0.46	−0.65*	−0.50
Insects	0.48	0.91**	0.77**

[a] Based on group A only, see text

* $p < 0.05$

** $p < 0.01$

travel least when leaves make up a large part of their feeding time. The relationship between insect feeding and travel distance is of interest because, unlike leaves, insects are generally consumed when ripe fruit is abundant (see Chapter 4); yet, none of the three measures of range use was significantly correlated to the amount of fruit in the diet.

Travel Order and Group Leadership

As an indicator of group leadership the order of group entry to and exit from major feeding trees was recorded whenever possible. Individual gibbons frequently used the same arboreal pathway when entering and exiting a tree, so it was often possible to determine the exact order of group progression. By contrast group progression during travel bouts was very difficult to establish. The *group leader* was defined as the first animal to either enter or exit a given tree. Group leadership was recorded on 293 occasions. On average, adult females were the first in progression 51% of the time (Table 5–4). This value was more than twice that of any other age-sex class. Juveniles were the second most likely to lead (25%), and adolescents the least likely (10%).

There was some variation in group leadership, depending on whether the group was entering or exiting a tree. Juveniles were more likely to lead progression when entering a tree (29%) than when exiting (21%). In group A the adult female and young juvenile were equally likely to be the first to enter a given feeding tree. It may be that younger juveniles, who generally maintain proximity to their mothers, anticipate the target tree once the adult female has laid out the direction of travel. Order of entry to a feeding site may also signify priority of access, in which case exit order may represent a more accurate measure of group leadership. Adult females of both groups were the first to exit feeding trees on far more occasions than any other group member.

DISCUSSION

Variation in Daily Path Length

The average distance gibbons traveled per day varied considerably over the annual cycle. For example gibbons traveled over two and a half times

Table 5–4 Group Leadership During Travel by Age-Sex Class

	Enter (%)	Exit (%)	Mean (%)
Adult Female	45	56	51
Juvenile	29	21	25
Adult Male	15	13	14
Adolescent	10	11	10

A juvenile gibbon follows the adult female during a travel bout.

farther in April than in November. Although it is likely that heavy rains limit group travel during some months, the main factor influencing daily travel distance by Khao Yai gibbons was resource abundance. The two social groups traveled less when ripe fruit was scarce. This conclusion is consistent with the lower overall time devoted to locomotion during the cool season (see Chapter 2). Furthermore the finding that gibbons alter travel in response to resource abundance is similar to observations made by Raemaekers (1980), who studied range use by white-handed gibbons and siamangs in the Krau Game Reserve, Malaysia. Raemaekers concludes that the strong correlation between food abundance and travel distance suggests that gibbons follow a "loss-cutting policy" when it comes to range use. As I have discussed in previous chapters optimal-foraging theory predicts that with the reduced availability of preferred foods, the best strategy is to limit search time (i.e., travel). A corollary of this prediction is that dietary selectivity falls, and the quality of the diet is diminished (Charnov 1976). For Khao Yai gibbons the negative correlation between day range and the quantity of leaves in the diet is consistent with this prediction.

In addition to fruit abundance there is good reason to suspect that gibbons modify patterns of range use in response to insect availability. Insects are an excellent source of readily accessible energy, and unlike ripe fruit they are also a valuable source of protein (Lambert 2007). Thus if they can be harvested easily, insects should represent a preferred food item. It, however, is not clear how increased rates of insectivory should impact range use. It is generally the case that insects are more evenly dispersed in the environment relative to plant resources. Consequently Robinson (1986:48) concludes that for capuchin monkeys (*Cebus olivaceus*) "foraging for invertebrates is not an important determinant of use of space because invertebrates are distributed relatively homogeneously in space." But the same may not hold true for range use by gibbons. If the insects exploited by gibbons are distributed homogenously throughout the forest, then there is no reason to assume that gibbons will cover greater distance when rates of insect feeding are highest. For example it is possible that gibbons would reduce travel rates (and ultimately, DPL) as they spend more time scanning foliage for prey. At Khao Yai DPL and travel distance between food patches correlate strongly with feeding time on insects. I suspect that this is in part because of gibbons traveling to favored insect foraging sites. Although they were not recorded as "feeding patches" per se, Khao Yai gibbons recurrently visited certain trees and woody climbers to forage for insects. One particular foraging patch was a large gymnosperm with an exceptional number of epiphytes that individuals combed through search-ing for insects. The gibbons also regularly returned to stands of trees with large numbers of climbers and searched through the dead vines and leaves trapped in tangles of vegetation. Because I made no attempt to measure insect abundance, the relationship between insect foraging time and range use is speculative; nevertheless the apparent impact of insec-tivory on the foraging behavior of gibbons suggests an important direc-tion for future research. A crucial first step is to monitor insect abundance along with fluctuations in the abundance of plant resources. Furthermore because not all forest insects exhibit the same pattern of availability (see Gursky 2000), every attempt should be made to identify the insect species consumed by gibbons at least to the level of their taxonomic order. Given the height at which gibbons forage, this will not be an easy task, but the results would potentially offer important insight into gibbon foraging decisions.

Home Range

Home-range sizes at Khao Yai, relative to that of other hylobatids, are small. Taking all species into account, average home-range size for gib-bons is approximately 40 ha [range = 15−87 ha (Bartlett 2007a)], which is nearly double the value reported in this study. One reason for this differ-ence may relate to the way range size is calculated by different observers. The use of superimposed grids of various sizes, previously the most common method used to determine home-range size, has the potential to overestimate range size by including unused areas at the periphery of the range. As I demonstrate earlier, the use of one-hectare quadrats can result in range-size estimates that are up to 43% larger than those based on MCPs. But even taking into account different measurement techniques, home-range sizes at Khao Yai are small. For example Raemaekers (1979) determined that home-range size for white-handed gibbons and siamangs at Krau Game Reserve, Malaysia, occupied home ranges of 47 and 57 ha, respectively. Significantly the home ranges of these two groups overlapped by 60% of their combined areas. And whereas Malayan siamangs are more folivorous than sympatric gibbons, siamangs also consume large amounts of fruit, especially figs. Thus it is likely that the larger ranges reported by Raemaekers are a consequence of these two species exploiting the same resources (Chivers 2001). But home-range sizes at Khao Yai are smaller even than those of congeners who occupy forest where larger apes are absent. Only silvery gibbons with a home range of 17 ha (Kappeler 1984) have smaller home ranges than those reported at Khao Yai. An additional factor accounting for small home-range sizes at Khao Yai may be the overall size of the primate community at other sites. Khao Yai gibbons share their range with only two other primate species, pig-tailed macaques and slow lorises. Whereas differences in the overall primate biomass may explain the relatively small home-range size at Khao Yai, range-size estimates for virtually all gibbon studies are based on a small number of groups at each site. A proper comparison of interspecific variation in gibbon range use must await additional data.

Seasonal Variation in Home-Range Use. Compared with DPL the portion of the home range used by gibbons each month was less influenced by fluctuations of resource abundance. For group A home-range size was smallest during November (11 ha) when fruit was scarce and greatest in April (20 ha) when fruit was abundant. But outside of these two months, variation in monthly home-range size was limited (range 14–18 ha). These findings are consistent with the prediction that territorial species should regularly use all parts of their range (Mitani and Rodman 1979).

Group Leadership

Although some frugivorous primates, notably chimpanzees and spider monkeys, frequently break up into small subgroups while foraging, this is rarely the case with gibbons. Feeding and travel are highly coordinated within social groups, and it is rare that Khao Yai gibbons ever lose sight of one another as they travel between feeding trees; consequently vocal cues to group movement are probably unnecessary. Instead group movement appears to be directed by adult females, who determine the timing and direction of travel. This is evident in that group members tend to converge on the female's night tree at the beginning of the day and in that adult females are regularly the first to enter, and especially the first to exit, feeding trees. The benefits of highly coordinated movement may lie in increased foraging efficiency (Terborgh 1983). Young animals benefit from the accumulated knowledge of older animals, and all group members avoid visiting recently depleted food sites. On the other hand foraging decision need not benefit all group members equally, and given the increased energetic demands of pregnant and lactating females, it is reasonable to expect that females would be more motivated to dictate the order and timing of feeding visits (Erhart and Overdorff 1999; Boinski 2000). Indeed a number of studies have shown that female gibbons lead most travel bouts (Chivers 1974; Tenaza 1975; Reichard and Sommer 1997), although this pattern is not universal. In one group of agile gibbons the female led group travel 36% of the time compared with 52% for the male (Gittins 1979 cited in Ahsan 2001). Also Ahsan (2001) found that the male of one of three hoolock social groups led travel slightly more often than the female. It appears in this case that the female was neither nursing nor lactating at the time. When this female subsequently died, she was "replaced" by the juvenile female of the same group. Under this new arrangement, the male's bias in group leadership increased. This finding highlights the possible role of individual knowledge and experience in determining foraging decisions (Boinski 2000; Overdorff et al. 2005). Future research on gibbon foraging behavior should focus on the extent to which newcomer females direct group movements.

CHAPTER SUMMARY AND CONCLUSIONS

Annually home-range size in Khao Yai gibbons is 23 ha, roughly half of which is used in any given month. Approximately 30% of the home range is shared with neighboring groups. When ripe fruit is scarce, gibbons limit the distance they travel, which is consistent with the characterization of gibbons as energy minimizers. Rather than spending more energy finding preferred foods, gibbons limit their travel and feed on less desirable items, such as leaves. Not only do gibbons travel farther when ripe fruit is abundant, but there is also a strong correlation between travel and the amount of time spent feeding on insects. Although unmeasured in this study, it is likely that the abundance and distribution of insect prey play an important role in the foraging decisions of these mostly frugivorous apes. Perhaps because of higher energetic demands related to lactation, adult female gibbons lead group movement far more often than males.

6

Territoriality and Intergroup Encounters

I couldn't be absolutely certain of the incentive for which these two gibbons were competing. There were two possibilities, the food or the female, which I suspected of being receptive. However, when the female left the tree and both males followed her, it became clear.

—*Carpenter (1940:172)*

As described in Chapter 5 a territory differs from a home range in that a territory represents a portion of the overall home range that is *actively defended* against encroachment by conspecifics from other groups (Burt 1943). By aggressively excluding neighbors, territorial animals maintain at least a portion of their range for their exclusive use. Discussions of the evolutionary benefits of defending a fixed territory typically focus on one of two purported functions: *resource defense* or *mate defense* (Cheney 1987). Although the two functions need not be mutually exclusive, the predictions of the two models differ in ways that can be addressed using observations from the field (van Schaik et al. 1992; Steenbeek 1999). Socioecological theory suggests that given the different levels of parental investment by males and females in most sexually reproducing animals, fitness in females is primarily limited by access to resources, whereas fitness in males is primarily limited by access to mates (Trivers 1972; Wrangham 1979). It follows, therefore, that if territoriality functions primarily as male mate defense, then (1) males should primarily be involved in range defense and advertisement and (2) males should always be intolerant of each other when they meet. A corollary of the second prediction is that males should be most aggressive when females in their group are in estrus (Fashing 2001). Alternatively if territoriality functions primarily as female resource defense, then (1) females should primarily be involved in range defense and advertisement and (2) home-range overlap should be small. The resource-defense theory also differs in that it does not assume that all encounters between neighbors are hostile, especially when resources are not easily monopolized. A variant of the resource-defense model posits that males defend resources on behalf of females who share their range (Rutberg 1983). In this way the interests of males and female are met simultaneously (Rubenstein 1986).

It is well known that gibbons are highly territorial, and the characteristics of gibbon encounters have been well documented (Gittins 1984; Kappeler 1984). In many previous studies, however, only a single social group was habituated. As a result, in some cases, encounters were concluded as soon as the observer was discovered. At Khao Yai the presence of habituated animals in several adjacent groups means that the diversity of gibbon encounters can be more fully described (Reichard and Sommer 1997). My goal in this chapter is to explore the structure and function of intergroup encounters by Khao Yai gibbons. Given the apparent contribution of gibbon vocal duets in advertising the location of gibbon territories (Raemaekers et al. 1984), I begin by describing patterns of gibbon vocal activity. I then turn to encounters between groups. As detailed in the following pages not all group encounters are hostile, thus it is unlikely that all encounters contribute to territorial maintenance. Similarly males and females do not participate equally in encounters between groups. These differences are considered in turn. Once I have described behavioral aspects of gibbon territoriality I describe the territories themselves, including size, degree of overlap, and defendability. Finally I close the chapter by evaluating alternative theories for territoriality that may account for territorial activity in Khao Yai gibbons.

OVERVIEW OF INTERGROUP ENCOUNTERS

During routine foraging all members of the social group tend to maintain visual contact with one another. In contrast during intergroup encounters the adult male often leaves the vicinity of the other members of the group. Depending on the composition of the social group, the adult male may be joined by an adolescent or subadult male. After detecting the presence of a neighbor in the vicinity of a territorial boundary, the adult male quietly approaches the border area. On reaching the territorial border the two opposing males sit or hang within view of one another uttering a quiet series of staccato hoots. As the encounter develops, the quiet hoots may grow into a louder and more-sustained full solo call. Generally one male will then displace the other by entering the other's tree. This continues back and forth until one of the males initiates a sudden but brief chase. After the aggressor has pursued his opponent some 20–40 m, he generally slows or turns back, thus providing an opportunity for the opponent to retaliate. Chasing alternates between the territories for as much as two hours. During this time the remaining group members will either wait and watch or continue to feed or forage. Over the course of the encounter females may sing great calls that go unanswered by their mate. Periodically the male returns to his group to feed or to groom with his mate before swinging off to rejoin the dispute. Foreign males too may approach a group while the resident is preoccupied by the dispute, although the sound of a returning resident male is generally enough to induce a retreat. When the dispute ends, both males move away from the boundary area and rejoin their social groups. Often the returning male then approaches his mate to be groomed. Usually within one half hour of the encounter the pair sings a duet. Although hostile encounters are the norm (at least between males), neighboring groups occasionally also meet in neutral or affiliative contexts. These will be described in later sections.

METHODS SPECIFIC TO THIS CHAPTER

The location and duration of all group encounters and vocalizations were recorded whenever they occurred. The durations of group vocalizations were recorded with a stopwatch to the nearest second, whereas the beginning and ending times of group encounters were recorded to the nearest minute. Analyses of both vocal behavior and intergroup encounters are based on full-day follows only ($N = 109$) so as to more accurately estimate rates of these activities.

Data Analysis

In the analysis of gibbon vocal behavior I include only group call bouts that include at least one complete great call sequence, that is, a female great call followed by a full, well-formed reply (or *coda*) from the male pair mate. This excludes female great calls sung in the absence of the male reply (i.e., female solos) and abnormal or interrupted sequences (usually of very short duration). Alarm calls, which are often sung in response to the alarms either of other species (e.g., squirrels and barking deer) or of other gibbon groups, are included because great-call sequences almost always make up a portion of gibbon alarm vocalizations. Whereas the structure of gibbon alarm calls initially differs from other gibbon songs, any attempt to exclude these from the analysis would be subjective. Raemaekers and co-workers (1984:179) summarize the difficulty in distinguishing normal group calls from alarm calls, or what they label "disturbed" calls, as follows: "A normal duet may become disturbed if the gibbons are upset during the course of the bout, and likewise a disturbed bout may normalize as the gibbons calm down" (but see Clarke et al. 2006). Finally male solo calls are not considered here. Male solos often begin before dawn, and it is likely that many solos were missed even during full-day follows; therefore, an accurate estimate of solo calling rates was not achieved. A more-thorough description of the calling behavior of Khao Yai gibbons, including solos, are provided in Raemaekers and co-workers (1984), Raemaekers and Raemaekers (1985), Reichard and Sommer (1997) and Clarke and co-workers (2006).

Territory size was calculated following Gittins (1982:51): "The territory was plotted by drawing a line-of-best-fit through the points where territorial disputes were observed." The relationship between home-range area and daily path length (DPL) is described using the *Index of Defendability* (D-index) (Mitani and Rodman 1979):

$$D = d/d'$$

where d is the average day range and d' is the diameter of a circle with an area equal to the observed home range A, [i.e., $d' = (4A/\pi)^{0.5}$]. This index describes the likelihood that a group will encounter its own range boundary as it moves around its range on an average day. Mitani and Rodman (1979) reason that animals that routinely approach their range boundary during normal travel will be able to monitor encroachment by neighboring animals with little extra cost. Monthly correlation between groups and between territorial activity and habitat characteristics (e.g., fruit abundance) is described using the Spearman's rank correlation coefficient (r_s) corrected for ties.

RESULTS

Gibbon Duets

On average gibbons sang 1.3 duets for a total of 17.5 min. per day. Compared across months there is a significant correlation between groups A and C for the total time spent calling per day ($r_s = 0.85, p = 0.005$), but not for the number of calling bouts ($r_s = 0.54, p = 0.071$). The mean call bout lasted 13.3 min. (SD = 10.6, range = 1.6–62.5, $N = 145$). The majority of duets were given during the mid-morning hours, with a considerable drop in calling after 1100 hours (Figure 6–1).

Monthly variation in duetting was high. On average the time spent calling per day in April (37.8 min.) was 16 times that of November (2.3 min.). In April I also recorded the highest number of calls per day (2.7) and in November, the fewest (0.4). Across months there is a strong correlation

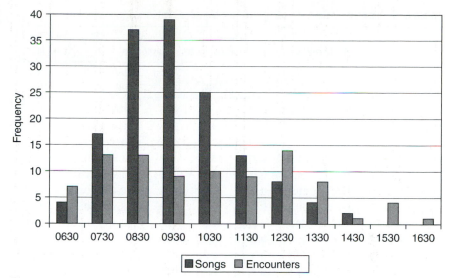

Figure 6–1 Start time of gibbon group calls and intergroup encounters.

between the abundance of ripe fruit in the environment and both the number of calls per day ($r_s = 0.66$, $p = 0.029$) and the time spent calling per day ($r_s = 0.85$, $p = 0.005$). There is also a significant correlation between the time spent calling each month and rainfall ($r_s = 0.62$, $p = 0.041$), although not between the number of call bouts and rainfall ($r_s = 0.43$, $p = 0.150$).

Intergroup Encounters

Overall I recorded 90 intergroup encounters during full-day follows. Averaged across months gibbons engaged in 0.85 encounter per day (Table 6–1). Taking all records together the average encounter lasted 53.9 min. (SD = 42.8; $N = 88$) with a range of 4 min. to 4 hr. 23 min. In the latter case groups A and C were involved in a protracted dispute over a very productive fig tree (*Ficus tinctoria*) that fruited in January. Similar to calling bouts encounters were high during the morning hours, but encounters also exhibited a second peak after midday (Figure 6–1).

One finding that I did not anticipate was that not all encounters between neighboring groups were agonistic (see Bartlett 2000, 2003). Neighbors sometimes ignored each other completely or, more surprisingly, engaged each other in affiliative interactions, including grooming and play. Whereas most encounters between groups are behaviorally diverse and may include vocal, agonistic, and affiliative elements (see Reichard and Sommer 1997), for the most part I had no difficulty assigning each encounter to one of four mutually exclusive categories—*agonistic,*

Table 6–1 Monthly Rates of Intergroup Encounters by Khao Yai Gibbons

	All Encounters		Friendly Encounters		Hostile Encounters		Resource Related Agonism	
	Bouts/ Day	Min./ Day	Bouts/ Day	Min./ Day	Bouts/ Day	Min./ Day	Bouts/ Day	Mins/ Day
February 1994	0.75	48.6	0.13	10.0	0.63	38.6	0.00	0.0
March 1994	1.63	57.4	0.25	9.0	1.38	48.4	0.50	31.6
April 1994	0.82	51.9	0.18	17.0	0.64	34.9	0.18	18.3
May 1994	1.56	95.0	0.22	13.2	1.33	81.8	0.44	25.3
June 1994	1.00	51.1	0.29	19.3	0.71	31.9	0.14	7.1
July 1994	0.75	19.9	0.25	9.5	0.50	10.4	0.00	0.0
August 1994	0.13	18.4	0.00	0.0	0.13	18.4	0.00	0.0
September 1994	1.00	60.3	0.40	17.0	0.60	43.3	0.10	0.4
October 1994	0.60	40.2	0.10	3.1	0.50	37.1	0.30	12.8
November 1994	0.36	15.8	0.00	0.0	0.36	15.8	0.27	10.4
December 1994	0.80	21.6	0.30	6.2	0.50	15.4	0.40	15.4
January 1995	0.67	46.0	0.11	5.8	0.56	40.2	0.22	29.8
Mean	0.85	43.9	0.19	9.2	0.65	34.7	0.21	12.6
SD	0.43	22.8	0.12	6.5	0.36	19.4	0.18	11.8

Note: Friendly Encounters is a category combining both affiliative and neutral encounters. Hostile Encounters combines vocal and agonistic encounters. Resource-Related Agonism represents agonistic encounters that occurred within 25 m of a feeding tree. See text for details.

vocal, neutral, or *affiliative.* Details of each class of encounter are provided in the following sections.

Agonistic Encounters. The majority of encounters, 52 out of 90 (57.8%), were characterized by vigorous chasing between members of neighboring groups. Agonistic encounters principally involved adult males, though subadults, adolescents, and even adult females occasionally joined disputes; 48% ($N = 25$) of all agonistic encounters occurred within 25 m of a major feeding site. In all such cases of *resource-related agonism* the contested tree was exploited for fruit or figs.

Vocal Encounters. The second most common encounters were those in which one or both males sang dispute vocalizations while in view of one another ($N = 18$, or 20%). These encounters share most of the elements of agonistic encounters but failed to escalate to the point of actual chasing.

Neutral Encounters. In five cases—5.6% of encounters—participants ostensibly ignored each other. In all cases this occurred as neighboring groups fed or foraged in the same patch. All but one of the neutral encounters I observed occurred in the same large fig tree (*Ficus altissima*) located in the area where the home ranges of gibbon groups A, B, and C overlap.

Affiliative Encounters.   During 15 of the 90 encounters (16.7%) members of neighboring groups engaged in affiliative interactions. All documented encounters occurred between group A and one of three neighbors: group B (N = 3), group C (N = 7), or group H (N = 5). In each case immature gibbons (juveniles and/or adolescents) engaged in bouts of play, especially chasing (see Table 6–2). Adults generally watched the social interactions of the younger animals while they rested in view of the adults of the neighboring group. On five occasions an adult male (Cassius, N = 2; Felix, N = 3) joined immatures in bouts of chase play, though adult females never did. During three encounters neighbors also engaged in grooming bouts. Once the A adolescent, Amadeus, briefly groomed (~5 sec.) the C juvenile, Caleba, on her head during a bout of wrestle play. In the two other cases the adult male of group H, Felix, groomed the immatures of group A. In the first of these Felix groomed Amadeus off and on for a period of approximately 22 min. during a 2-hour encounter in April. At the end of the encounter Amadeus returned to the tree occupied by the A adults and was

Table 6–2 Affiliative Intergroup Encounters Between Gibbon Group A and Neighboring Groups

Group	Date	Interaction	Duration
B	March 21, 1994	Immatures play chase; A adolescent briefly grooms B juvenile.	20 min.
B	March 28, 1994	Immatures play chase, wrestle.	52 min.
B	May 24, 1994	Immatures play chase.	25 min.
C	February 20, 1994	Immatures play chase.	1 hr. 20 min.
C	June 28, 1994	Immatures play chase.	1 hr. 33 min.
C	July 23, 1994	Immatures play chase; C male joins play.	44 min.
C	July 25, 1994	Immatures play chase; C male joins play.	32 min.
C	July 17, 1994	Juveniles play chase; groups A and C feed.	40 min.
C	September 26, 1994	Juveniles play chase.	44 min.
C	September 28, 1994	Immatures play chase.	16 min.
H	April 24, 1994	Immatures play chase; H male grooms the two A immatures.	1 hr. 59 min.
H	5/24, 1994	H male grooms A juvenile; H male/A adolescent play chase.	1 hr. 34 min.
H	June 25, 1994	Juveniles play chase; H male joins play.	42 min.
H	October 27, 1994	H male and A juvenile play chase.	31 min.
H	January 25, 1995	Immatures play chase.	52 min.

From Thad Bartlett, "Intragroup and Intergroup Social Interactions in White-Handed Gibbons," *International Journal of Primatology* 24, no. 2 (2003): 239–259. Reproduced with kind permission of Springer Science and Business Media.

immediately groomed by the male, Fearless. Felix also groomed the juvenile Aran for approximately 8 min. during the same encounter. During an encounter between the same two groups the following month, Felix again groomed Aran. As in the previous case this was made possible by Fearless's tolerance of Felix, who entered the tree occupied by the animals of group A repeatedly during the encounter. Earlier that same day Aran and Amadeus had played chase with the immatures of group B. Although the majority of group encounters were agonistic all encounters I witnessed between groups A and H were affiliative ($N = 5$) (Table 6–3).

Interactions Between Males and Females During Encounters

Adult females were involved in territorial chases on only five occasions. All but one of these instances involved the female of group B, who was without an infant during the entire study period (see Table 2–3). In the fifth case the two A adults together chased the two B adults away from a territorial border. Even though females were not actively involved in most disputes, males regularly approached neighboring females during encounters. On 17 occasions I observed an adult male approach a female of a neighboring group within a few meters and in 5 cases that male made

Table 6–3 Frequency of Group Encounters by Encounter Type for Social Groups A and C

Group	Agonistic	Vocal	Neutral	Affiliative	Total
		Group A			
B	9	2	1	3	15
C	16	4	1	6	27
H	—	—	—	5	5
M	4	—	—	—	4
N	5	2	—	—	7
Total	34	8	2	14	58
		Group C			
A	7	4	2	1	14
B	8	1	1	—	10
K	7	4	—	—	11
Unknown	3	1	—	—	4
Total	25	10	3	1	39

Note: Some encounters involved multiple groups, so totals exceed the number of total encounters observed ($N = 90$).

From Thad Bartlett, "Intragroup and Intergroup Social Interactions in White-Handed Gibbons," *International Journal of Primatology* 24, no. 2 (2003): 239–259. Reproduced with kind permission of Springer Science and Business Media.

physical contact with her. In four of these Cassius touched the A female, Andromeda, on either the head or the hand. For example once Cassius approached Andromeda from above, slowly pursuing her down the trunk of a small tree, he reached down and brushed his hand through the fur on her head, as if grooming. Andromeda reacted by squealing, then charged at Cassius and fled from the tree.

Females were also approached in a more overtly hostile manner. Twice, the N male charged Andromeda during an agonistic encounter, and on one occasion Fearless pursued the C female, Cassandra, jumped on her back, and briefly grappled with her before she turned and chased Fearless from the area. The two females were carrying their infants when these encounters occurred. All male–female encounters occurred while the resident male was out of visual contact with his mate. In every case where the resident male returned during an encounter, the rival male was chased from the area.

Monthly Variation in Encounter Rates

The frequency of intergroup encounters varied considerably over the course of the year (Table 6–1). Encounters were most frequent in March (1.63 per day) and least frequent in August (0.13 per day). The pattern differs somewhat in the case of total time devoted to encounters, in which case the peak time devoted to encounters was May (95.0 min./day) and the lowest point was November (15.8 min./day). When all encounters are considered together, there is a positive correlation between fruit availability and both the number of encounters per day ($r_s = 0.61$, $p = 0.042$) and the total time devoted to encounters per day ($r_s = 0.63$, $p = 0.037$). Because not all encounters constitute territorial activity, however, I further grouped encounters into *friendly* (affiliative and neutral) and *hostile* (vocal and agonistic). When these two categories were each compared separately with fruit availability, significance was maintained only for the number of minutes devoted to friendly encounters ($r_s = 0.62$, $p = 0.039$). In other words, gibbons devoted more time to friendly encounters when ripe fruit was abundant, but the same was not true of hostile encounters, which showed no discernable pattern across months.

Resource-Related Agonism. As I indicated earlier approximately half of all agonistic encounters occurred within 25 m of feeding trees. These encounters differ from all others in that they result, at least in the short term, in the exclusive access to a feeding site. Significantly the time devoted to such encounters also differs from the general activity pattern exhibited by gibbons at Khao Yai. Although there was a peak in resource-related agonism during the hot season (March to May), there was a second peak beginning at the end of the wet season, in October, and continuing through January (see Table 6–1). In other words during a time of year when gibbons limited

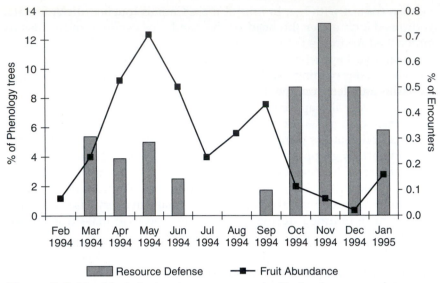

Figure 6–2 Monthly fruit abundance compared with the frequency of resource-related agonistic encounters (i.e., resource defense) expressed as a percentage of all intergroup encounters.

their activity (including vocal, social, and travel time) conflicts over resources were relatively high. Furthermore as a percentage of all encounters, conflicts at feeding trees were most common during periods of fruit scarcity. Annually resource-related agonism accounted for 26.2% (25/90) of all encounters, but from October to January it accounted for 52.1% (13/24) of encounters on average (Figure 6–2). During this period gibbons defended two foods exclusively: *Choerospondias axillaris* trees ($N = 3$) and *Ficus* trees ($N = 10$). This is not surprising given the importance of these two fruit sources during periods of overall fruit scarcity (see Chapter 4).

Territory Size

The locations of all intergroup encounters for groups A and C are shown in Figure 6–3. The approximate home-range boundaries of all neighboring groups are indicted by dashed lines. Figure 6–4 shows the plotted territories for the two groups based on a line of best fit drawn through the location of all encounters (see Gittins 1982). In the areas where territorial boundaries were not actively defended, territorial boundaries follow home-range boundaries. Territory sizes for groups A and C were 20.3 and 18.2 ha, respectively. These values represent 80% and 85% of the respective group's annual home-range size (Table 6–4).

As defined earlier, territory does not imply an area of exclusive use because areas of the home range that are at times actively defended will

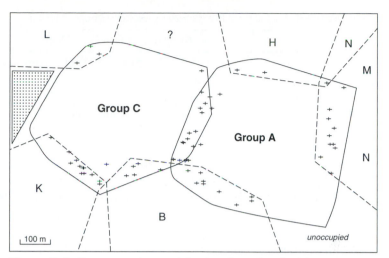

Figure 6–3 Range overlap and the location of territorial encounters. The shaded area on the left of the map indicates disturbed habitat not entered by gibbons. Groups M and N were known to forage together occasionally, thus the boundary between these two groups is ill defined.

simply be visited when a neighbor is too far away to detect incursion (cf. Pitelka 1959). By contrast an *area of exclusive use* (AEU) denotes a portion of the range never visited by neighboring animals. A precise measure of AEU would require constant monitoring; nevertheless the AEU for groups A and C can be estimated by calculating the area within each group's home

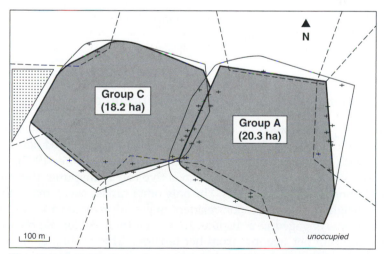

Figure 6–4 Territory size for study groups A and C based on a line of best fit (Gittins 1982:51).

Table 6–4 Measures of Range Size by Gibbon Groups A and C

	Group A	Group C	Mean
Home Range	25.4	21.4	23.4
Territory	20.3 (80)	18.2 (85)	19.3 (83)
Area of Exclusive Use	16.7 (66)	16.7 (78)	16.7 (72)

Note: Percentage of total home range is give parenthetically.

range delineated by the borders of the home ranges of all neighboring groups (see Figure 6–3). As indicated in Table 6–4 AEU for the two main study groups is the same, 16.7 ha, yielding an average of 72% of home-range size.

Index of Defendability

The average D-index for Khao Yai gibbons is 2.29, which is the same as the value Mitani and Rodman (1979) calculated for *Hylobates lar* based on information in Chivers (1972). Hypothetically a D-index of 1.0 allows animals to cross from one side of their range to the other in a single day. Accordingly Mitani and Rodman determined that no territorial species had a D-index of less than 1.0. They hypothesize that this is the threshold below which territorial maintenance is impossible. To investigate intra-annual variation in defendability for Khao Yai gibbons I also calculated the D-index for each month separately for each group. Though D was greater than 1 in all months, values varied greatly between months (group A: mean = 2.04, SD 0.57, range = 1.27–2.91; group C: mean = 2.55, SD = 0.80, range = 1.19–3.69). For the both groups defendability was greatest in April and lowest in November.

DISCUSSION

Male and Female Behavior During Group Encounters

The primary role played by gibbon males in territorial disputes is well documented, and the behavior of Khao Yai gibbons described here is consistent with previous findings (e.g., Reichard and Sommer 1997). In the few cases where adult females took an active role in disputes, the females acted in consort with their mates. The only other times I saw female gibbons chase a neighbor was when non-resident males approached a female while her mate was engaged in a dispute. And even then the female chased the male only from her tree, not from her territory. This finding alone argues against accepting female resource defense as a primary explanation for territoriality in gibbons. On the other hand the frequency of male–male aggression in gibbons is consistent with either male mate defense or male resource defense on behalf of females.

Based on data presented here it is clear that resident males defend females against the approaches of other males. This was true even though neither female under study was sexually receptive during the observation period. Yet resident males often expelled trespassing males after the fact once they had already achieved close contact with their mates. It might be argued that this is a byproduct of the reproductive condition of the two females under study. Males with unreceptive mates may be less vigilant about guarding their partners. Nevertheless observations of EPCs involving the group A female, Andromeda, by Reichard (1995) attests to the inefficiency of male mate defense at least in this population, and likely among gibbons in general (see Chapter 1). Moreover gibbon males were not invariably intolerant of would-be rivals as predicted by the male mate defense hypothesis. Resident males tolerated the presence of neighbor males during 22% of encounters. As I have described elsewhere (Bartlett 2003) in the case of groups A and H, the high level of male–male tolerance can be explained by the fact that these males, Fearless and Felix, are siblings who emigrated together from group F into group A in 1983, with Felix subsequently emigrating to group H five years later (see Brockelman et al. 1998; Chambers et al. 2002). Male–male tolerance, however, was not limited to these two groups alone. For example Fearless often tolerated the presence of the males of groups B and C as well. Though at other times, these same males reacted aggressively toward one another. On three occasions groups A and C engaged each other in separate friendly and hostile encounters on the same day. In other words male–male intolerance is situation dependent, and this dependency cannot be explained in terms of the sexual condition of either of the two females, neither of which was sexually receptive.

On the other hand situational tolerance of neighboring males is consistent with male resource defense in at least two contexts: (1) when groups meet in the absence of feeding patches or (2) when resources are not easily defended—such as very large fruiting trees. For example a single large fruiting fig tree (*Ficus altissima*) located in an area shared by groups A, B, and C was the site of six separate intergroup encounters in December 2004. Whereas half of these encounters were agonistic, the other half were neutral, two groups foraged together in the same tree and departed without interacting. Another large-crowned fruit tree of the species *Aphananthe cuspidate* was the location of four separate encounters in September. During two of the encounters immatures played together while the other group members fed on fruit. In the other two cases the adult males sang dispute calls, although ultimately they never chased one another. In the case of these two feeding trees, I suspect their physical size and their continuity with other canopy trees made it difficult to forcibly exclude other groups from them.

A large *Ficus tinctoria* tree on the border of the territories of group A and C provides an interesting contrast. Owing to its location along a streambed, the crown of this free-standing tree could be entered via a single arboreal pathway only. In November and January this tree was the site of five separate encounters all of which where agonistic. On more than one occasion Cassius sang conflict vocalizations in an adjacent tree while group A fed. Chasing occurred when Fearless exited the crown of the fig tree at the point of entry and chased Cassius from his position in the adjacent tree. Based on these examples it is clear that the nature of group encounters (hostile versus friendly) is determined in part by the degree to which local resources (i.e., fruit patches) are able to be monopolized by a single group.

Home-Range Overlap

Another prediction of the male resource defense model is that home-range overlap should be small. In my analysis a distinction is drawn between territory and AEU. Gibbons often defend areas that are visited by neighbors in their absence, thus the two terms are not interchangeable. On average territory size for groups A and C amounted to 83% of home range. The degree to which areas of truly exclusive use exists is uncertain. Among gibbons adult males of rival groups will occasionally penetrate very deep into a neighbor's territory, although these incursions tend to be brief. Reichard and Sommer (1997) conclude, based on their work on the same gibbon population, that "only about one-third of a group's range was exclusively used" (p. 1141).

In the present analysis AEU was calculated in two ways. First, by multiplying the known overlap area between groups A and C by the total number of neighbors for each of the two groups. Based on this estimate, Khao Yai gibbons used 71% of their range exclusively (see Chapter 5). The second estimate of exclusive range involved measuring the area delineated by the approximate home-range boundaries of each neighbor. Based on this method the average AEU was almost identical, 72%. These values are comparable with those reported for other gibbon species. According to Chivers (1984) with all species taken into account, "about 75 per cent of the home range is defended against neighboring conspecifics for the exclusive use of the resident group" (p. 271). Reichard and Sommer (1997), who provide little detail on how home-range size was measured, apparently used 0.25 ha quadrats to calculate range size. Thus methodological differences may account, in part, for differences in the estimated overlap between their study and mine. It is also possible that their focus on male behavior could have led to increased estimates of home-range overlap as males may penetrate deeper into neighboring ranges on occasion. One means of dealing with this problem in the future would be to calculate male and female range sizes independently (see Vasey 2006).

Monthly Variation in Territorial Activity

If territoriality in gibbons is the product of resource defense, we might expect encounter rates to increase when favored resources are most scarce (Reichard and Sommer 1997). As we have seen in previous chapters, however, fluctuations in resource abundance have a marked impact on gibbon activity budgets. Consistent with this pattern there is a significant relationship between food availability and the time devoted to encounters. But as I described, it is unlikely that all encounters contribute equally to territorial maintenance. If we consider friendly encounters independently of hostile ones, we find a significant positive correlation with fruit abundance for friendly encounters only. In other words intergroup affiliation follows the same pattern as that seen with intragroup affiliation (see Chapter 3). Although hostile encounters did peak during the fruit-abundant hot season, the frequency of hostile encounters was relatively high in some fruit-poor months as well. This is likely because of high levels of resource-related agonism during periods of fruit scarcity. For example from October 1994 to January 1995 Khao Yai gibbons engaged in 13 disputes over access to fruit trees; 3 of these involved *Choerospondias axillaris*, whereas the remaining 10 involved fruiting fig trees.

The lack of a clear relationship between fruit abundance and resource defense is likely a consequence of energetic considerations. As first observed by Brown (1964) territoriality is best considered in terms of "economic defendability." If the costs of territoriality, either in energy or in reproductive output, outweigh the benefits, territoriality will not evolve. Because resources fluctuate in terms of abundance, the costs and benefits of territoriality will also fluctuate during the year. Although some resource defense models predict that resource defense should be highest when resources are scarce (Reichard and Sommer 1997), others have argued that territorial activity should be greatest when resource abundance is not too high and not too low (Waser and Wiley 1979; Ostfeld 1990). According to the latter argument when resource abundance is very high, the loss of food to competitors has little effect on overall supply. Alternatively when resources are scarce, the gain in resource access will not be able to offset the energy expended in defense. Kinnaird (1992) concludes that resource defense among Tana River crested mangabeys fits this pattern. She found that aggressive encounters at food trees were most common when resources were abundant, but patchily distributed. The pattern I observed with Khao Yai gibbons presents another scenario. Resource-related agonism was high in the hot season when fruit were abundant and again during the cool season when fruit was scarce. I suspect that gibbons differ from mangabeys because gibbons defend a fixed territory year-round. Active range defense during periods of abundance serves to establish not only access to specific feeding trees but also a territorial border, the benefits of which may be realized at other times of the year. Alternatively when resources are scarce, the benefits of aggressive defense of resources are realized immediately. As I described in Chapter 4 gibbons feed longer per patch during the dry season. This suggests that they are depleting patches more quickly, which makes immediate access to preferred feeding trees worth fighting for.

Defendability

Defendability is typically measured based on the average annual day range length. But presumably territorial borders need to be monitored year-round, or they risk losing their integrity. Given the annual fluctuations in DPL, it follows that defendability too may fluctuate. It is clear from the data presented here that gibbon day ranges remain high enough in all months to effectively monitor territorial boundaries. Nevertheless the D-index approached the threshold below which territoriality is theoretically impracticable. This raises the possibility that gibbon home-range size is constrained by periods (e.g., months, seasons, years) when resource abundance is low. Thus whereas it might be possible for gibbon males to defend much larger ranges when resources are abundant, these range boundaries could not be effectively defended at other times of the year. This is significant given the widespread speculation that gibbon males should be able to simultaneously defend the ranges of several adult females at once (van Schaik and Dunbar 1990; Reichard 2003; see Chapter 7 for further discussion of this point).

Territorial Calls

Like other aspects of territoriality, gibbon duets have been interpreted as contributing to both mate defense and resource defense (Wich and Nunn 2002). These two purported functions of gibbon calls are hard to tease apart because by singing together gibbon pair mates simultaneously announce their presence within a given territory and their relationship to one another. Further complicating matters is the possibility that singing may serve different purposes for males and females, whereby female songs serve a territorial function while male songs indicate that the resident female is paired (Cowlishaw 1992). If duets act, at least in part, as a form of resource defense, we might expect monthly variation in vocal activity to change with resource abundance. As was the case with resource-related agonism, we might expect a relative or absolute increase in duetting when ripe fruit is scarce. Instead duetting by Khao Yai gibbons exhibited a pattern of distribution similar to other nonsubsistence behaviors, such as grooming and affiliative intergroup encounters. That is, gibbons sang most when ripe fruit was abundant and almost not at all when ripe fruit was scarce.

These findings appear to undermine the link between duetting and resource defense, but as with territorial defense generally, duetting must be examined in terms of energetic constraints. Although duetting is a costly behavior, it is almost certainly less costly than spending time in agonistic encounters. Thus the benefit of duetting is that it signals a willingness to defend a territory without having to expend energy in actual conflict (Cowlishaw 1992). But duetting is economical only if it is likely to preclude potential disputes. Given the low overall rate of hostile encounters during the dry season, time devoted to vocal activity may be wasted. It does not make economic sense to sing to forestall encounters that will not occur anyway. An additional consideration is that the majority of encounters during fruit-poor months (October to January) were conflicts over feeding sites. Given the immediate payoff of such encounters it may be that vocal displays have little potential to prevent conflict in such contexts.

CHAPTER SUMMARY AND CONCLUSIONS

On average Khao Yai gibbons occupied home ranges of 23 ha, 83% of which were defended against encroachment by neighboring animals. Gibbon pairs sang duets 1.3 times per day and engaged in intergroup encounters 0.9 times per day. Although calling and encounters were more common when ripe fruit was abundant, resource-related agonism accounted for half of all encounters when ripe fruit was scarce. This finding suggests that resource defense is an important aspect of territoriality in gibbons. Though the majority of intergroup encounters were hostile, involving chasing and vocal displays, surprisingly, males of neighboring groups were mutually tolerant during 22% of encounters. During 17% of encounters, animals from neighboring groups, especially juveniles, came together in affiliative bouts of play and grooming. Mutual male tolerance is likely dependent on many factors, including female reproductive condition, kinship, resource abundance, and the ability of males to monopolize individual feeding trees.

7

Gibbon Socioecology

It was found that the family pattern with limited variations characterized gibbon societies. The term "monogamous mateship" might be used as suggested by Alverdes but this description may be an overgeneralization.

—Carpenter (1940:218)

Gibbons are unusual among primates in that they form socially monogamous family groups. As illustrated by the epigraph of this chapter the extent to which social monogamy entails mating monogamy has long been a subject of debate. In any case monogamous social systems are rare among mammals and have generated considerable theoretical interest (Table 7–1). Here I am mostly interested in the evolutionary determinants of social monogamy, which I define as a stable association between one male, one female, and affiliated young that share a common home range or territory. Although mating monogamy, or exclusive sexual access, is not a necessary corollary of social monogamy, primate *social structure*[1] (the size and composition of social groups) is closely tied to primate *social organization* (the patterns of interactions between group members) because it determines the availability of social partners (Eisenberg et al. 1972; Terborgh and Janson 1986). This is especially true in two-adult groups, in which most of an adult's time is spent in proximity to a single member of the opposite sex. Given the constraints that a two-adult social structure

Table 7–1 Hypotheses for the Evolution of Monogamous Social Systems in Primates and Other Mammals

Explanation for Monogamy	References
Female Dispersion	Emlen and Oring 1977; Wrangham 1979
Male Mate Guarding	Wittenberger and Tilson 1980; Palombit 1996, 1999
Male Parental Care	Kleiman 1977; Wittenberger and Tilson 1980
Male Service to Females	
Infanticide Defense	Wrangham 1987; van Schaik and Dunbar 1990
Resource Defense	Ellefson 1974; Raemaekers and Chivers 1980; Rutberg 1983

places on the reproductive options of socially monogamous pair mates, it follows that an important first step in understanding the evolution of gibbon social organization is examining ecological factors that limit group size.

According to socioecological theory group size in primates is constrained minimally by two factors: (1) predator pressure, which drives animals to live in permanent groups, and (2) intragroup feeding competition, which depending upon the size and abundance of food resources will set a limit to the size of group wherein animals may live (Terborgh 1983; van Schaik and van Hooff 1983; but see Johnson et al. 2002; Sussman et al. 2005). In the case of gibbons it has been argued that a preference for ripe fruit in small, scattered patches leads to high rates of female feeding competition, which limits group size to a single adult pair and offspring (Leighton 1987). To evaluate this assertion, it is crucial first to demonstrate that food resources are limiting for gibbons and thus play a significant role in shaping their adaptive strategies (Chivers 1984; van Schaik and Dunbar 1990). Observations in seasonal environments such as Khao Yai National Park provide an excellent setting in this regard because animals that are nutritionally challenged are less able to devote time and energy to reproductive activity, which may have important consequences for their fitness (Gaulin and Konner 1977; Cant and Temerin 1984).

I begin this chapter by summarizing the impact of seasonality in resource abundance on the feeding ecology of Khao Yai gibbons. Throughout their range white-handed gibbons and their close relatives have been shown to maintain highly frugivorous diets. I describe in detail the foraging patterns that make such dietary stability possible and I compare the foraging behavior of Khao Yai gibbons to that of other species. I then turn to a consideration of gibbon socioecology. As the name implies, socioecology is the study of how physical aspects of the environment, such as the distribution and abundance of preferred resources, influence species-specific aspects of group size, composition, and social dynamics (Overdorff and Parga 2007). Many competing models have been proposed to account for monogamous social systems, and I will briefly review these before taking a closer look at the role of resource defense and food-patch size in the evolution of gibbon social structure.

SEASONAL ECOLOGY OF WHITE-HANDED GIBBONS

Seasonal Variation in Diet

Central Thailand, which includes Khao Yai National Park, experiences three seasons based on the influence of two monsoons, or seasonal winds: the hot season from March to May; the wet season from June to October; and the cool season from November to February (see Chapter 2). Although seasonal boundaries can be somewhat arbitrary and may change from year to year because of prevailing weather patterns, phenological productivity during my study varied more or less in accordance with these three recognized seasons. The hot season was a period of fruit abundance, the wet season, which exhibited a secondary fruiting peak, represented a period of transition, and the cool season, which was the peak period of flowering and leaf flush, was marked by low fruit abundance (see Figure 2–4).

On a monthly basis fruit abundance in 1994 varied from a high of just over 12% of sampled trees in May to a low of less than 1% of trees in December (Table 2–2). Not surprisingly nonfig fruit consumption by gibbons also varied considerably over the year largely in accordance with abundance, ranging from 82% of the diet in June to 5% in November (Table 4–2). But whereas the amount of nonfig fruit in the gibbon diet correlates significantly with overall fruit abundance, this is not the case with fig fruit, which was eaten most often during periods of overall fruit scarcity. For example during November when nonfig fruit feeding was at its lowest, figs accounted for 53% of the gibbon diet on average. In fact fig feeding during the cool season never fell below 30% of feeding time. In contrast figs accounted for 0%–15% of the diet during the remaining months, when fruit was more plentiful. These findings suggest that as a food class, figs are not preferred by Khao Yai gibbons, as has been suggested for gibbons in other forests (e.g., Palombit 1997). Rather figs represent a *fallback food,* one that is eaten most heavily when favored foods are unavailable (Leighton and Leighton 1983; Marshall and Leighton 2006).

This distinction in no way undermines the importance of figs to gibbon population dynamics. There is no doubt that *Ficus* spp. represent a keystone plant resource that is vital to the survival of gibbons as well as other species within the Khao Yai frugivore community (Poonswad et al. 1998). Nevertheless the difference between preferred and fallback foods may have important implications for understanding gibbon foraging adaptations because they have been hypothesized to exert different selection pressures. In particular Marshall and Wrangham (2007) argue that whereas preferred foods are more likely to shape *harvesting* adaptations, such as those related to detection and navigation [e.g., color vision (Regan et al. 2001), brachiation (Temerin and Cant 1983)], fallback foods are more likely to influence *processing* abilities, such as mastication and digestion. If so, a valuable avenue for future research might be to look at the different digestive challenges posed by figs versus nonfig fruit. Leighton (1993) found that relative to other fruits, *Ficus* spp. in Kutai National Park were high in fiber and low in digestible carbohydrates, protein and fat. As such, species that rely heavily on figs during parts of the year may require different anatomical or physiological specializations than those of species that rely on different fallback foods. That said, Khao Yai gibbons also respond to shortages of ripe fruit in other ways, such as feeding more heavily on young leaves, a food item that may present greater processing challenges than figs.

The amount of leaves in the diet of Khao Yai gibbons correlates positively with their abundance in the environment; thus it is not clear that young leaves represent a fallback food in the same way that figs do. Young leaves provide nutrients, including amino acids, that are lacking in most ripe fruits, and, therefore, their inclusion in the diet in all months (range 6%–39%) may be necessary for proper dietary balance (Milton 2000). It is relevant in this context that there is a significant negative correlation between feeding on insects compared with leaves, suggesting these two foods may represent alternative sources of dietary protein. Nevertheless given the structural difficulties in digesting young leaves and the lower overall nutritional quality of young leaves, it is unlikely that young leaves would be as highly selected as fruit or insects. It is probable therefore that the marked increase in young leaves in the diet, beginning in October and continuing through January (see Table 4–2), represents a shift in diet induced, at least in part, by the drop in fruit abundance.

Shoots and flowers, although never a major component of the diet, were also consumed most heavily in the cool season. Based both on the contribution of different food classes to the diet and on the number of different species consumed, the gibbon diet was most diverse during this period, a finding that is consistent with diet breadth models (MacArthur and Pianka 1966; Charnov 1976). The contribution of insects to the gibbon diet also varied on a monthly basis (range 2%–19%), although in the case of insects they were eaten most heavily during the hot season when fruit, and also probably insects themselves, were most abundant (see Chapter 4).

Diet Shift in Other Populations. The general pattern of shifting the diet to alternative foods during periods of fruit scarcity is generally common among primates and has also been documented in some other gibbon populations (Hemingway and Bynum 2005). Leighton and Leighton (1983) recorded a shift in diet among Bornean gibbons at the Kutai Nature

Reserve. Despite lacking a prolonged dry season, the authors determined that Kutai exhibits a clear pattern of resource abundance, which is "marked by a single large peak in supply followed by a prolonged period of resource scarcity" (p. 187). During their study not only gibbons but also macaques (*Macaca fascicularis*), orangutans (*Pongo pygmaeus*), squirrels (*Callosciurus prevostii*), and three species of hornbill all turned increasingly to figs when other fruits were scarce. In contrast to Khao Yai, however, Leighton and Leighton (1983) found that, in aggregate, fruits of the family Annonaceae (which are important to the gibbon diet at both sites) produced fruit more or less all through the year. The aseasonal availability of this fruit source may reduce the impact of resource seasonality at Kutai relative to Khao Yai.

During her study of hybrid gibbons at Barito Ulu in central Borneo, Bricknell (1999) also documented a shift in diet. Study animals consumed more figs and leaves when nonfig fruit was scarce. On the other hand McConkey and co-workers (2003), working at the same site, found no such relationship. They speculate that gibbons, because of their close knowledge of their resource base, were able to identify sources of ripe fruit even during periods of general resource scarcity. Instead McConkey and co-workers conclude that flowering peaks had the greatest effect on the gibbon diet. When flowers were abundant, gibbons consumed them in the place of ripe fruit. Nevertheless the authors allow that greater fluctuations in fruit availability than they observed during their study might require gibbons to shift to alternative or backup foods.

A second line of evidence that demonstrates the ability of gibbons to alter their diet in response to resource availability comes from comparing the annual diet of white-handed gibbons with that of congeners in other forests. Table 7–2 lists the annual diets of *Hylobates* spp. at 10 field sites. The range of fruit (50%–72%), leaves (2%–39%), and insects (0%–25%) in the diet at these 10 sites approximates the monthly variation seen in the diet of Khao Yai gibbons: fruit (52%–82%), leaves (6%–39%), insects (2%–19%). The only food class for which the annual range across sites markedly exceeds the monthly range from Khao Yai is flowers, which accounted for 13% of the annual diet at Barito Ulu but made up a maximum of 5% of the monthly diet at Khao Yai. Flowers, which are a good source of carbohydrates and soluble sugars (Strier 2000), are often a more than adequate nutritional substitute for fruit in the diet. Their availability, however, is strongly seasonal, and this factor may account for their relatively small contribution to the diet of most gibbon species. The comparatively high rate of flower feeding at Barito Ulu was apparently the consequence of an "El Nino–induced drought" that led to a mast flowering event (McConkey et al. 2003:26).

According to Hemingway and Bynum (2005) there is no clear pattern across primate species as to "whether dietary flexibility in general or

Table 7-2 Comparison of Gibbon Diets (*Hylobates* spp.) Across 10 Populations

Species	Study Site	Diet				
		Fruit (Fig)	Leaves	Flowers	Insects	Source
H. agilis	Sungai Dal, W. Malaysia	57 (17)	39	3	1	Gittins 1982
H. klossii	Paitan, Siberut, Indonesia	72 (23)	2	0	25	Whitten 1984
H. lar	Tanjon Triang, W. Malaysia	67 (—)	33	0	0	Ellefson 1968
	Kuala Lompat, W. Malaysia	50 (22)	29	7	13	Raemaekers 1979
	Ketambe, Sumatra, Indonesia	71 (45)	4	1	24	Palombit 1997
	Mo Singto, Khao Yai, Thailand	66 (19)	24	1	9	This Study
H. moloch	Ujong Kulan, Java, Indonesia	61 (—)	38	1	0	Kappeler 1984
H. muelleri	Kutai, Kalimantan, Indonesia	62 (24)	32	4	2	Leighton 1987
H. muelleri x agilis	Barito Ulu, Central Kalimantan, Indonesia	62 (17)	24	13	1	McConkey et al. 2002
H. pileatus	Khao Soi Dao, Thailand	71 (26)	13	0	15	Srikosamatara 1984

reliance on particular keystone resources is more important to seeing primates through resource bottlenecks" (p. 88). Khao Yai gibbons show elements of both patterns, but in any case, the alterations to the diet occurred at the expense of resource quality. Consequently gibbons also altered ranging behavior to accommodate resultant energy deficits.

Flexible Versus Stable Foraging in Primates

Despite alterations to their diet, most gibbons, like most apes in general, maintain a fruit-dominated diet throughout the year (Temerin and Cant 1983; Hemingway and Bynum 2005). Investigators have speculated that the ability of gibbons to maintain a fruit-rich diet is the product of their particular success in tracking rare foods (Leighton 1987; McConkey et al. 2003). As described by Gittins and Raemaekers (1980) "gibbons have to travel relatively long distances each day to obtain their food. Their wide and regular coverage of the home range enables them also to monitor the condition of imminent food sources" (p. 99). Garber (1993) describes a remarkably similar pattern of foraging in a mixed-species group of tamarins (*Saguinus mystax* and *S. fuscicollis*) at the Rio Blanco Field Site in northeastern Peru. Although the animals he studied ate equal amounts of fruit and insects, he found that the fruit component of the diet varied by no more than 11% across seasons (*S. mystax*, dry season—38%, wet season—49%; *S. fuscicollis*, dry season—34%, wet season—40%). Garber attributes this dietary consistency to their ability to track preferred resources:

> *Instead of restricting activities to a single or circumscribed part of the forest, daily travel paths took the form of long progressive arcs. . . . Over the course of a typical 3-day period, 60%–75% of quadrats in the entire range were visited. This pattern of habitat utilization may enable the tamarins to collect and update information on the location and phenology of highly ephemeral feeding sites (pp. 159–160).*

According to Garber similarly stable patterns of foraging have been documented in a number of species (e.g., lemurs, titis, macaques, baboons, colobus, and siamang). Consequently he concludes, "there is evidence that the feeding ecology of certain primate species is extremely stable and that patterns of foraging and habitat utilization may vary minimally throughout the year" (p. 162). Garber speculates that stable foraging strategies may be the product of what Sussman (1987) calls "species-specific dietary patterns." As described by Sussman the basic diet of a species (i.e., the proportion of plant parts in the diet) is constrained by aspects of the species' anatomy and physiology. Although the particular plant species that comprise the diet may change, the overall dietary makeup in terms of plant parts will remain stable. Under these constraints it might be that species evolve foraging strategies to maintain relatively stable diets both throughout their range and throughout the year. But although a link between stable diet and stable foraging might prove to characterize gibbon populations in less-seasonal habitat [e.g., Barito Ulu, Kalimantan (McConkey et al. 2003); Kutai, Kalimantan (Leighton and Leighton 1983)], such a connection is not supported by data from Khao Yai.

Flexible Foraging and Resource Abundance in Gibbons. Although all forests show seasonal fluctuations in productivity, wet forests typically show less-pronounced drops in resource abundance. Recall that in Borneo, Leighton and Leighton (1983) found that fruiting among species of one plant family, Annonaceae, was more or less aseasonal. In contexts such as these, careful tracking of individual fruit patches may indeed lead to stable patterns of resource use including dietary consistency. In more seasonal forests, on the other hand, where fruiting peaks are more synchronized and resource deficits are more pronounced, stable foraging strategies are bound to break down because no amount of travel will increase fruit yield. At this point animals are forced to switch to alternative forms of food with attendant changes in range use and activity budgets (van Schaik and Brockman 2005). For Khao Yai gibbons seasonal fluctuations in resource availability resulted in a mixed foraging strategy. During most of the year gibbon foraging resembled the stable pattern described by Garber (1993). Gibbons traveled long distances and visited multiple feeding sites in succession (Figure 5–2). The particular food species consumed rotated month to month in concert with availability (Figure 4–8), but the fruit component of the diet was consistently high (Figure 4–4). During the cool season when ripe fruit was scarce, on the other hand, gibbons were forced to rely more heavily on young leaves and figs (Figure 4–4) and to expand their diet to include a greater variety of species (Figure 4–6). Although the addition of figs to the diet made it possible to maintain high rates of fruit (*sensu latu*) in the diet, cool season foraging revealed a pattern of energy conservation. Although gibbons actually spent more of their activity time feeding, they retired to night trees earlier and limited time devoted to nonsubsistence behaviors, including grooming and play (Figure 3–5), singing, and friendly intergroup encounters (Table 6–1). In addition patch visits were longer (Figure 4–3) and the time spent traveling (Table 3–1) and daily path lengths (DPLs; Figure 5–1) reached their minimum values.

In the absence of direct measures of metabolism, it is impossible to know if gibbons entered negative energy balance during this period, but based on activity patterns alone it appears likely that Khao Yai gibbons experienced an energy deficit at the beginning of the cool season. Data from the phenology transect identified November and December as two of the three most fruit-poor months of the year. These were also the only two months during which no fruiting food species were identified in the three-hectare botanical plot (Table 2–2). Concomitant with this drop in fruit abundance, several parameters of gibbon activity rates and foraging behavior reached their minimum values. Activity levels in November appear to have been particularly affected, with annual lows in travel, social activity, singing, and overall activity time. During the same month DPLs were their shortest and gibbons entered night trees four hours before sunset. Although circumstantial, these findings argue that gibbons, despite foraging in small social groups for which intragroup feeding competition is expected to be low, do experience periods of nutritional stress that may be expected to have important consequences for their fitness (but see King and Murphy 1985). It is appropriate, therefore, that reliable access to sources of ripe fruit has featured prominently in discussions of gibbon socioecology.

THE EVOLUTION OF MONOGAMOUS SOCIAL SYSTEMS

Contemporary models for the evolution of primate social systems start from the premise that fitness in females is principally limited by access to food, whereas fitness in males is principally limited by access to reproductive females (Trivers 1972; Wrangham 1979). Consequently male behavior is often described as a response to the feeding strategies of females. Further most models for the evolution of monogamous social systems, in particular, begin with the supposition that the optimal strategy for females is to forage alone (i.e., without other females) in order to avoid resource competition (e.g., van Schaik and Dunbar 1990; Komers and Brotherton 1997). As explained by Wrangham (1979)

> *An individual accompanied by others suffers feeding competition whenever food sources are too small to satiate the whole party. The cost may be in extra travel time to satisfy the day's food requirement, in energy spent racing for the best feeding site, in too rapid, and hence inefficient, selection of food items etc. (p. 346).*

Building from these preconditions, four non-mutually exclusive models for the evolution of social monogamy have been described: (1) female dispersion, (2) male mate guarding, (3) male parental care and (4) male service to females (Table 7–1). The first two of these are similar in that they consider females to be resources that may or may not be monopolized by male consumers. By contrast the latter two focus on the potential benefit of male assistance to the reproductive success of the two sexes.

Females-as-Resource Models

Female Dispersion.   As described by van Schaik and Dunbar (1990) the female dispersion hypothesis rests on the premise that females are an "overdispersed resource" that males are unable to monopolize. Males would associate with multiple females if possible, but given the distribution of females into separate ranges, defending access to more than one is impossible (see Emlen and Oring 1977; Wrangham 1979). Males, therefore, are reduced to traveling with a single female. Presumably this is a costly arrangement for females because it means that they must share valuable and potentially limiting resources with a competitor, but their inability to exclude males means that they have no choice—"males cannot be avoided since they do not have the costs of rearing infants, which limit the females' ability to defend the territory against them" (Wrangham 1979:352). According to van Schaik and Dunbar (1990) one weakness of the female dispersion hypothesis as applied to gibbons is that long DPLs relative to home-range size indicate that gibbon males could readily defend the territories of multiple females. Recall from Chapter 6 that the D-index for Khao Yai gibbons was well above the value of 1.0 that Mitani and Rodman (1979) hypothesize is necessary for territoriality to be economical. To estimate the maximum number of female territories a male could potentially defend given his observed DPL, van Schaik and Dunbar (1990) invert the formula for the D-index to derive the maximum defendable area. Using range use data from 11 gibbon populations, they conclude that gibbon males of 7 of the 11 populations ranged far enough on average to defend two or more female ranges. They therefore reject the female-dispersion model.

The argument that gibbon males should be able to effectively defend access to multiple females has recently been revisited by Reichard (2003) using data from Khao Yai. But as I explain in Chapter 6 calculating maximum defendable areas based on *annual* DPLs may overestimate defendability. Although territory size remains stable throughout the year, DPL varies considerably between months. As a result defendability for Khao Yai gibbons approached the Mitani–Rodman threshold during the cool season. Consequently the maximum number of females a gibbon male could expect to maintain access to will also fall during this period, to a level below two (Bartlett 2007b). Thus for Khao Yai gibbons the maximum number of females is actually consistent with social monogamy. In any case a more-serious weakness of the female dispersion hypothesis is that without relying on "secondarily derived" mechanisms it fails to explain why male–female associations persist outside periods of female receptivity.

Male Mate Guarding. In some ways the male mate guarding hypothesis resembles the female dispersion hypothesis in reverse. In the latter monogamous males are characterized as having failed in their attempts at polygyny (Barlow 1988), whereas in the former, polygyny may be said to have failed them. That is, it is assumed that males could potentially maintain ranges large enough to encompass multiple female territories (as van Schaik and Dunbar 1990 argue), but in so doing they could not ensure exclusive reproductive access to *any* of the females whose ranges they overlap. By monopolizing breeding access to a single female, males increase their average reproductive output even though the number of partners may be lower (Wittenberger and Tilson 1980). Although such a strategy does not require permanent groups, Palombit (1999) argues that by keeping his pair mate away from other males even outside of estrus, a paired male can also limit his mate's ability to acquire knowledge about other potential partners, thereby further increasing his fitness by increasing the likelihood of siring subsequent offspring. Although the hypothetical benefits of mate guarding to males are clear, in the absence of some form of male parental care or other service, the benefits of male-imposed social monogamy to females are incidental at best. As stated by Palombit (1999:126) "it is simply less costly for the female to tolerate his presence than to attempt to expel him from the territory."

There is no doubt that gibbon males do guard their mates against the approach of neighbor males. This fact was clearly described by Carpenter (1940) and is consistent with my own observation that resident males regularly chased neighbors who approached their mates (see Chapter 6). On the other hand, males frequently leave the proximity of females precisely when mate guarding should be most intense—during intergroup encounters (Brockelman 2005). In at least some cases we know that EPCs are the result (Palombit 1994b; Reichard 1995). Although it does not necessarily follow that extra-pair paternity is achieved, the fact that males leave females unguarded in order to defend territorial borders suggests that territorial defense and mate defense are at least partially distinct phenomena (contra Reichard and Sommer 1997).

Male Assistance Models

Male Parental Care. The most common form of male assistance cited in considering primate monogamy is direct parental care, such as carrying offspring (Kleiman 1977). Indeed parental-care models have regularly been invoked to explain social monogamy in New World primates, such as titi monkeys (*Callicebus* spp.) and owl monkeys (*Aotus* spp.), for which it is common for males to carry infants (Wright 1986; Fuentes 2002). The absence of infant-carrying behavior in all but siamangs has led some investigators to dismiss this explanation for gibbon monogamy outright (e.g., van Schaik and Dunbar 1990). But direct male parental care need not be subject to so narrow an interpretation. In fact Kleiman (1977) defines male care as also including infant defense (from predators or conspecifics), grooming, and socialization, each of which is among proposed benefits offered by socially monogamous male pair mates (Tenaza 1975; Dunbar and Dunbar 1980; Wittenberger and Tilson 1980; Brockelman and Srikosamatara 1984). In the case of gibbons it is likely that each of these benefits is relevant.

As I noted in Chapter 3 males are the only age-sex class among Khao Yai gibbons that spend more time at rest than they do feeding. One interpretation of this finding is that gibbon males exhibit higher rates of vigilance relative to other group members. Although Uhde and Sommer (2002) conclude that male gibbons do not actively scan the environment more than females do, the possibility that male gibbons are more attentive to potential threats is supported by two preliminary forms of evidence. First, at Khao Yai it is my impression that male gibbons rested lower in the canopy, especially when other animals were engaged in feeding or foraging. Despite my careful attempts to evenly distribute observations across all age-sex classes, for each group I ended up with somewhat more data for males than for other group members (see Table 2–5). It is likely that their low position in the canopy gives males an unencumbered view of the surrounding area, including potential avenues of approach by predators. It also gave me an unencumbered view of them. Second, although I discerned no difference in effort between age-sex classes devoted to singing alarm calls, males do appear to take a lead role in investigating perceived threats. On a return trip to Khao Yai I once saw the gibbons of group A

Fearless scanning the environment.

alarm at what I suspect was a snake in a tree they were about to enter. (Although I carefully inspected the tree with the aid of binoculars I was never able to confirm the target of their alarm). Whereas the female and juvenile circumvented the tree in question, the adult male remained at the site calling for some time before making a series of approaches and then finally leaping into a mass of vines that covered the trunk, by which time the threat apparently had passed. This observation is consistent with Uhde and Sommer's (2002) conclusion that male gibbons take a more-vigorous role when mobbing predators. The lead role played by gibbon males in predator defense is also described by Kappeler (1981), who observed the behavior of silvery gibbons in the presence of a leopard: "Occasionally one of the group members (mostly the adult male) swang down to a lower level of the forest (10–15 m.), glanced at the leopard and swang upwards again." Similarly Tenaza (1975), who studied heavily hunted Kloss' gibbons on the island of Siberut, was approached on six occasions by male gibbons, which circled above him for up to 30 minutes. Taken together, these observations suggest that male gibbons play an important role in predator defense, although they must often abandon this role when feeding, foraging, or when engaged in intergroup encounters.

In addition to their possible role in predator defense, gibbon males invest heavily in grooming the immatures of their group. At Khao Yai male gibbons spent more time grooming than did females (Table 3–4). This difference may partly or even wholly be the product of the presence of dependant infants in both groups. Dependant young were not scored as social partners so it is likely that rates of grooming by females were under-estimated. Nevertheless in both groups males spent more time grooming immatures (juveniles and adolescents combined) than they did grooming their mate (Table 3–5). This highlights the important role gibbon males play in the social development of older offspring or at least in helping maintain adequate hygiene. Gibbon males (as well as females) also play with immatures, although in Khao Yai rates were very low.

Although male gibbons (aside from siamangs) do not provide the kind of care seen in some other species, including infant carrying or food shar-ing, it is likely that the extent of care by male gibbons has been underesti-mated. But to what degree male parental care is essential to gibbon social organization remains to be determined. The fact that social monogamy has often evolved in the absence of any involvement by males in taking care of offspring has led many investigators to conclude that the benefits of biparental care could only be realized once stable pair living had already evolved via some other mechanism [e.g., female dispersion (Barlow 1988); infanticide defense (van Schaik and Kappeler 2003); mate guarding (Broth-erton and Komers 2003); resource defense (Raemaekers and Chivers 1980)].

Male Service to Females.   Besides helping females in the care of infants, males may offer other forms of assistance that lead directly or indirectly to infant survival. One proposed form of aid is protection against strange males that might kill unknown infants. According to van Schaik and Kappeler (1993, 1997) because of long periods of infant dependence, females of all infant-carrying primates are at risk of having their offspring targeted by strange males. Unweaned infants are specifically at risk because when they die, females become sexually receptive sooner than they other-wise might. Consequently infanticidal males who subsequently mate with a victim's mother improve their relative fitness. Females can reduce their risk by affiliating with a single male provided he is able to thwart attempted infanticidal attacks by rival males. In species where females are mutually intolerant, as in gibbons, social monogamy is expected to be the result.

Evaluating the infanticide defense hypothesis for gibbons is especially problematic in light of the lack of direct evidence of its occurrence. With the exception of a single brief report (Alfred and Sati 1991), infanticide has never been witnessed among wild gibbons. This fact greatly undermines the infanticide defense hypothesis for gibbon monogamy (Fuentes 2002;

Brotherton and Komers 2003; Bartlett 2007a). Nevertheless to some investigators the rarity of the act is seen as a demonstration of the effectiveness of pair living as an infanticide prevention strategy (van Schaik and Dunbar 1990; Reichard and Sommer 1997). Obviously these two interpretations are in conflict. For example whereas Fuentes (2002) concludes that there is little support for the infanticide defense hypothesis, van Schaik and Kappeler (2003) assert it is the "best supported" explanation.

Perhaps the most often cited form of assistance that males are thought to offer female pair mates is territorial resource defense (Ellefson 1974; Wrangham 1979; Gittins and Raemaekers 1980; Rutberg 1983; Brockelman and Srikosamatara 1984; Fuentes 2000; Fashing 2001). According to this hypothesis by taking the lead role in territorial defense, males free females to spend more time foraging, which increases reproductive output and offspring survival. Although males and females need not forage together for females to benefit from the exclusive access to a resource base, foraging in cohesive groups may have additional benefits in the form of increased foraging efficiency. For example pair mates may share knowledge about the location of resources (Brockelman and Srikosamatara 1984), and foraging together may ensure that resources are not unknowingly depleted by adults foraging alone (Terborgh 1983).

Significantly the resource defense hypothesis is the only model for the evolution of social monogamy that also offers an explanation of why gibbon males defend stable territories year after year—namely that the regular use of stable territories promotes foraging efficiency through the improved knowledge of the spatial and temporal availability of resources. This aspect alone does not discount competing models; nevertheless any hypothesis that aims to explain gibbon social organization must also address why gibbon males defend stable territories. Within the primate literature, resource defense models have further focused on the importance of resource-patch size. According to Chivers (2001:22) "All gibbon field workers know that gibbons are monogamous, because they are adapted to surviving on small fruiting trees." Whereas this statement is clearly incorrect (see Palombit 1999; Sommer and Reichard 2000; this study), it is true that models for the evolution of monogamy in gibbons and other primates have often invoked small feeding patches (Wrangham 1979; Raemaekers and Chivers 1980; Terborgh 1983; MacKinnon and MacKinnon 1984; Wright 1986; Leighton 1987).

MONOGAMY, PATCH SIZE, AND RESOURCE DEFENSE TERRITORIALITY

As conceived by Raemaekers and Chivers (1980) the small-patch model for the evolution of gibbon monogamy builds on the observation that gibbons rely more heavily on ripe fruit than do sympatric primates. Because

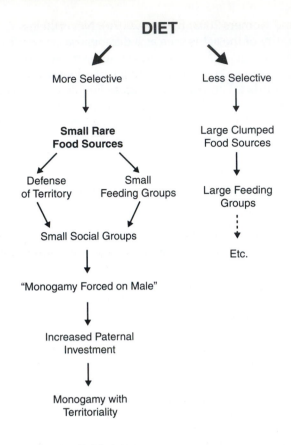

Figure 7–1 The "small-patch model" for the evolution of male resource defense monogamy, linking the evolution of small group size to intragroup feeding competition in small feeding patches (following Raemaekers and Chivers 1980:295).

species with less-selective diets, which feed in larger groups, will often exclude gibbons from large food patches, the gibbon niche is comprised of "rare, scattered, and often small, sources of food" (Raemaekers and Chivers 1980:291). This feeding niche constrains gibbon foraging behavior in a number of ways (Figure 7–1):

(1) intragroup feeding competition within small food patches will limit foraging group size;
(2) at the same time, a preference for rare sources of food will promote defense of stable territories because (a) detailed knowledge of a small range will reduce travel costs and (b) individuals will save time by not visiting sites recently depleted by others; and

(3) the economic constraints on defendability will limit social group size to a single adult male, a single adult female, and her offspring.

The small-patch model differs from the female dispersion model in that it does not presuppose territoriality by females. Instead, by defending a shared territorial border, males perform a service to females that enhances the reproductive fitness of both sexes. As explained by Raemaekers and Chivers (1980) "The female cannot defend a territory and raise young alone, so the male must remain with the female and assume the bulk of territorial behavior so as to ensure the survival of his offspring" (pp. 292–293). Finally, as with other models, male parental care develops only after the formation of two adult groups, with female intrasexual aggression intensifying as a result. This is consistent with both female intrasexual aggression exhibited during playback experiments (Mitani 1984, 1985) and the limited role played by females in home-range defense.

Are Gibbons Small-Patch Specialists?

Despite the apparent logic of the small-patch model, patch use by gibbons has rarely been quantified and the available data, including that described in this study, undermine the view of gibbons as small-patch specialists. First, in Khao Yai, comparison of the distributions of the gibbon feeding patches with the distribution of patch sizes in the forest as a whole shows that the average feeding tree visited by gibbons is larger than 90% of the trees available in the forest (see Chapter 4). In fact Khao Yai gibbons appear to avoid small patches except when feeding on leaves (see Figure 4–9). The small-patch model is further undermined by the routine exploitation by gibbons of large fig trees (MacKinnon and MacKinnon 1980; Chivers and Raemaekers 1986; Palombit 1992). When compared with other food parts, fig patches are larger (see Figure 4–9), fed in longer per visit (see Figure 4–2), and are occupied by more individuals during feeding bouts (see Chapter 4).

Further the small-patch model assumes that small social groups are able to exploit small feeding patches that are too small to simultaneously accommodate larger social groups. But research on a variety of species has shown that it is routine for primates to modify group size in response to food-patch size (Strier 2000). Most well known are the variable foraging strategies of fission-fusion species [e.g., *Ateles* spp. (Symington 1988; Chapman 1990); *Pan* spp. (Ghiglieri 1984; White and Wrangham 1988)]; however, many other species modify foraging behavior in more subtle ways. Milton (1980) reports that howler monkey troops (*Alouatta palliata*) often break up to feed simultaneously on leaves from a number of trees located within the same concentrated area. Leighton and Leighton (1982) found that howlers also break into feeding subgroups when entering fruit patches, with different subgroups feeding on different species, and Norconk and Kinzey (1994) report similar findings for bearded sakis (*Chiropotes satanas*), which are far more frugivorous than howlers. Gibbon groups are smaller on average than those of the above species, but similarly alter their foraging dynamics in response to the abundance of food within a patch as when feeding on young leaves. In other words gibbons appear to exploit small food patches in the same way as other primates, by modifying foraging group size. Furthermore the ability to exploit small patches does not imply that small groups cannot effectively exploit large patches (Terborgh 1983). As described by Gittins and Raemaekers (1980) a preference for large patches should result in reduced travel costs: "functionally, large food sources are attractive to gibbons, because they spend less time and energy in travel, finding and revisiting one large source, than they would over several smaller sources for the same amount of food" (p. 94). This suggests that in some contexts large-patch exploitation might be especially advantageous for small foraging groups (see following section).

Group Size and Patch Size in Other Primates

Monogamy and small-patch use have also been linked in monogamous New World monkeys. Terborgh (1983), in a now-classic study of the socioecology of five sympatric New World primates, identified a positive correlation between group size, dependence on figs, home-range size, and mean fruit-tree size. Based on this pattern he concludes that primates exhibit species-typical patch-size preferences. Terborgh's findings were confirmed by Wright (1986), who compared patch preferences of pair-living titi monkeys (*Callicebus moloch*) and owl monkeys (*Aotus trivigatus*) to similar-sized squirrel monkeys (*Saimiri sciureus*) that forage in much larger groups. Wright reports that titis spent the least amount of time foraging in large crowned trees (5%) and squirrel monkeys spent the most (55%); Owl monkeys fell in-between (33%). Wright (1986) concludes that her data "support the prediction that the monogamous primate species would rely on small, predictable, evenly spaced resources" (p. 164). Although both Terborgh and Wright draw comparisons to gibbons, data from Khao Yai diverge in many ways from the pattern identified by these investigators. This point is punctuated by the fact that Khao Yai gibbons reverse the trend identified by Terborgh (1983)—despite small group size, gibbons used relatively large patches and relied heavily on figs. Also Wright (1984) observes that *traplining*, visiting multiple patches of the same species in succession (see Janson et al. 1981), is common among titi monkeys, which is consistent with the view that foraging groups regularly deplete the patches they enter (Chapman and Chapman 2000). Khao Yai gibbons, on the other hand, rarely trapline (Bartlett and Brockelman 2002) and the fact that the study groups regularly revisited feeding sites during the same day undermines the view that they deplete the patches they enter during a single visit (see Grether et al. 1992).

Social Monogamy and Resource Density

The differences in the foraging behavior of gibbons and monogamous New World primates described above may indicate that the social systems of these two groups evolved in the context of very different ecological pressures. Alternatively, the differences described may simply reflect the fact that patch size is only one of several influences on primate foraging decisions. In describing what they refer to as the *ecological constraints* (EC) model, Chapman and Chapman (2000) assert that a more important determinant of group size in primates is habitat-wide food availability, which is determined not only by patch size but also by the density and distribution of resources (see Denham 1971; S. Altmann 1974; Emlen and Oring 1977; van Schaik and van Hooff 1983). A key element of the EC model is its explicit focus on travel costs as a measure of intragroup feeding competition. Larger groups will deplete patches more quickly and therefore sustain increased travel costs as they are forced to travel further in search of enough food to satisfy all group members. With respect to gibbon foraging behavior this approach has several advantages over the more narrowly focused small-patch model delineated earlier. First, the EC model recognizes that intragroup feeding competition constrains foraging in both large and small feeding patches. Large groups can reasonably exploit small patches as long as those patches are close together, but as the distance between patches and therefore the cost of reaching them increase, so does the advantage of small group size *regardless of patch size*, because small groups deplete patches more slowly. Second, the EC model highlights the importance of seasonal fluctuations in resource availability to the understanding of primate socioecology. According to Chapman and Chapman (2000)

> If food patches are clumped, scarce, and found in either large or small patches, animals may not be constrained from being in large groups in the short term, but may be forced to live in small groups if those resource conditions persist on a longer temporal scale (p. 33).

Finally, the EC model provides a framework for comparing a broad range of species. Raemaekers and Chivers (1980) consider gibbon monogamy in reference only to socially polygynous Malayan species with less-selective diets. As a result they never explicitly account for why gibbon social systems differ from those of other fruit pulp specialists. For example fission-fusion social systems, such as those exhibited by spider monkeys or chimpanzees, might be equally efficient at exploiting rare, scattered (if not small) food patches. In fact as Robbins and co-workers (1991) observe, gibbons and spider monkeys, in particular, share many striking similarities:

> Both are almost exclusively arboreal, use suspensory posture and locomotion, and are heavily reliant on ripe fruits, particularly figs. They have similar mean group sizes and individual home ranges. Based on these similarities, it might be expected that the two species would have similar patterns of social organization (p. 301).

But they do not, and the question posed by Robbins and co-workers is, Why? Based on a comparison of Mueller's gibbons and spider monkeys (*Ateles geoffroyi*), they exclude patch size as a primary ecological determinant because foraging groups in both species exploit similar-sized patches. Instead they propose that the principle reason that gibbons exhibit stable groups rather than a fission-fusion organization "is that their environments do not exhibit sufficient variability in food abundance and peak levels of food abundance are lower" (p. 304).[2] Given the potential for high levels of intraspecific variation in diet and foraging in both gibbons and spider monkeys, conclusions based on the comparison of just two populations must be approached with caution. Nevertheless Robbins and co-workers' (1991) findings do suggest a provisional modification of the small-patch model, one that emphasizes foraging efficiency (i.e., ecological constraints) over patch size per se while still recognizing the importance of the male role in resource defense (see Chapter 6).

According to a revised male resource defense model (Figure 7–2) temporal stability in the abundance of rare foods promotes small stable foraging groups because small groups require fewer patch visits per day. Foraging effort is further optimized through the defense of a fixed territory because the detailed knowledge of a small home range will further reduce travel costs and therefore individuals will save time by not visiting sites recently depleted by others. Thus the constraints of territorial economics—rather than patch size—impose a maximum limit on group size. Typically an adult male will be unable to defend sufficient resources to sustain more than a single adult female and her offspring. Males and females both benefit from the reduced travel costs, which is the result of a predictable resource base. Cost saving may be realized in a number of ways, including more-active resource defense by males and improved reproductive output in females. Ultimately social monogamy—including pair-bonding—evolves from small social groups because of intrasexual competition that is intensified (in females) by the secondary emergence of male paternal care. By contrast in areas where fruit abundance is more variable, periods of superabundance will allow much larger aggregates, at least temporarily, whereas extreme resource deficits would force animals to seek increasingly rare food patches beyond the borders of their defendable range. In committed frugivores, fission-fusion social

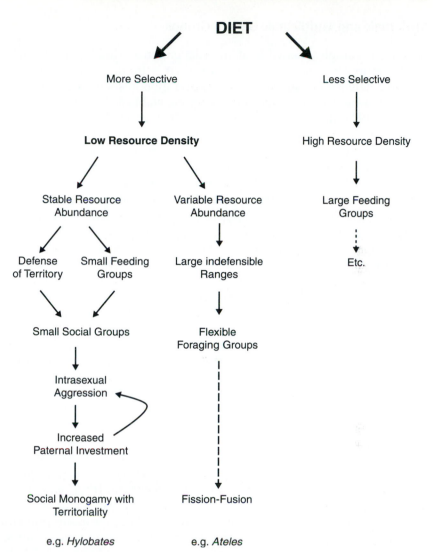

Figure 7–2 A revised model for the evolution of male resource defense monogamy, which focuses on the foraging benefits of small group size irrespective of patch size (see Robbins et al. 1991; Chapman and Chapman 2000).

systems are likely to develop as a result. This model is consistent with scenarios, based on phylogenetic analysis, which conclude that pair living in infant-carrying species, such as gibbons, evolved from small, mixed-sex groups rather than solitary foragers (Fuentes 2000; van Schaik and Kappeler 2003).

Multimale and Multifemale Gibbon Groups

Given the complex network of interdependence—linking territoriality, small group size, and biparental care—that is fundamental to the male resource defense model, we should expect gibbon social organization to be highly resistant to change and, therefore, stable across all populations (Ellefson 1974; Raemaekers and Chivers 1980; Brockelman 1984). Indeed two-adult social groups are clearly the modal pattern for hylobatids; nevertheless most long-term gibbon field studies have documented social groups with extra adults (for reviews, see Fuentes 2000; Sommer and Reichard 2000; Reichard 2003). One possible explanation for this finding is that recent habitat disturbance, a condition seen at many gibbon study sites, has resulted in elevated population densities that limit dispersal opportunities for maturing offspring (e.g., Lan et al. 1990; Bleisch and Chen 1991; Chivers 2001, 2005). In such cases emigrating subadults may remain with their natal group longer than usual and/or dispersing animals will often have no alternative but to join an already established group. This scenario is likely to explain at least some instances in which more than two adults have been recorded in gibbon groups. For example Ahsan (2001) observed a single hoolock gibbon group that had one adult male and two adult females living in disturbed forest at Lawachara in the West Bhanugach Reserve, Bangladesh. The lone male mated with both females; however, the three-adult grouping arrangement was temporary, and the remaining female failed to reproduce until she had forced the second female from the group. Most observers would agree that occasional episodes, such as this one, do little to undermine the characterization of gibbons as socially monogamous or to undermine the male resource defense model for gibbon monogamy. On the other hand multiadult groups have also been recorded in less-disturbed habitat [e.g., Khao Soi Dao (Srikosamatara and Brockelman 1987); Khao Yai (Brockelman et al. 1998, Sommer and Reichard 2000); Way Canguk Research Station, Sumatra (Lappan 2007b)], a finding that ostensibly violates the assumption that gibbon males are incapable of defending sufficient resources to support more than a single pair and associated offspring (e.g., Fuentes 2000). But on closer inspection the occurrence of multiadult gibbon groups is consistent with the model under certain conditions.

Social Polygyny in Crested Gibbons.   First, because male resource-defense monogamy is predicated on the idea that group size is limited by the foraging costs associated with a dietary preference for ripe fruit, populations that exhibit low rates of frugivory—either on an annual or seasonal basis—might be expected to diverge from the monogamous pattern. Consequently it is perhaps no coincidence that black-crested gibbons (*Nomascus concolor*), which are the most folivorous of all hylobatids, are also the species most commonly reported to exhibit polygyny in some groups (Delacour 1933; Haimoff et al. 1987; Jiang et al. 1999; Fan et al. 2006). To date, the most pertinent data come from two mountainous wildlife reserves, Mt. Ailao and Mt. Wuliang, in Yunnan Province, China, where fruit is estimated to constitute less than a quarter of the annual diet [Mt. Ailao, 24% (Chen 1995); Mt. Wuliang, 21% (Lan 1993)]. The low rates of frugivory are apparently the result of a very long dry season marked by occasional snowfall and a complete absence of fruit in the environment for over half of the year (Haimoff et al. 1987; Chen 1995). Available data also indicate that gibbons in these two reserves occupy much larger home ranges than other species [Mt. Ailao, 87 ha (Chen 1995); Mt. Wuliang, 100–200 ha (Sheeran et al. 1998)]. Although claims of social polygyny have often been dismissed as a product of habitat disturbance (e.g., Bleisch and Chen 1991; Sheeran et al. 1998), recent reports provide compelling evidence that polygyny is a viable alternative to social monogamy among black-crested gibbons. Jiang and co-workers (1999), for example, conducted complete group counts at two sites at Mt. Ailao and one at Mt. Wuliang and found that three of the nine groups censused had two breeding females. In two groups the evidence that both females had reproduced was based on the presence of two infants of similar size, whereas in a third group both females were carrying infants at the time of the census. In addition Fan and co-workers (2006), based on their observations at a separate site within the Wuliang Nature Reserve, found that all five groups under study had two adult females. In three of the groups the two females gave birth or carried infants at the same time. Relations between co-resident females were apparently amicable at both Mt. Ailao and Mt. Wuliang. This last point stands in contrast to Srikosamatara and Brockelman's (1987) description of a multifemale group of pileated gibbons at Khao Soi Dao, Thailand. In the group they observed the larger of the two females clearly dominated the smaller, and although the two females were initially observed carrying infants, the smaller female's infant disappeared between observations and was presumed dead.

Although it would be premature to exclude anthropogenic factors, such as habitat loss or low predator densities, as a potential cause of reported cases of multifemale groups in black-crested gibbons, social polygyny is consistent with the distinct ecological constraints confronted by gibbons in the mountainous regions of Yunnan, and perhaps throughout their range (Jiang et al. 1999). Because of the absence of high-quality resources during much of the year, groups are forced to range farther in search of food, making territoriality impractical. As a result (some) males will be able to improve reproductive success by pursuing a polygynous mating strategy. Because females no longer benefit from exclusive access to defended resources, female intrasexual aggression will abate. The loss of exclusive male parental care in the form of predator protection and socialization is more than compensated for by the presence of additional females and age mates. It remains to be determined if the distinct ecology of black-crested gibbons is simply the expression of the flexible foraging exhibited, to some degree, by all gibbons or if it is a species-specific adaptive pattern (perhaps related to their digestive physiology) that allows them to survive in highly seasonal environments. In either case, the occurrence of social polygyny among black-crested gibbons should not be viewed as a challenge to the male resource defense monogamy model because the preconditions of the model do not appear to apply in this context.

Social Polyandry and Male Kin Networks. From the standpoint of territorial economics the presence of multiple males in gibbon social groups is more readily accommodated by the male resource defense model. Although the addition of a second male should increase intragroup feeding competition, it is reasonable to expect that the loss of resources would be offset by his contribution to territorial defense. Groups with more males should be able to maintain larger or more-exclusive ranges. The energetic benefits might be realized in terms of reduced interbirth intervals, higher survival rates, or healthier offspring. In fact this argument has been proposed to explain the delayed dispersal of subadult males in Khao Yai gibbons (Brockelman et al. 1998). Nevertheless assistance during territorial encounters does not explain a resident male's tolerance of a reproductive competitor, except in the case wherein (a) the resident male is unable to maintain the territory alone (Savini and Reichard 2004) or (b) males are close genetic relatives (Lappan 2007a). The analysis of defendability in Chapter 6 suggests that Khao Yai males are able to defend ranges without the aid of additional males. On the other hand multimale groups have formed through the immigration of male siblings on at least two occasions. The first occurred in 1983 when Fearless emigrated from group F into group A, accompanied by what are believed to be his two younger brothers, Felix and Frodo (Brockelman et al. 1998). The second instance occurred in the years since the main phase of my field study was completed, when Christopher (by then fully adult) replaced Fearless as resident male in group A and was subsequently joined by his brother, Chiku (born in 1996), and father, Cassius (Brockelman et al. 2001; Brockelman pers. comm.). As of July 2004 when I last visited Khao Yai National Park, group A consisted of Andromeda and the three C males all of which fed and foraged as a cohesive unit.[3] These remarkable events suggest that in some cases of multimale gibbon groups (i.e., social polyandry), mutual male tolerance is the direct result of close genetic relatedness among coresident males. In this context resident males that are excluded from parenting infants during their residence may benefit because of inclusive fitness. This interpretation is supported by the evidence that neighbor males are often close relatives. Available data from Khao Yai (Brockelman et al. 1998) as well as Way Canguk (Lappan 2007a) suggest that male-dispersal distances are quite low among gibbons. Although comparable data on female dispersal is mostly lacking, this suggestion raises the intriguing possibility that gibbon neighborhoods represent "dispersed male networks," such as Bradley and co-workers (2004) describe for western gorillas (*Gorilla gorilla*). Genetic analysis of hair samples collected from gorilla nests demonstrated that resident males were usually related to at least one neighboring male, leading the investigators to conclude that the close genetic relationships between neighboring males accounted for the often "peaceful" intergroup encounters they observed. Although admittedly speculative, close male kinship may likewise explain mutual male tolerance between, and occasionally within, gibbon social groups (Bartlett 2003).

Significantly, multimale gibbon groups have also formed in the absence of any apparent kin relationship between coresidents. For example when the C group subadult male, Chet, dispersed in April 1994 (see Chapter 3), he was subsequently discovered in the neighboring group B (Bartlett and Brockelman 1996). In this case the B male, Bard, was initially hostile to Chet and regularly chased him from the group's vicinity. Yet Chet always returned and soon after joining the group began singing during duets, including singing simultaneous replies to the B female's (Bridget) great calls. Eventually Bard stopped singing his portion of the duet and was replaced by Chet as Bridget's primary grooming partner. Nevertheless the two males were observed mating with Bridget during their period of coresidence, which lasted roughly three years (Sommer and Reichard 2000). Based on these events Sommer and Reichard (2000) conclude that social polyandry may be an evolutionarily stable strategy for males living at high population densities. Older males, they suggest, are simply unable to rebuff the persistent advances of younger males, particularly in contexts where females are receptive to the company of both males, as Bridget was.

For now the question as to whether coresident males in socially polyandrous gibbon groups are commonly close kin is unresolved. Although additional data on male-dispersal patterns will be helpful in addressing this issue, more complete data on patterns of female emigration are also needed. Sommer and Reichard (2000) estimate that as much as a quarter of gibbon groups in saturated habitat have multiple males. Assuming an equal socionomic sex ratio in gibbons at birth, we are left to determine why there are not an equal number of multifemale groups in the same populations. Perhaps one reason is that females face higher predation pressure because, unlike males, they typically leave their neighborhoods when dispersing.

Mating Monogamy in Gibbons

As I indicated at the beginning of this chapter a species' social structure will limit the patterns of social interaction—including mating—among group members. With regard to social monogamy in particular, mating will often be restricted to a single reproductive partner. Accordingly all the models describing the evolution of social monogamy described in this chapter assume some degree of fidelity on the part of females (but see Gowaty 1996b). From a theoretical standpoint this is particularly important to male-service models because males that invest heavily in unrelated offspring will suffer fitness costs (Trivers 1972). Nevertheless it is a mistake to view sexual fidelity as a species-typical, or sex-typical, behavioral trait; rather, mating behavior in primates is best viewed as the product of sexual access, which is limited by, but independent of, social structure. So although the large majority of gibbon social groups are comprised of only two fully adult animals, both males and females may seek matings with multiple partners when conditions permit (Palombit 1994b; Reichard 1995; Ahsan 2001; Lappan 2007b). The clear benefit of multiple mating to males is the possibility of siring greater numbers of offspring. There is less consensus as to the principle benefit of multiple mating to females, although increasing the probability of conception has been identified as a possible cause (Hrdy 1981; Small 1993; Gowaty 1996a). In any case, clearly, females exercise considerable control over male reproductive behavior, and hence females should not be dismissed simply as a "resource" to be exploited by males (Roughgarden et al. 2006). This suggestion is especially true for gibbons because females are of similar body size to males and are therefore less likely to be coerced. For example the A female, Andromeda, chased the C male, Cassius, from her tree during an intergroup encounter, despite the fact that she carried a young infant, whereas at other times she allowed the approach of neighbor males and engaged in EPCs (see the following section). In fact the reproductive history of Andromeda represents an interesting case study in the investigation of gibbon mating patterns.

The Sex Life of Andromeda: A Case Study.   When I began my preliminary observations of group A in 1993, Andromeda was in the advanced stages of pregnancy. But despite being clearly paired with Fearless, the paternity of her offspring was uncertain (among the human observers at least). As described by Reichard (1995) at the beginning of 1993 Andromeda copulated with both Fearless and Cassius, a neighboring male, during the period when her infant Akira was conceived. Throughout my field study Andromeda was nursing this infant and never engaged in any form of mating behavior. In fact without the careful observations of Reichard, there would be little reason to question her fidelity, although Brockelman and co-workers' (1998) long-term observations had already established that Fearless was at least Andromeda's second pair mate. Then in 2000–2001 Andromeda took a third mate, Christopher (Brockelman et al. 2001), and I observed this new couple mate, exclusively to my knowledge,

Andromeda with her infant, Akira, in 1994.

during my brief visit to the park in 2002. Finally Andromeda and Christopher subsequently formed a socially polyandrous group with the addition of Cassius and Chiku in 2004 (see the previous section). Although she was paired first with Christopher, who was also her duet partner, Andromeda copulated with all three males (Brockelman pers. comm.). In one instance, which I observed when I revisited the group in July 2004, Andromeda (who I had seen copulate with Christopher on several occasions) copulated with the subadult Chiku during an intergroup encounter. Initially both Christopher and Chiku were involved in a border dispute with the group B male, Chet. As the dispute continued, Chiku quietly traveled to the tree where Andromeda rested. As soon as he entered her tree, Andromeda presented to the young male, who mounted her dorsoventrally and initiated a series of thrusts. This copulation followed several prior attempts (made over several days of observation) that were interrupted when Christopher threatened or chased Chiku away. In each case Andromeda was receptive to Chiku's advances, although even the successful copulation I observed was truncated when Christopher rushed back from the border to displace Chiku from Andromeda's side. Surprisingly in this case Christopher did not chase the subadult from the tree, perhaps owing to the ongoing border dispute.

This series of events, although drawn from the history of a single female, nevertheless illustrates the complexities of gibbon social systems.

A polyandrous gibbon group. Andromeda grooms the auxiliary male Chiku as her pair mate, Christopher, watches. Andromeda mated with both males.

First, the multiple mating by Andromeda demonstrates the conflicting reproductive interest of males and females and illustrates the important role of female choice in the reproductive patterns of even socially monogamous primates. Andromeda repeatedly allowed the approach of the auxiliary males in the group despite Christopher's interference. Second, Christopher's behavior during the encounter exemplifies the multiple-selection pressures faced by gibbon males. Social monogamy demands the maintenance of stable territories, whereas mating monogamy demands constant mate guarding. The compromises made by male gibbons reflect these conflicting aims, reinforcing the now well-established view, which bears repeating here, that social structure and mating systems are not the same (e.g., Anzenberger 1992; Gowaty 1996a; Overdorff and Parga 2007). Consequently, the fact that gibbons are not the paragons of virtue they were once thought to be should in no way diminish our interest in the evolution of social monogamy in this species.

CONCLUSION

As I have detailed in this chapter social monogamy in gibbons is likely the outcome of a dietary preference for rare but stable resources that make territorial defense possible and advantageous because of the fitness benefits of improved foraging efficiency. Tests of this model ultimately rest on the ability to operationalize concepts such as *scarcity, stability,* and *density* in ways that can be reliably compared across species and study sites (see Robbins et al. 1991; Fuentes 2000; Overdorff and Parga 2007). Unfortunately despite some circumstantial evidence (e.g. Brockelman et al. 1973; O'Brien et al. 2003), it continues to be the case that essential data on the relationship between resource defense and reproductive success is almost completely absent (Chivers 1984; van Schaik and Dunbar 1990). Nevertheless I contend that provisional support for a model of social monogamy based on foraging efficiency tied to male resource defense territoriality may be found in the way that gibbons alter foraging in response to seasonal fluctuations in resource abundance. If so, I hope that the research I have presented here serves as a first step.

ENDNOTES

1. The distinction between social structure and social organization presented here follows Rowell (1972, 1979). Kappeler and van Schaik (2002) reverse these labels. For additional discussion see Fuentes (2007).
2. But see Knott (2007) for a discussion of the impact of *mast fruiting* (the synchronous fruiting of very large numbers of trees) on the socioecology of orangutans, which share part of their habitat with gibbons. She argues that solitary foraging in orangutans is a response to the large swings in fruit availability that mast fruiting produces.
3. Although this group is composed predominantly of animals from group C, it retains the designation "group A" because of its geographic locale. The location of the A territory changed little in 10 years (1994–2004) despite extensive changes to group composition.

CHAPTER

8

Summary and Directions for Future Research

Like most studies made under natural conditions, this one is incomplete on some subjects. The picture can be further filled in by laboratory work and by more prolonged work in the field.

—Carpenter (1940:266)

Khao Yai gibbons can be described as fruit-pulp specialists that maintain a fruit-dominated diet year-round by switching to lower-quality fallback foods—namely figs—when the overall abundance of ripe fruit is low. During the fruit-rich hot season the study animals traveled long distances, visiting multiple fruiting trees in succession and foraging more heavily on insects than during other times of the year. At the same time gibbons exhibited high rates of nonsubsistence behavior, including grooming, play, and friendly interactions with neighboring groups. When ripe fruit was scarce, gibbons coped by exhibiting an economical foraging strategy that optimized energy use by increasing feeding time while limiting time devoted to nonsubsistence behaviors and the distance traveled per day. In contrast to many other populations Khao Yai gibbons recurrently visited large feeding patches (including both figs and nonfig fruit trees) throughout the year. These findings indicate that from the standpoint of primate socioecology it is important to decouple group size and patch size. In Khao Yai the importance of patch size to gibbons appears to lie not in their ability to jointly exploit small food patches, but in their ability to recurrently exploit and defend large patches, thereby minimizing search effort

148

while maximizing energy gain. Because such benefits can be realized only if animals have reliable access to known food sources, territoriality has evolved in concert with the gibbon's dietary preference for ripe fruit. Ultimately social monogamy in gibbons likely emerged in response to male parental care, at first indirectly in the form of resource defense territoriality and second, in the form of direct parental care as exhibited by predator protection and grooming.

NUTRITIONAL AND COGNITIVE ECOLOGY IN GIBBONS

The approach I have adopted in this study focuses on energy balance and the way the availability of preferred (i.e., high-energy) foods influences gibbon activity patterns. It is important to keep in mind, however, that energy content is only a part of the overall value of a food item. In addition to necessary caloric intake, all animals must consume an adequate balance of vitamins, minerals, and amino acids while at the same time avoiding/limiting exposure to chemical defenses (e.g., tannins) that plants employ to inhibit digestion (Milton 1980; Lambert 2007). Consequently primate foraging patterns will also be shaped by their need to maintain nutritional balance (Milton 2000). For Khao Yai gibbons the abundance of ripe fruit in the environment correlates significantly with several measures of energy expenditure; nevertheless fruit-feeding peaks were out of phase with fruiting peaks, suggesting that factors other than caloric content influence gibbon food choice (see Vasey 2002). One possibility is that gibbons were responding to the need to maintain adequate levels of protein in the diet (a nutrient in which ripe fruit is often lacking). This is suggested, in part, by the negative correlation between feeding time devoted to insects compared with leaves (both of which may serve as sources of essential amino acids), but validating this conclusion will require a different approach.

An important first step will be to employ nutritional analyses of the food items gibbons actually consume (see Vellayan 1981). This is particularly important given the variation in nutrient content within broadly defined food classes, such as "fig fruit," which is often characterized as a low-quality food (see references in Wrangham et al. 1993; Wendeln et al. 2000). For example Leighton (1993) concludes, based on an analysis of *Ficus* species consumed by Bornean orangutans in Kutai National Park, that "almost all fig species produced nutritionally poor fruits" (p. 300). Specifically he showed that figs, compared with nonfig fruit, had very low levels of digestible carbohydrates, fats, and protein, as well as "much higher tannin content and nearly twice the fiber." But Wendeln and co-workers (2000), who analyzed nutrient values for 14 *Ficus* species from Barro Colorado Island, Panama, documented considerable variation between species in the levels of most nutritionally significant constituents. One species (*F. insipida*) had very high concentrations of protein and most amino acids, whereas another (*F. bullenei*) had high levels of both lipids and carbohydrates. And although tannin levels likely present digestive challenges to hylobatids, Vellayan (1981) determined that gibbons at Kuala Lompat, Malaysia, selected fig species with low tannin content, a pattern similar to that identified by Leighton (1993) for orangutans. So whereas as a food class figs may indeed be nutritionally poor, individual species compare favorably with nonfig fruits with regard to nutrient content and density. Such variation in nutritional quality recalls Janzen's (1979) warning: "A *fig* is not a FIG is not a **fig**" (p. 41, emphasis in original), a warning that applies equally to other food classes [e.g., fruit (Matsumoto-Oda and Hayashi 1999); leaves (Janson and Chapman 1999); insects (Gursky 2000)].

A second goal for future research into gibbon feeding ecology should be to integrate the nutritional content of specific foods with data on the temporal and spatial distribution of feeding patches to better relate patch value to gibbon foraging decisions. If gibbon social structure evolved in response to foraging constraints related to resource density, then gibbons should exhibit cognitive adaptations that promote search efficiency (Milton 1981; Garber 2000). Previous studies on spatial foraging in a variety of arboreal New World primates [e.g., *Saguinus* spp. (Garber 1989; Garber and Hannon 1993); *Cebus apella* (Janson 1998); *Ateles belzebuth* (Suarez 2003)] suggest effective approaches for evaluating the efficiency of gibbon route selection, for example, by comparing the routes actually traveled by gibbons with those derived from computer models based on random or systematic search strategies. An additional consideration with regard to the foraging behavior of gibbons would be to compare the location of feeding trees and travel routes with the location of territorial borders in order to better understand the relationship between resource distribution and territorial defense. In 2001 Brockelman and colleagues completed mapping, tagging, and identifying all trees on the Mo Singto forest dynamics plot (a task begun in 1994; see Chapter 2). The 28.6 ha area contains the entire group A home range, making Mo Singto an ideal setting for continued research on the feeding and ranging behavior of white-handed gibbons (Brockelman et al. 2001).

WILDLIFE CONSERVATION

As with all primates the future of gibbon research will depend on the conservation of the tropical environments where gibbons live. I was fortunate to work at a site that was well protected from human encroachment, and during my periodic revisits to Khao Yai in 1998, 2002, and 2004, the forest and the gibbons were much the same as I left them (with the exception of the growing number of gibbon researchers roaming the trails). The most visible impact on the area was in the form of intermittent poaching of mai hom, the aromatic wood of the aloewood tree (*Aquilaria crassna*) which is processed for use in perfumes and medicinal products sold worldwide. To

Aloewood poachers harvest resin-infused wood by hollowing out the trunks of standing *Aquilaria crassna* trees, as shown here.

harvest the wood, poachers hack into the broad base of the tree and shear away layers of resin-infused wood, leaving a still-standing but badly scarred trunk. When I first arrived in Khao Yai in 1993, most of the large *Aquilaria* trees in the study area were scarred, but I never encountered poachers nor saw evidence that mai hom was being actively harvested within the study area. According to Srikosamatara and Brockelman (2002), however, mai hom poaching, which can be very lucrative, increased in the park following the 1997 collapse of the Thai baht. *Aquilaria* fruit constitutes a very small part of the gibbon diet so the direct impact of mai hom poaching on gibbons is probably minimal. Of greater concern is opportunistic hunting by mai hom poachers during their forays into the forest. Thus far the gibbon population around the park head quarters has been unaffected, but increased traffic in mai hom brings increased risk to all forms of wildlife, including gibbons (Kantawatanakid et al. 2002; Vejpongsa 2006). Thai law strictly prohibits extraction and use of all forest products, but enforcement is difficult because of the large number of villages circling the park boundary as well as the easy access to the park interior the paved road provides. Also of growing concern is the increased development within park—including new restaurants and lodging, a 300-seat conference center, and wider roads—which prompted one editorial in the *Bangkok Post* to facetiously refer to the park as Khao Yai City (Kongsanit 2001).

Fortunately the growing popularity of the park has also spurred increased efforts to curb development and reduce illegal exploitation (Srikosamatara and Brockelman 2002). In 2000 The Khao Yai Conservation Project (KYCP) was established as a joint effort by the Thai Royal Forest Department, the Wildlife Conservation Society (WCS), and WildAid (now Wildlife Alliance) to improve environmental law enforcement. With financial assistance from the U.S. Department of State, KYCP provided Khao Yai rangers with training and technology, including GPS receivers, to assist them in tracking poachers deep within the park. At the same time WildAid and WCS instituted outreach and education programs that provided funds to help expoachers to develop alternative sources of income and to raise awareness in the wider community. Today Wildlife Alliance (2007) claims that poaching in the park is down 70% since the inception of the program. Even if the actual figure is substantially less [i.e., 17–27% (Wildlife Conservation Society 2007)], it is a major accomplishment and reason for hope.

Conservation efforts have also been buoyed by the recent declaration of the Dong Phayayen–Khao Yai Forest Complex as a World Heritage Site. This complex, which includes Khao Yai National Park in addition to the adjacent Thap Lan National Park and three smaller protected areas, comprises 615,500 ha (UNESCO 2007). But despite international recognition of the importance of this ecosystem to global diversity, future development projects are already planned for Khao Yai, including further widening of the road through the park (from two lanes to four) to facilitate the movement of industrial goods between Bangkok and the Northeast provinces (Khao Yai road works 'Destroying' the National Park 2006). As is the case the world over, in Thailand conservation and economic interests are at odds. Only time will tell if the awareness and goodwill fostered by conservation programs such as those implemented by Wildlife Alliance and WCS are sufficient to stand up to the challenges posed by the powerful economic interests that continue to threaten Khao Yai National Park and other protected areas in Thailand.

References

Ahsan, M. F. 2001. Socio-Ecology of the Hoolock Gibbon (*Hylobates hoolock*) in Two Forests of Bangladesh. In *The Apes: Challenges for the 21st Century*, Conference Proceedings, Chicago Zoological Society, 286–299.

Aldrich-Blake, F. P. G., and D. J. Chivers. 1973. On the Genesis of a Group of Siamang. *American Journal of Physical Anthropology* 38(2): 631–636.

Alfred, J. R. B., and J. P. Sati. 1991. On the First Record of Infanticide in the Hoolock Gibbon (*Hylobates hoolock*) in the Wild. *Records of the Zoological Survey of India*, 89(1–4): 319–321.

Altmann, J. 1974. Observational Study of Behavior: Sampling Methods. *Behavior* 49(3): 227–267.

———. 1980. *Baboon Mothers and Infants*. Cambridge: Harvard University Press.

Altmann, S. 1974. Baboons, Space, Time and Energy. *American Zoologist* 14(1): 221–248.

Altmann, S., and J. Altmann. 1970. *Baboon Ecology*. Chicago: University of Chicago Press.

Anzenberger, G. 1992. Monogamous Social Systems and Paternity in Primates. In *Paternity in Primates: Genetic Tests and Theories*, ed. R. D. Martin, A. F. Dixson, and E. J. Wickings, 203–224. Basel: Karger.

Barlow, G. W. 1988. Monogamy in Relation to Resources. In *The Ecology of Social Behavior*, ed. C. N. Slobodchikoff, 55–79. San Diego: Academic Press, Inc.

Bartlett, T. Q. 2000. In the Field: Close Encounters of the Friendly Kind. In *Primate Diversity*, ed. D. Falk, 268–269. New York: W. W. Norton.

———. 2002. Social Behavior and Social Organization (and Social Traditions?) in White-Handed Gibbons. *Abstracts of the XIXth Congress of the International Primatological Society*, Beijing, China, 114. Beijing: Mammalogical Society of China.

———. 2003. Intragroup and Intergroup Social Interactions in White-Handed Gibbons. *International Journal of Primatology* 24(2): 239–259.

———. 2007a. The Hylobatidae: Small Apes of Asia. In *Primates in Perspective*, ed. C. J. Campbell, A. Fuentes, K. C. MacKinnon, M. Panger and S. K. Bearder, 274–289. Oxford: Oxford University Press.

———. 2007b. Seasonal Home Range Use and Defendability in White-Handed Gibbons (*Hylobates lar*) in Khao Yai National Park, Thailand. *American Journal of Physical Anthropology* (Supplement) 44: 69.

Bartlett, T. Q., and W. Y. Brockelman. 1996. Gradual Replacement of a Male Pairmate in White-Handed Gibbons (*Hylobates lar*) in Khao Yai National Park, Thailand. *American Journal of Physical Anthropology* (Supplement) 22: 66.

———. 2002. Foraging and Patch Use in White-Handed Gibbons. *American Journal of Physical Anthropology* (Supplement) 34: 40.

Bates, B. C. 1970. Territorial Behavior in Primates: A Review of Recent Field Studies. *Primates* 11: 271–284.

Begun, D. R. 2002. The Pliopithecoidea. In *The Primate Fossil Record*, ed. W. C. Hartwig, 221–240. Cambridge: Cambridge University Press.

Bingham, H. C. 1932. *Gorillas in a Native Habitat*. Washington: Carnegie Institute of Washington Publication 426, 1–66.

Bleisch, W. V., and N. Chen. 1991. Ecology and behavior of wild black-crested gibbons (*Hylobates concolor*) in China with a Reconsideration of Evidence for Polygyny. *Primates* 32(4): 539–548.

Boinski, S. 1987. Habitat Use by Squirrel Monkeys (*Saimiri oerstedi*) in Costa Rica. *Folia Primatologica* 49: 151–167.

———. 2000. Social Manipulation within and between Troops Mediates Primate Group Movement. In *On the Move*, ed. S. Boinski and P. A. Garber, 411–469. Chicago: University of Chicago Press.

Boinski, S., and N. L. Fowler. 1989. Seasonal Patterns in a Tropical Lowland Forest. *Biotropica* 21(3): 223–233.

Bradley, B. J., D. M. Doran-Sheehy, D. Lukas, C. Boesch, and L. Vigilant. 2004. Dispersed Male Networks in Western Gorillas. *Current Biology* 14(6): 510–513.

Bricknell, S. J. 1999. Hybridisation and Behavioral Variation: A Socio-Ecological Study of Hybrid Gibbons (*Hylobates agilis albibarbis × H. muelleri*) in Central Kalimantan, Indonesia. Ph.D. dissertation, Australian National University, Canberra.

Brockelman, W. Y. 1975. Gibbon Populations and Their Conservation in Thailand. *Natural History Bulletin of the Siam Society* 26: 133–157.

———. 2004. Inheritance and Selective Effects of Color Phase in White-Handed Gibbons (*Hylobates lar*) in Central Thailand. *Mammalian Biology* 69(2): 73–80.

———. 2005. Review of *Monogamy: Mating Strategies and Partnerships in Birds, Humans and Other Mammals*, ed. U. H. Reichard and C. Boesch. *Primates*, 46(2): 151–153.

Brockelman W. Y., and S. P. Gittins. 1984. Natural Hybridization in the *Hylobates lar* Species Group: Implications for Speciation in Gibbons. In *The Lesser Apes: Evolutionary and Behavioural Biology*, ed. H. Preuschoft, D. J. Chivers, W. Y. Brockelman, and N. Creel, 498–532. Edinburgh: Edinburgh University Press.

Brockelman, W. Y., B. A. Ross, and S. Pantuwatana. 1973. Social Correlates of Reproductive Success in the Gibbon Colony on Ko Klet Kaeo, Thailand. *American Journal of Physical Anthropology* 38(2): 637–640.

Brockelman, W. Y., A. Natalang, P. Charoenchai, C. Nan, T. Santisuk, C. Suckaseam, G. Gale, and J. F. Maxwell. 2001. Study of Forest Biodiversity at Mo Singto Forest Dynamics Plot, Khao Yai National Park. *BRT Research Reports 2001*, 218–224, The Biodiversity Research and Training Program, Bangkok.

Brockelman, W. Y., U. Reichard, U. Treesucon, and J. J. Raemaekers. 1998. Dispersal, Pair Formation and Social Structure in Gibbons (*Hylobates lar*). *Behavioral Ecology and Sociobiology* 42(5): 329–339.

Brockelman, W. Y., and D. Schilling. 1984. Inheritance of Stereotyped Gibbon Calls. *Nature* 312: 634–636.

Brockelman, W. Y., and S. Srikosamatara. 1993. Estimation of Density of Gibbon Groups by Use of Loud Songs. *American Journal of Primatology* 29(2): 93–108.

———. 1984. Maintenance and Evolution of Social Structure in Gibbons. In *The Lesser Apes: Evolutionary and Behavioural Biology*, ed. H. Preuschoft, D. J. Chivers, W. Y. Brockelman, and N. Creel, 298–323. Edinburgh: Edinburgh University Press.

Brockman, D., and C. P. van Schaik. 2005. *Primate Seasonality: Implications for Human Evolution*. Cambridge: Cambridge University Press.

Brotherton, P. N. M., and P. E. Komers. 2003. Mate Guarding and the Evolution of Social Monogamy in Mammals. In *Monogamy: Mating Strategies and Partnerships in Birds, Humans, and Other Mammals*, ed. U. H. Reichard, and C. Boesch, 42–58. Cambridge: Cambridge University Press.

Brown, J. L. 1964. The Evolution of Diversity of Avian Territorial Systems. *Wilson Bulletin.* 76: 160–169.

Burt, W. H. 1943. Territoriality and Home Range Concepts as Applied to Mammals. *Journal of Mammalogy.* 24: 364–352.

Byers, J. A., and C. Walker. 1995: Refining the Motor Training Hypothesis for the Evolution of Play. *The American Naturalist* 146: 25–40.

Caine, N. G. 1987. Vigilance, Vocalizations, and Cryptic Behavior at Retirement in Captive Groups of Red-Bellied Tamarins. *American Journal of Primatology* 12: 241–250.

Cant, J., and A. L. Temerin. 1984. A Conceptual Approach to Foraging Adaptations in Primates. In *Adaptations for Foraging in Nonhuman Primates: Contributions to an Organismal Biology of Prosimians, Monkeys, and Apes*, ed. P. S. Rodman and J. G. H. Cant, 304–342. New York: Columbia University Press.

Carpenter C. R. 1934. A Field Study of the Behavior and Social Relations of Howling Monkeys (*Alouatta palliata*). *Comparative Psychology Monographs* 10: 1–168.

———. 1935. Behavior of the Red Spider Monkey (*Ateles geoffroyi*) in Panama. *Journal of Mammalogy* 16: 171–180.

————. 1938. *A Survey of Wild Life Conditions in Atjeh North Sumatra: With Special Reference to the Orang-Utan.* Amsterdam, Netherlands Committee for International Nature Protection, Communications No. 12, 1–34.

————. R. 1940. A Field Study in Siam of the Behavior and Social Relations of the Gibbon (*Hylobates lar*). *Comparative Psychology Monographs* 16: 1–212. Reprinted in Naturalistic Behavior of Nonhuman Primates. University Park, Pennsylvania State University Press. 1964. 145–271.

————. 1964. *Naturalistic Behavior of Nonhuman Primates.* University Park: Pennsylvania State University Press.

Chambers, K., L. Vigilant, C. Boesch, and U. Reichard. 2002. Within Group Relatedness and Genetic Mating Systems in White-Handed Gibbons (*Hylobates lar*). *American Journal of Physical Anthropology* (Supplement) 34: 52–53.

Chapman, C. 1988. Patterns of Foraging and Range Use by Three Species of Neotropical Primates. *Primates* 29(2): 177–194.

Chapman, C. 1990. Ecological Constraints on Group Size in Three Species of Neotropical Primates. *Folia Primatologica* 55(1): 1–9.

Chapman, C. A., L. J. Chapman, R. Wrangham, K. Hunt, D. Gebo, and L. Gardner. 1992. Estimators of Fruit Abundance of Tropical Trees. *Biotropica* 24(4): 527–531.

Chapman, C. A., and L. J. Chapman. 2000. Determinants of Group Size in Primates: The Importance of Travel Costs. In *On the Move: How and Why Animals Travel in Groups,* ed. S. Boinski and P. A. Garber, 24–42. Chicago: University of Chicago Press.

Charnov, E. L. 1976. Optimal Foraging: The Marginal Value Theorem. *Theoretical Population Biology* 9: 129–136.

Chen, N. 1995. *Ecology of the Black-Crested Gibbon* (Hylobates concolor) *in the Ailao Mt. Reserve, Yunnan, China.* M.A. thesis, Mahidol University, Bangkok, Thailand.

Chivers, D. J. 1972. The Siamang and the Gibbon in the Malay Peninsula. *Gibbon and Siamang* 1: 103–135.

————. 1974. The Siamang in Malaya: A Field Study of a Primate in Tropical Rain Forest. *Contributions to Primatology* 4: *i–ix*, 1–335.

————. 1977. The Lesser Apes. In *Primate Conservation,* ed. Prince Rainier of Monaco and G. H. Bourne, 539–598. New York: Academic Press.

————. 1980. Introduction. In *Malayan Forest Primates: Ten Years' Study in Tropical Rain Forest,* ed. D. J. Chivers, 1–27. New York: Plenum Press.

————. 1984. Feeding and Ranging in Gibbons: A Summary. In *The Lesser Apes: Evolutionary and Behavioural Biology,* ed. H. Preuschoft, D. J. Chivers, W. Y. Brockelman and N. Creel, 267–281. Edinburgh: Edinburgh University Press.

————. 2001. The Swinging Singing Apes: Fighting for Food and Family in the Far-East Forests. In *The Apes: Challenges for the 21st Century,* Conference Proceedings, Chicago Zoological Society, 1–28.

————. 2005. Review of *Monogamy: Mating Strategies and Partnerships in Birds, Humans and Other Mammals,* ed. U. R. Reichard and C. Boesch. Cambridge: Cambridge University Press. *Folia Primatologica* 76: 184.

Chivers, D. J., and J. J. Raemaekers. 1986. Natural and Synthetic Diets of Malayan Gibbons. In *Primate Ecology and Conservation,* ed. J. G. Else and P. C. Lee, 39–56. New York: Cambridge University Press.

Clarke E., U. H. Reichard, and K. Zuberbüler. 2006. The Syntax and Meaning of Wild Gibbon Songs. *PLoS ONE* 1(1): 1–10.

Clutton-Brock, T. H. 1975. Ranging Behaviour of Red Colobus (*Colobus badius tephrosceles*) in Gombe National Park. *Animal Behaviour* 23: 706–722.

Clutton-Brock, T. H. 1977. Some Aspects of Intraspecific Variation in Feeding and Ranging Behaviour in Primates. In *Primate Ecology,* ed. T. H. Clutton-Brock, 539–556. London: Academic Press.

Cowlishaw, G. 1992. Song Function in Gibbons. *Behaviour* 121(1–2): 131–153.

Dawkins, R. 1996. *Climbing Mount Improbable.* New York: W. W. Norton.

Defler, T. R. 1995. The Time Budget of a Group of Wild Woolly Monkeys (*Lagothrix lagotricha*). *International Journal of Primatology* 16(2): 107–120.

Delacour, J. 1933. On the Indochinese Gibbons (*Hylobates concolor*). *Journal of Mammology* 14: 71–73.

Denham, W. W. 1971. Energy Relations and Some Basic Properties of Primate Social Organization. *American Anthropologists* 73(1): 77–95.

DeVore, I. 1965. *Primate Behavior: Field Studies of Monkeys and Apes.* New York: Holt Rinehart Winston.

Di Fiore, A. 2003. Ranging Behavior and Foraging Ecology of Lowland Woolly Monkeys (*Lagothrix lagotricha poeppigii*) in Yasuní National Park, Ecuador. *American Journal of Primatology* 59: 47–66.

Di Fiore, A., and P. S. Rodman. 2001. Time Allocation Patterns of Lowland Woolly Monkeys (*Lagothrix lagotricha poeppigii*) in a Neotropical Terra Firma Forest. *International Journal of Primatology* 22: 449–480.

Doran, D. M. 1997. The influence of Seasonality on Activity Patterns, Feeding Behavior, Ranging, and Grouping Patterns in Tai chimpanzees. *International Journal of Primatology* 18: 183–206.

Dunbar, R. I. M. 1992. Time: A Hidden Constraint on the Behavioural Ecology of Baboons. *Behavioral Ecology and Sociobiology* 31: 35–49.

Dunbar, R. I. M., and E. P. Dunbar. 1980. The Pairbond in Klipspringer. *Animal Behaviour* 28: 219–229.

Edwards, A. A. R., and J. D. Todd. 1991. Homosexual Behavior in Wild White-Handed Gibbons (*Hylobates lar*). *Primates* 32(2): 231–236.

Eisenberg, J. F., N. A. Muckenhirn, and R. Rudran. 1972. The Relation between Ecology and Social Structure in Primates. *Science* 176: 863–874.

Ellefson, J. O. 1974. A Natural History of White-Handed Gibbons in the Malayan Peninsula. In *Gibbon and Siamang*, Vol. 3, ed. D. M. Rumbaugh, 1–136. Basel: S Karger.

Emlen, S. T., and L. W. Oring. 1977. Ecology, Sexual Selection and the Evolution of Mating Systems. *Science* 197: 215–223.

Erhart E. M., and D. J. Overdorff. 1999. Female Coordination of Travel in Wild *Propithecus diadema* and *Eulemur*. *International Journal of Primatology* 20: 927–940.

Fagen, R. 1993. Primate Juveniles and Primate Play. In *Juvenile Primates: Life History, Development, and Behavior*, ed. M. E. Pereira and L. A. Fairbanks. New York: Oxford University Press.

Fan, P., X. Jiang, C. Liu, and W. Luo. 2006. Polygynous Mating System and Behavioural Reason of Black Crested Gibbon (*Nomascus concolor jingdongensis*) at Dazhaizi, Mt. Wuliang, Yunnan, China. *Zoological Research* 27(2): 216–220.

Fashing, P. J. 2001. Male and Female Strategies during Intergroup Encounters in Guerezas (*Colobus guereza*): Evidence for Resource Defense Mediated through Males and a Comparison with Other Primates. *Behavioral Ecology and Sociobiology* 50(3): 219–230.

Fooden, J. 1971. Color and Sex in Gibbons. *Bulletin* (Field Museum of Natural History) 42(6): 2–7.

Fowler, J., L. Cohen, and P. Jarvis. 1998. *Practical Statistics for Field Biologists*. Chichester: John Wiley & Sons.

Freeland, W. J. 1976. Pathogens and the Evolution of Primate Sociality. *Biotropica* 8: 12–24.

Fuentes, A. 1998. Reevaluating Primate Monogamy. *American Anthropologist* 100(4): 890–907.

———. 2000. Hylobatid Communities: Changing Views on Pair Bonding and Social Organization in Hominoids. *Yearbook of Physical Anthropology* 43: 33–60.

———. 2002. Patterns and Trends in Primate Pair Bonds. *International Journal of Primatology* 23(5): 953–978.

———. 2007. Social Organization: Social Systems and the Complexities in Understanding the Evolution of Primate Behavior. In *Primates in Perspective*, ed. C. Campbell, A. Fuentes, K. C. MacKinnon, M. Panger and S. K. Bearder, 609–621. Oxford: Oxford University Press.

Garber, P. A. 1987. Foraging Strategies among Living Primates. *Annual Review of Anthropology* 16: 339–364.

———. 1989. Role of Spatial Memory in Primate Foraging Patterns: *Saguinus mystax* and *Saguinus fuscicollis*. *American Journal of Primatology* 19: 203–216.

———. 1993. Seasonal Patterns of Diet and Ranging in Two Species of Tamarin Monkeys: Stability versus Variability. *International Journal of Primatology* 14(1): 145–166.

———. 2000. Evidence for the Use of Spatial, Temporal, and Social Information by Some Primate Foragers. In *On the Move*, ed. S. Boinski and P. A. Garber, 261–298. Chicago: University of Chicago Press.

Garber, P. A., and B. Hannon. 1993. Modeling Monkeys: A Comparison of Computer Generated and Naturally Occurring Foraging Patterns in Two Species of Neotropical Primates. *International Journal of Primatology* 14: 827–852.

Garza, J. C., and D. S. Woodruff. 1992. A Phylogenetic Study of the Gibbons (*Hylobates*) Using DNA Obtained Non-Invasively from Hair. *Molecular Phylogenetics and Evolution* 1: 202–210.

Gaulin, S. J. C., and M. Konner. 1977. On the Natural Diet of Primates, Including Humans. In *Nutrition and the Brain*, Vol. 1, ed. R. J. Wurtman and J. J. Wurtman, 1–86. New York: Raven Press.

Gautier-Hion, A., J. P. Gautier, and R. Quris. 1981. Forest Structure and Fruit Availability as Complementary Factors Influencing Habitat Use by a Troop of Monkeys (*Cercopithecus cephus*). Revue d'Ecologie (la Terre et la Vie) 35: 511–536.

Geissmann, T. 1984. Inheritance of Song Parameters in the Gibbon Song, Analysed in Two Hybrid Gibbons (*Hylobates pileatus × H. lar*). *Folia Primatologica*. 42: 216–235.

———. 1993. Evolution of Communication in Gibbons (Hylobatidae). Ph.D. dissertation, Universitaet Zuerich, Zuerich.

———. 1995. Gibbon Systematics and Species Identification. *International Zoo News* 42: 467–501.

———. 2000. Gibbon Songs and Human Music from an Evolutionary Perspective. In *The Origins of Music*, ed. N. Wallin, B. Merker and S. Brown, 103–123. Cambridge, MA: MIT Press.

———. 2002. Duet-Splitting and the Evolution of Gibbon Songs. *Biological Reviews* 77: 57–76.

———. 2004. *The Gibbons (Hylobatidae): An Introduction*. Retrieved September 14, 2004 from, http://www.tiho-hannover.de/gibbons/main/index.html

Geissmann, T., and M. Orgeldinger. 2000. The Relationship between Duet Songs and Pair Bonds in Siamangs, *Hylobates syndactylus*. *Animal Behaviour* 60: 805–809.

Ghiglieri, M. P. 1984. *The Chimpanzees of Kibale Forest: A Field Study of Ecology and Social Structure*. New York: Columbia University Press.

Gilbert, L. E. 1980. Food Web Organization and the Conservation of Neotropical Diversity. In *Conservation Biology*, ed. M. E. Soule and B. A. Wilcox, 11–33. Sunderland, Mass. Sinauer Associates, Inc.

Gittins, S. P. 1979. The Behaviour and Ecology of the Agile Gibbon (*Hylobates agilis*). Ph.D. dissertation, Cambridge University.

———. 1982. Feeding and Ranging in the Agile Gibbon. *Folia Primatologica*. 38: 39–71.

———. 1984. Territorial Advertisement and Defense in Gibbons. In *The Lesser Apes*, ed. H. Preuschoft, D. J. Chivers, W. Y. Brockelman, and N. Creel, 420–424. Edinburgh: Edinburgh University Press.

Gittins, S. P., and J. J. Raemaekers. 1980. Siamang, Lar, and Agile Gibbons. In *Malayan Forest Primates: Ten Years' Study in Tropical Rain Forest*, ed. D. J. Chivers, 63–105. New York: Plenum Press.

Goodman, M., C. A. Porter, J. Czelusniak, S. L. Page, H. Schneider, J. Shoshani, G. Gunnell, and C. P. Groves. 1998. Toward a Phylogenetic Classification of Primates Based on DNA Evidence Complimented by Fossil Evidence. *Molecular Phylogenetics and Evolution* 9: 585–598.

Gowaty, P. A. 1996a. Battles of the Sexes and Origins of Monogamy. In *Partnerships in Birds: The Study of Monogamy*, ed. J. M. Black, 21–52. Oxford University Press.

———. 1996b. Multiple Mating by Females Selects for Males That Stay: Another Hypothesis for Social Monogamy in Passerine Birds. *Animal Behavior* 51: 482–484.

Gray, D., C. Piprell, and M. Graham. 1991. *National Parks of Thailand*. Bangkok: Communications Resources (Thailand) Ltd.

Grether, G. F., R. A. Palombit, and P. S. Rodman. 1992. Gibbon Foraging Decisions and the Marginal Value Model. *International Journal of Primatology* 13(1): 1–17.

Groves, C. P. 1972. Systematics and Phylogeny of Gibbons. In *Gibbon and Siamang*, Vol. 1, ed. D. M. Rumbaugh, 1–89. Basel: Karger.

———. 1984. A New Look at the Taxonomy and Phylogeny of the Gibbons. In *The Lesser Apes: Evolutionary and Behavioural Biology*, ed. H. Preuschoft, D. J. Chivers, W. Y. Brockelman and N. Creel, 542–561. Edinburgh: Edinburgh University Press.

———. 2001. *Primate Taxonomy*. Washington, DC: Smithsonian Institution Press.

Gursky, S. 2000. Effect of Seasonality on the Behavior of an Insectivorous Primate *Tarsius spectrum*. *International Journal of Primatology* 21(3): 477–495.

Haimoff, E. H., D. J. Chivers, S. P. Gittins, and A. J. Whitten. 1982. A Phylogeny of Gibbons (*Hylobates* spp.) Based on Morphological and Behavioural Characters. *Folia Primatologica* 39: 213–237.

Haimoff, E. H., X.-J. Yang, S.-J. He, and N. Chen. 1987. Preliminary Observations of Wild Black-Crested Gibbons (*Hylobates concolor concolor*) in Yunnan Province, People's Republic of China. *Primates* 28(3): 319–335.

Hall, L. M., D. S. Jones, and B. A. Wood. 1998. Evolution of Gibbon Subgenera Inferred from Cytochrome *b* DNA Sequence Data. *Molecular Phylogenetics and Evolution* 10: 281–286.

Halle, S., and N. S. Stenseth, eds. 2000. *Activity Patterns in Small Mammals—An Ecological Approach*. Berlin: Springer Verlag.

Hanya, G., M. Kiyono, A. Yamada, K. Suzuki, M. Furukawa, Y. Yoshida, and A. Chijiiwa. 2006. Not Only Annual Food Abundance But Also Fallback Food Quality Determines the Japanese Macaque Density: Evidence from Seasonal Variations in Home Range Size. *Primates* 47: 275–278.

Haraway, D. 1989. *Primate Visions: Gender, Race, and Nature in the World of Science*. New York: Rutledge.

Harrison, T., J. Kringbaum, and J. Manser. 2006. Primate Biogeography and Ecology on the Sunda Shelf Islands: A Paleontological and Zooarchaeological Perspective. In *Primate Biogeography*, ed. S. M. Lehman and J. G. Fleagle, 331–372. New York: Springer.

Hemingway, C., and N. Bynum. 2005. The Influence of Seasonality on Primate Diet and Ranging. In *Seasonality in Primates*, ed. D. K. Brockman and C. P. van Schaik, 57–104. Cambridge University Press.

Hrdy, S. B. 1981. *The Woman That Never Evolved*. Cambridge, MA: Harvard University Press.

Iwamoto, T., and R. I. M. Dunbar. 1983. Thermoregulation, Habitat Quality, and the Behavioural Ecology of Gelada Baboons. *Journal of Animal Ecology* 52: 357–66.

———. 1998. Experimental Evidence for Spatial Memory in Foraging Wild Capuchin Monkeys, *Cebus apella*. *Animal Behavior* 55: 1129–1143.

Janson, C. H., and C. A. Chapman. 1999. Resources and Primate Community Structure. In *Primate Communities*, 237–260. Cambridge: Cambridge University Press.

Janson, C. H., J. Terborgh, and L. H. Emmons. 1981. Non-Flying Mammals as Pollinating Agents in the Amazonian Forest. *Biotropica* 13 (Supplement 2): 1–6.

Janzen, D. H. 1979. How To Be a Fig. *Annual Review of Ecology and Systematics* 10: 13–51.

Jiang, X, Y. Wang, and Q. Wang. 1999. Coexistence of Monogamy and Polygyny in Black-Crested Gibbons (*Hylobates concolor*). *Primates* 40(4): 607–611.

Johnson, D. D. P., R. Kays, P. G. Blackwell, and D. W. McDonald. 2002. Does the Resource Dispersion Hypothesis Explain Group Living? *Trends in Ecology and Evolution* 17(12): 563–570.

Kantawatanakid, C., A. J. Lynam, S. R. Galster, A. Chugaew, K. Kaewplung, and C. Suckaseam. 2002. Mixing Science, Security and Community Outreach for the Conservation of Biological Diversity at Khao Yai National Park, Thailand. *Abstracts of the Society for Conservation Biology 16th Annual Meeting, July 14–19 2002*. Retrieved August 2007 from http://www.conbio.org/Activities/Meetings/2002/abstracts/Thursday/mpatwo.cfm

Kaplin, B. A 2001. Ranging Behavior of Two Species of Forest Guenons (*Cercopithecus mitis doggetti* and *C. l'hoesti*) in the Nyungwe Forest Reserve, Rwanda. *International Journal of Primatology* 22(4): 521–548.

Kappeler, M. 1981. The Javan Silvery Gibbon (*Hylobates lar moloch*). Ph.D. dissertation, University of Basel. Retrieved August 22, 2006, from http:// www.markuskappeler.ch/gib/gibs/chapter5.html

———. 1984. Diet and Feeding Behavior of the Moloch Gibbon. In *The Lesser Apes: Evolutionary and Behavioural Biology*, ed. H. Preuschoft, D. J. Chivers, W. Y. Brockelman and N. Creel, 228–241. Edinburgh: Edinburgh University Press.

Kappeler, P. M., and C. P. van Schaik. 2002. Evolution of Primate Social Systems. *International Journal of Primatology* 23(4): 707–740.

Khao Yai Road Works 'Destroying' the National Park. 2006, May 3. *Bangkok Post*. Retrieved August 2007 from http://www.ecologyasia.com/news-archives/ 2006/may-06/bp_060503_1.htm

King, J. R., and M. E. Murphy. 1985. Periods of Nutritional Stress in the Annual Cycles of Endotherms: Fact or Fiction. *American Zoologist* 25: 955–964.

Kinnaird, M. F. 1992. Variable Resource Defense by the Tana River Crested Mangabey. *Behavioral Ecology and Sociobiology* 31: 115–122.

Kitamura, S., T. Yumoto, P. Poonswad, P. Chuailua, K. Plongmai, T. Maruhashi, and N. Noma. 2002. Interactions between Fleshy Fruits and Frugivores in a Tropical Seasonal Forest in Thailand. *Oecologia* 133: 559–572.

Kleiman, D. 1977. Monogamy in Mammals. *Quarterly Review of Biology* 52: 39–69.

Knott, C. D. 1998. Changes in Orangutan Caloric Intake, Energy Balance, and Ketones in Response to Fluctuating Fruit Availability. *International Journal of Primatology* 19: 1061–1077.

———. 2007. Orangutans in Perspective: Forced Copulations and Female Mating Reistance. In *Primates in Perspective*, ed. C. J. Campbell, A. Fuentes, K. C. MacKinnon, M. Panger and S. K. Bearder, 290–305. Oxford: Oxford University Press.

Koenig A., C. Borries, S. Suarez, N. Kreetiyutanont, and J. Prabnasuk. 2004. Socio-Ecology of Phayre's Leaf Monkeys (*Trachypithecus phayrei*). *Journal of Wildlife Thailand* 12: 150–163.

Komers, P. E., and P. N. M. Brotherton. 1997. Female Space Use Is the Best Predictor of Monogamy in Mammals. *Proceedings of the Royal Society of London, Series B*, 264: 1261–1270.

Kongsanit, P. 2001, March 26. Concrete Jungle. *Bangkok Post*. Retrieved August 2007, from http://www.ecologyasia.com/news-archives/2001/mar-01/bangkokpost_260301_Outlook01.htm

Lambert, F. R., and A. G. Marshall. 1991. Keystone Characteristics of Bird-Dispersed *Ficus* in a Malaysian Lowland Rain Forest. *Journal of Ecology* 79: 793–809.

Lambert, J. E. 2007. Primate Nutritional Ecology: Feeding Biology and Diet at Ecological and Evolutionary Scales. In *Primates in Perspective,* ed. C. J. Campbell , A. Fuentes, K. C. MacKinnon, M. A. Panger and S. K. Bearder, 482–495. Oxford: Oxford University Press.

Lan, D. Y. 1993. Feeding and Vocal Behaviours of Black Gibbons (*Hylobates concolor*) in Yunnan: A Preliminary Study. *Folia Primatologica* 60: 94–105.

Lan, D. Y., S. He, and L. D. Shu. 1990. Preliminary Observations on the Group Composition of the Wild Concolor Gibbons (*Hylobates concolor*) in Yunnan, China. *Primate Report* 26: 89–96.

Lappan, S. 2007a. Patterns of Dispersal in Sumatran Siamangs (Symphalangus syndactylus): Preliminary *mt*DNA Evidence Suggests More Frequent Male than Female Dispersal to Adjacent Groups. *American Journal of Primatology* 69: 692–698.

———. 2007b. Social Relationships among Males in Multifemale Siamang Groups. *International Journal of Primatology* 28: 369–387.

Lee, P. C. 1987. Nutrition, Fertility and Maternal Investment in Primates. *Journal of Zoology, London*. 213: 409–422.

Leighton, D. R. 1987. Gibbons: Territoriality and Monogamy. In *Primate Societies,* ed. B. B. Smuts, D. L. Cheney, R. M. Seyfarth, R. W. Wrangham, and T. T. Struhsaker, 135–145. Chicago: Chicago University Press.

Leighton, M. 1993. Modeling Dietary Selectivity by Bornean Orangutans: Evidence for Integration of Multiple Criteria in Fruit Selection. *International Journal of Primatology* 14: 257–313.

Leighton, M., and D. R. Leighton. 1982. The Relationship of Size of Feeding Aggregate to Size of Food Patch: Howler Monkeys (*Alouatta palliata*) Feeding in *Trichilia cipo* Fruit Trees on Barro Colorado Island. *Biotropica* 14(2): 81–90.

———. 1983. Vertebrate Responses to Fruiting Seasonality within a Bornean Rain Forest. In *Tropical Rain Forest Ecology and Management,* ed. S. L. Sutton, T. C. Whitmore and A. C. Chadwick, 181–196. Oxford: Blackwell Scientific Publications.

Lekagul, B., and P. Round. 1991. *A Guide to the Birds of Thailand.* Bangkok: Saha Karn Nhaet Co. Ltd.

Li, Z., and E. Rogers. 2004. Habitat Quality and Activity Budgets of White-Headed Langurs in Fusui, China. *International Journal of Primatology* 25(1): 41–54.

MacArthur, R. H., and E. R. Pianka. 1966. On Optimal Use of a Patchy Environment. *American Naturalist* 100:603–609.

MacKinnon, J. R., and K. S. MacKinnon. 1980. Niche Differentiation in a Primate Community. In *Malayan Forest Primates: Ten Years' Study in Tropical Rain Forest,* ed. D. J. Chivers, 167–190. New York: Plenum Press.

———. 1984. Territoriality, Monogamy and Song in Gibbons and Tarsiers. In *The Lesser Apes: Evolutionary and Behavioural Biology,* ed. H. Preuschoft, D. J. Chivers, W. Y. Brockelman and N. Creel, 291–297. Edinburgh: Edinburgh University Press.

Marks, J. 2000. Sherwood Washburn 1911–2000. *Evolutionary Anthropology,* 9(6): 225–226.

Marsh, C. W. 1981. Ranging Behaviour and Its Relation to Diet Selection in Tana River Red Colobus (*Colobus badius rufomitratus*). *Journal of Zoology, London* 195: 473–492.

Marshall, A. J., and M. Leighton. 2006. How Does Food Availability Limit the Population Density of White-Bearded Gibbons? In *Feeding Ecology in Apes and Other Primates: Ecological, Physical and Behavioral Aspects,* ed. G. Hohmann, M. M. Robbins, and C. Boesch, 311–333. Cambridge: Cambridge University Press.

Marshall, A. J., and R. W. Wrangham. 2007. Evolutionary Consequences of Fallback Foods. *International Journal of Primatology* 28(6): 1219–1235.

Marshall, J. T., and E. R. Marshall. 1976. Gibbons and Their Territorial Songs. *Science* 193: 235–238.

Marshall, J., and J. Sugardjito. 1986. Gibbon Systematics. In *Comparative Primate Biology,* Vol. 1, *Systematics, Evolution, and Anatomy,* ed. D. R. Swindler, and J. Erwin, 137–185. New York: Liss.

Marshall, J. T. Jr., B. A. Ross, and S. Chantharojvong. 1972. The Species of Gibbons in Thailand. *Journal of Mammalogy* 53(3): 479–486.

Martin, P., and P. Bateson. 1986. *Measuring Behavior: An Introductory Guide.* Cambridge: Cambridge University Press.

Maruhashi, T., S. Kitamura, T. Yumoto, and P. Poonswad. 2002. Socio-Ecological Study of Pig-Tail Macaque in Khao Yai National Park, Thailand. *Abstracts of the XIXth Congress of the International Primatological Society,* 223. Beijing, China: Mammalogical Society of China.

Mather, R. J. 1992. A Field Study of Hybrid Gibbons in Central Kalimantan, Indonesia. Ph.D. dissertation, University of Cambridge.

Matsumoto-Oda, A., and Y. Hayashi. 1997. Nutritional Aspects of Fruit Choice by Chimpanzees. *Folia Primatologica* 70(3): 154–162.

Matsumoto-Oda, A., and R. Oda. 1998. Changes in the Activity Budget of Cycling Female Chimpanzees. *American Journal of Primatology* 46(2): 157–166.

McConkey, K. R., F. Aldy, A. Ario, and D. J. Chivers. 2002. Selection of Fruit by Gibbons (*Hylobates muelleri* × *H. agilis*) in the Rain Forests of Central Borneo. *International Journal of Primatology* 23(1): 123–145.

McConkey, K. R., A. Ario, F. Aldy, and D. J. Chivers. 2003. Influence of Forest Seasonality on Gibbon Food Choice in the Rain Forests of Barito Ulu, Central Kalimantan. *International Journal of Primatology* 24(1): 19–32.

McKey, D., and P. G. Waterman. 1982. Ranging Behaviour of a Group of Black Colobus (*Colobus satanas*) in the Douala-Edea Reserve, Cameroon. *Folia Primatologica* 39: 264–304.

Meijaard, E., and C. P. Groves. 2006. The Geography of Mammals and Rivers in Mainland Southeast Asia. In *Primate Biogeography*, ed. S. M. Lehman and J. G. Fleagle, 305–329. New York: Springer.

Milton, K. 1980. *The Foraging Strategy of Howler Monkeys.* New York: Columbia University Press.

———. 1981. Diversity of Plant Foods in Tropical Forests as a Stimulus to Mental Development in Primates. *American Anthropologist* 83: 534–548.

———. 2000. Quo Vadis? Tactics of Food Search and Group Movement in Primates and Other Animals. In *On the Move*, ed. S. Boinski and P. A. Garber, 375–417. Chicago: University of Chicago Press.

Mitani, J. C. 1984. The Behavioral Regulation of Monogamy in Gibbons (*Hylobates muelleri*). *Behavioral Ecology and Sociobiology* 15(3): 225–229.

———. 1985. Location-Specific Responses of Gibbons (*Hylobates muelleri*) to Male Songs. *Zeitschrift fuer Tierpsychology* 70: 219–224.

Mitani, J. C., and P. S. Rodman. 1979. Territoriality: The Relation of Ranging Pattern and Home Range Size to Defendability, with an Analysis of Territoriality among Primate Species. *Behavioral Ecology and Sociobiology* 5(3): 241–251.

Montgomery, G. M. 2005. Place, Practice and Primatology: Clarence Ray Carpenter, Primate Communication and the Development of Field Methodology, 1931–1945. *Journal of the History of Biology* 38(3): 495–533.

Mootnick, A. R., and C. Groves. 2005. A New Generic Name for the Hoolock Gibbon (Hylobatidae). *International Journal of Primatology* 26(4): 971–976.

Müller S., M. Hollatz, and J. Wienberg. 2003. Chromosomal Phylogeny and Evolution of Gibbons (Hylobatidae). *Human Genetics* 113: 493–501.

Nissen, H. W. 1931. A Field Study of the Chimpanzee. *Comparative Psychological Monographs* 8(1): 1–122.

Norconk, M. A., and W. G. Kinzey. 1994. Challenge of Neotropical Frugivory: Travel Patterns of Spider Monkeys and Bearded Sakis. *American Journal of Primatology* 34: 171–183.

———. 1987. Food Distribution and Foraging Behavior. In *Primate Societies*, ed. B. B. Smuts, D. L. Cheney, R. M. Seyfarth, R. W. Wrangham and T. T. Struhsaker, 197–209. Chicago: University of Chicago Press.

O'Brien, T. G., and M. F. Kinnaird. 1997. Behavior, Diet, and Movements of the Sulawesi Crested Black Macaque (*Macaca nigra*). *International Journal of Primatology* 18(3): 321–351.

O'Brien, T. G., M. F. Kinnaird, A. Nurcahyo, M. Prasetyaningrum, and M. Iqbal. 2003. Fire, Demography and the Persistence of Siamang (*Symphalangus syndactylus*: Hylobatidae) in a Sumatran Rainforest. *Animal Conservation* 6: 115–121.

Ostfeld, R. S. 1990. The Ecology of Territoriality in Small Mammals. *Trends in Ecology and Evolution* 5(12): 411–415.

Overdorff, D. J. 1993. Similarities, Differences, and Seasonal Patterns in the Diets of *Eulemur rubriventer* and *Eulemur fulvus rufus* in the Ranomafana National Park, Madagascar. *International Journal of Primatology* 14(5): 721–753.

———. 1996. Ecological Correlates to Activity and Habitat Use of Two Prosimian Primates: *Eulemur rubriventer* and *Eulemur fulvis rufus* in Madagascar. *American Journal of Primatology* 40(4): 327–342.

Overdorff, D., and J. Parga. 2007. The New Era of Primate Socioecology: Ecology and Intersexual conflict. In *Primates in Perspective*, ed. C. J. Campbell, A. Fuentes, K. C. MacKinnon, M. A. Panger and S. K. Bearder, 466–482. Oxford: Oxford University Press.

Overdorff, D. J., E. M. Erhart, and T. Mutschler. 2005. Does Female Dominance Facilitate Feeding Priority in Black-and-White Ruffed Lemurs (*Varecia variegata*) in Southeastern Madagascar? *American Journal of Primatology* 66(1): 7–22.

Palombit, R. A. 1992. Pair Bonds and Monogamy in Wild Siamang (*Hylobates syndactylus*) and White-Handed Gibbon (*Hylobates lar*) in Northern Sumatra. Ph.D. dissertation, University of California, Davis.

————. 1993. Lethal Territorial Aggression in a White-Handed Gibbon. *American Journal of Primatology* 31(4): 311–318.

————. 1994a. Dynamic Pair Bonds in Hylobatids: Implications Regarding Monogamous Social Systems. *Behaviour* 128(1–2): 65–101.

————. 1994b. Extra-Pair Copulations in a Monogamous Ape. *Animal Behavior* 47(3): 721–723.

————. 1995. Longitudinal Patterns of Reproduction in Wild Female Siamang (*Hylobates syndactylus*) and White-Handed Gibbons (*Hylobates lar*). *International Journal of Primatology* 16(5): 739–760.

————. 1996. Pair Bonds in Monogamous Apes: A Comparison of the Siamang *Hylobates syndactylus* and the White-Handed Gibbon *Hylobates lar*. *Behaviour* 133(5–6): 321–356.

————. 1997. Inter- and Intraspecific Variation in the Diets of Sympatric Siamang (*Hylobates syndactylus*) and Lar Gibbons (*Hylobates lar*). *Folia Primatologica* 68(6): 321–337.

————. 1999. Infanticide and the Evolution of Pair Bonds in Nonhuman Primates. *Evolutionary Anthropology* 7(4): 117–129.

Parr, J. 2003. *A Guide to the Large Mammals of Thailand*. Bangkok: Sarakadee Press.

Peres, C. A. 1989. Costs and Benefits of Territorial Defense in Wild Golden Lion Tamarins *Leontopithecus rosalia*. *Behavioral Ecology and Sociobiology* 25(3): 227–233.

Pianka, E. R. 1988. *Evolutionary Ecology*, 4th ed. New York: Harper and Row.

Pitelka, F. 1959. Numbers, Breeding Schedule, and Territory in Pectoral Sandpipers of Northern Alaska. *The Condor* 61(4): 233–264.

Pollock, J. I. 1977. The Ecology and Sociology of Feeding in *Indri indri*. In *Primate Ecology*, ed. T. H. Clutton-Brock, 37–69. London: Academic Press.

Poonswad, P., P. Chuailua, K. Plongmai, and S. Nakkuntod. 1998. Phenology of Some *Ficus* Species and Utilisation of *Ficus* Sources in Khao Yai National Park, Thailand. In *The Asian Hornbills: Ecology and Conservation*, ed. P. Poonswad, 227–252. Bangkok: Biodiversity Research and Training Program, National Center for Genetic Engineering and Biotechnology.

Preuschoft, H., D. J. Chivers, W. Y. Brockelman, and N. Creel, eds. 1984. *The Lesser Apes: Evolutionary and Behavioural Biology*. Edinburgh: Edinburgh University Press.

Prouty, L. A., P. D. Buchanan, W. S. Pollitzer, and A. R. Mootnick. 1983a. A Presumptive New Hylobatid Subgenus with 38 Chromosomes. *Cytogenetics and Cell Genetics* 35(2): 141–142.

————. 1983b. *Bunopithecus*: A Genus-Level Taxon for the Hoolock Gibbon (*Hylobates hoolock*). *American Journal of Primatology* 5(1): 83–87.

Quiatt, D. 1985. The "Household" in Non-Human Primate Evolution: A Basic Linking Concept. *Anthropologea Contemporanea* 3: 187–193.

————. 1987. A-Group: One Example of Gibbon Social Organization. Videotape available from the Primate Center Library, Wisconsin Regional Primate Research Center, Madison, WI.

Quiatt, D., and J. Kelso. 1987. The Concept of the Household: Linking Behavior and Genetic Analyses. *Human Evolution* 2(5): 429–435.

Raaum, R. L., K. N. Sterner, C. M. Noviello, C. B. Stewart, and T. R. Disotell. 2005. Catarrhine Primate Divergence Dates Estimated from Complete Mitochondrial Genomes: Concordance with Fossil and Nuclear DNA Evidence. *Journal of Human Evolution* 48(3): 237–257.

Raemaekers, J. J. 1977. Gibbons and Trees: Comparative Ecology of the Siamang and Lar gibbons. Ph.D. dissertation, Cambridge University.

————. 1979. Ecology of Sympatric Gibbons. *Folia Primatologica* 31: 227–245.

Raemaekers, J. J., and D. J. Chivers. 1980. Socio-Ecology of Malayan Forest Primates. In *Malayan Forest Primates: Ten Years' Study in Tropical Rain Forest*, ed. D. J. Chivers, 279–316. New York: Plenum Press.

Raemaekers, J. J., and P. M. Raemaekers. 1984. Vocal Interactions between Two Male Gibbons, *Hylobates lar*. *Natural History Bulletin of the Siam Society* 32(2): 95–106.

————. 1985. Field Playback of Loud Calls to Gibbons (*Hylobates lar*): Territorial, Sex-Specific, and Species-Specific Responses. *Animal Behavior* 33: 481–493.

————. 1990. *The Singing Ape: A Journey to the Jungles of Thailand*. Bangkok: The Siam Society.

Raemaekers, J. J., P. M. Raemaekers, and E. H. Haimoff. 1984. Loud Calls of the Gibbon (*Hylobates lar*): Repertoire, Organization and Context. *Behaviour* 91: 146–189.

Redford, K. H., G. A. Bouchardet da Fonesca, and T. E. Lacher Jr. 1984. The Relationship between Frugivory and Insectivory in Primates. *Primates* 25(4): 433–440.

Regan, B. C., C. Juliot, B. Simmen, F. Viénot, P. C. Charles-Dominique, and J. D. Mollon. 2001. Fruits, Foliage and the Evolution of Primate Colour Vision. *Philosophical Transactions of the Royal Society B* 356: 229–283.

Reichard, U. 1995. Extra-Pair Copulations in a Monogamous Gibbon (*Hylobates lar*). *Ethology* 100(2): 99–112.

———. 1998. Sleeping Sites, Sleeping Places, and Presleep Behavior of Gibbons (*Hylobates lar*). *American Journal of Primatology* 46(1): 35–62.

———. 2003. Social Monogamy in Gibbons: The Male Perspective. In *Monogamy: Mating Strategies and Partnerships in Birds, Humans, and Other Mammals*, ed. U. H. Reichard and C. Boesch, 190–213. Cambridge: Cambridge University Press.

Reichard, U., and V. Sommer. 1994. Grooming Site Preferences in Wild White-Handed Gibbons (*Hylobates lar*). *Primates* 35(3): 369–374.

———. 1997. Group Encounters in Wild Gibbons (*Hylobates lar*): Agonism, Affiliation, and the Concept of Infanticide. *Behavior* 134: 1135–1174.

Richard, A. F. 1985. *Primates in Nature*. New York: W. H. Freeman and Co.

Robbins, D., C. A. Chapman, and R. W. Wrangham. 1991. Group Size and Stability: Why Do Gibbons and Spider Monkeys Differ? *Primates* 32(3): 301–305.

Robinson, J. G. 1986. Seasonal Variation in Use of Time and Space by the Wedge-Capped Capuchin Monkey, *Cebus olivaceus*: Implications for Foraging Theory. *Smithsonian Contributions to Zoology* 431: 1–60.

Rodman, P. S. 1977. Feeding Behaviour of Orangutans of the Kutai Nature Reserve, East Kalimantan. In *Primate Ecology*, ed. T. H. Clutton-Brock. London: Academic Press.

Roos, C., and T. Geissmann. 2001. Molecular Phylogeny of the Major Hylobatid Divisions. *Molecular Phylogenetics and Evolution* 19(3): 486–494.

Roughgarden, J., M. Oishi, and E. Akcay. 2006. Reproductive Social Behavior: Cooperative Games to Replace Sexual Selection. *Science* 311: 965–969.

Rowell, T. E. 1972. Social Behaviour of Monkeys. Middlesex: Penguin Press.

———. 1979. How Would We Know If Social Organization Were *Not* Adaptive? In *Primate Ecology and Human Origins: Ecological Influences on Social Organization*, ed. I. S. Bernstein and E. O. Wilson, 1–22. New York: Garland.

Rubenstein, D. I. 1986. Ecology and Sociality in Horses and Zebras. In *Ecological Aspects of Social Evolution*, ed. D. I. Rubenstein and R. W. Wrangham, 282–302. Princeton: Princeton University Press.

Rutberg, A. T. 1983. The Evolution of Monogamy in Primates. *Journal of Theoretical Biology* 104: 93–112.

Savini, T., and U. H. Reichard. 2004. Does Ecological Home Range Quality Influence the Development of Social Polyandry in White-Handed Gibbons? Feeding Ecology in Apes and other Primates, *Conference Abstracts*, 20. Leipzig: Max Plank.

Schoener, T. W. 1971. Theory of Feeding Strategies. *Annual Review of Ecology and Systematics* 2: 369–404.

Schultz, A. H. 1938. To Asia after Apes. *Johns Hopkins Alumni Magazine* 26(2): 37–46.

———. 1939. Notes on Diseases and Healed Fractures of Wild Apes. *Bulletin of the History of Medicine* 7(6): 571–582.

Shanahan, M., S. So, S. G. Compton, and R. T. Corlett. 2001. Fig-Eating by Vertebrate Frugivores: A Global Review. *Biological Reviews* 76: 529–572.

Schneider, G. 1906. Ergebnisse Zoologischer Forschungsreisen in Sumatra. Zoologisch Jahrbücher. *Abteilung Systematik, Geographie und Biologie der Tiere* 23: 1–172.

Sheeran, L. K., Y. Zhang, F. E. Poirier, and D. Yang. 1998. Preliminary Report on the Behavior of the Jingdong Black Gibbon (*Hylobates concolor furvogaster*). *Tropical Biodiversity* 5: 113–125.

Siegel, S. 1956. *Non-Parametric Statistics for the Behavioral Sciences*. New York: McGraw-Hill.

Small, M. F. 1993. *Female Choices: Sexual Behavior of Female Primates*. Ithaca: Cornell University Press.

Sommer, V., and U. Reichard. 2000. Rethinking Monogamy: The Gibbon Case. In *Primate Males: Causes and Consequences of Variation in Group Composition*, ed. P. M. Kappeler, 159–168. Cambridge: Cambridge University Press.

Spinka, M., R. C. Newberry, and M. Bekoff. 2001. Mammalian Play: Training for the Unexpected. *Quarterly Review of Biology* 76(2): 141–168.

Srikosamatara, S. 1984. Ecology of Pileated Gibbons in South-East Thailand. In *The Lesser Apes: Evolutionary and Behavioural Biology*, ed. H. Preuschoft, D. J. Chivers, W. Y. Brockelman and N. Creel, 242–257. Edinburgh: Edinburgh University Press.

Srikosamatara, S., and W. Y. Brockelman. 1987. Polygyny in a Group of Pileated Gibbons via a Familial Route. *International Journal of Primatology* 8(4): 389–393.

——. 2002. Conservation of Protected Areas in Thailand: A Diversity of Problems, A Diversity of Solutions. In *Making Parks Work: Strategies for Preserving Tropical Nature,* ed. J. Terborgh, C. van Schaik, L. Davenport and M. Rao, 218–231. Washington, DC: Island Press.

Srikosamatara, S., and T. Hansel. 1996. *Mammals of Khao Yai National Park.* World Wildlife Fund, Thailand.

Stanford C. B. 1991. The Capped Langur in Bangladesh: Behavioral Ecology and Reproductive Tactics. *Contributions to Primatology* 26. Basel: Karger.

Steenbeek, R. 1999. Tenure Related Changes in Wild Thomas's Langurs I: Between-Group Interactions. *Behaviour* 136(5): 595–625.

Strier, K. B. 1987a. Activity Budgets of Woolly Spider Monkeys, or Muriquis *(Brachyteles arachnoids). American Journal of Primatology* 13: 385–395.

——. 1987b. Ranging Behavior of Woolly Spider Monkeys, or Muriquis, *(Brachyteles arachnoids). International Journal of Primatology* 8(6): 575–591.

——. 1989. Effects of Patch Size on Feeding Associations in Muriquis *(Brachyteles arachnoids). Folia Primatologica* 52: 70–77.

——. 2000. *Primate Behavioral Ecology.* New York: Allyn and Bacon.

Strum S. C., and L. M. Fedigan. 2000. *Primate Encounters: Models of Science, Gender and Society.* Chicago: University of Chicago Press.

Suarez, S. A. 2003. Spatio-Temporal Foraging Skills of White-Bellied Spider Monkeys *(Ateles belzebuth belzebuth)* in the Yasuni National Park, Ecuador. Ph.D. dissertation, Stony Brook University, Stony Brook, New York.

Sussman, R. W. 1987. Morpho-Physiological Analysis of Diets: Species-Specific Dietary Patterns in Primates and Human Dietary Adaptations. In *The Evolution of Human Behavior: Primate Models,* ed. W. G. Kinzey, 151–179. Albany, NY: State University of New York Press.

——. 2007. A Brief History of Primate Field Studies. In *Primates in Perspective,* ed. C. J. Campbell , A. Fuentes, K. C. MacKinnon, M. A. Panger, and S. K. Bearder, 6–10. Oxford: Oxford University Press.

Sussman, R. W., P. A. Garber, and J. Cheverud. 2005. The Importance of Cooperation and Affiliation in the Evolution of Primate Sociality. *American Journal of Physical Anthropology* 128(1): 84–97.

Suwannakerd, S., and N. Aggimarangsee. 2001. Variation in the Diets of White-Handed Gibbons *(Hylobates lar). The Journal of Wildlife Thailand* 9(1): 58–62.

Suwanvecho, U. 2003. Ecology and Interspecific Relations of Two Sympatric Hylobates species *(H. lar* and *H. pileatus)* in Khao Yai National Park, Thailand. Ph.D. dissertation, Mahidol University, Thailand.

Symington, M. M. 1988. Food Competition and Foraging Party Size in the Black Spider Monkey *(Ateles paniscus chamek). Behavior* 105(1–2): 117–134.

Tanaka, L. K., and S. K. Tanaka. 1982. Rainfall and Seasonal Changes in Arthropod Abundance on a Tropical Oceanic Island. *Biotropica* 14(2): 114–123.

Tangtham, N. 1991. Khao Yai Ecosystem: The Hydrological Role of Khao Yai National Park. *Proceedings of International Workshop on Conservation and Sustainable Development, 22–26 April 1991,* 345–363. AIT/Bangkok and Khao Yai National Park, Thailand.

Temerin, L. A., and J. G. H. Cant. 1983. The Evolutionary Divergence of Old World Monkeys and Apes. *The American Naturalist* 122(3): 335–351.

Tenaza, R. R. 1975. Territory and Monogamy among Kloss' Gibbons *(Hylobates klossii)* in Siberut Island, Indonesia. *Folia Primatologica* 24: 60–80.

Tenaza, R. R., and W. J. Hamilton III. 1971. Preliminary Observations of the Mentawai Islands Gibbon, *Hylobates klossii. Folia Primatologica* 15(3): 201–211.

Tenaza, R., and R. L. Tilson. 1985. Human Predation and Kloss's Gibbon *(Hylobates klossii)* Sleeping Trees in Siberut Island, Indonesia. *American Journal of Primatology* 8(4): 299–308.

Terborgh, J. 1983. *Five New World Primates.* Princeton: Princeton University Press.

——. 1986. Keystone Plant Resources in the Tropical Forest. In *Conservation Biology,* ed. M. Soulé, 330–344. Sunderland, MA: Sinauer Associates Publishers.

Terborgh, J., and C. H. Janson. 1986. The Socioecology of Primate Groups. *Annual Review of Ecology and Systematics* 17: 111–136.

Tilson, R. L. 1979. Behavior of Hoolock Gibbons *(Hylobates hoolock)* during Different Seasons in Assam, India. *Journal of Bombay Natural History Society* 76: 1–16.

————. 1980. Monogamous Mating Systems of Gibbons and Langurs in the Mentawai Islands, Indonesia. Ph.D. dissertation, University of California, Davis.

————. 1981. Family Formation Strategies of Kloss's Gibbons. *Folia Primatologica* 35(4): 259–287.

Tilson, R. L., and R. R. Tenaza.1982. Interspecific Spacing between Gibbons (*Hylobates klossii*) and Langurs (*Presbytis potenziani*) on Siberut Island, Indonesia. *American Journal of Primatology* 2(4): 355–361.

Treesucon, U. 1984. Social Development of Young Gibbons (*Hylobates lar*) in Khao Yai National Park Thailand. M.S. thesis. Mahidol University, Bangkok.

Treesucon, U., and Raemaekers, J. J. 1984. Group Formation in Gibbons through Displacement of an Adult. *International Journal of Primatology* 5: 387.

Trivers, R. L. 1972. Parental Investment and Sexual Selection. In *Sexual Selection and the Descent of Man,* ed. B. Campbell, 136–179. Chicago: Aldine-Atherton.

Tutin, C. E. G., R. M. Ham, L. J. T. White, and M. J. S. Harrison. 1997. The Primate Community of the Lope Reserve, Gabon: Diets, Responses to Fruit Scarcity, and Effects on Biomass. *American Journal of Primatology* 42(1): 1–24.

Uhde, N. L., and V. Sommer. 2002. Antipredatory Behavior in Gibbons (*Hylobates lar*), Khao Yai/Thailand. In *Eat or Be Eaten: Predator Sensitive Foraging among Primates,* ed. L. E. Miller, 268–291. Cambridge: Cambridge University Press.

UNESCO. 2007. Dong Phayayen-Khao Yai Forest Complex. Retrieved August 2007, from http://whc.unesco.org/en/list/590.

van Schaik, C. P., and D. K. Brockman. 2005. Seasonality in Primate Ecology, Reproduction, and Life History: An Overview. In *Seasonality in Primates,* ed. D. K. Brockman and C. P. van Schaik, 3–20. Cambridge: Cambridge University Press.

van Schaik, C. P., and R. I. M. Dunbar. 1990. The Evolution of Monogamy in Large Primates: A New Hypothesis and Some Crucial Tests. *Behaviour* 115(1–2): 30–62.

van Schaik C. P., and P. M. Kappeler. 1993. Life History and Activity Period as Determinants of Lemur Social Systems. In *Lemur Social Systems and Their Ecological Basis,* ed. P. M. Kappeler and J. U. Ganzhorn, 241–260. New York: Plenum Press.

————. 1997. Infanticide Risk and the Evolution of Male–Female Association in Primates. *Proceedings of the Royal Society of London B* 264(1388): 1687–1694.

————. 2003. The Evolution of Social Monogamy in Primates. In *Monogamy: Mating Strategies and Partnerships in Birds, Humans, and Other Mammals,* ed. U. H. Reichard and C. Boesch, 59–80. Cambridge: Cambridge University Press.

van Schaik, C. P., and van Hooff, J. A. R. A. M. 1983. On the Ultimate Causes of Primate Social Systems. *Behaviour* 85(1–2): 91–117.

van Schaik, C. P., P. R. Assink, and N. Salafsky. 1992. Territorial Behavior in Southeast Asian Langurs: Resource Defense or Mate Defense? *American Journal of Primatology* 26(4): 233–242.

Vasey, N. 2002. Niche Separation in *Varecia variegata rubra* and *Eulemur fulvus albifrons*: II. Intraspecific Patterns. *American Journal of Physical Anthropology* 118(2): 169–183.

————. 2005. Activity Budgets and Activity Rhythms in Red Ruffed Lemurs (*Varecia rubra*) on the Masoala Peninsula, Madagascar: Seasonality and Reproductive Energetics. *American Journal of Primatology* 66: 23–44.

————. 2006. Impact of Seasonality and Reproduction on Social Structure, Ranging Patterns, and Fission-Fusion Social Organization in Red Ruffed Lemurs. In *Lemurs: Ecology and Adaptation,* ed. L. Gould and M. L. Sauther, 275–304. New York: Springer.

Vejpongsa, T. 2006, February 7. Turning Villagers from Poachers to Gamekeepers. *Bangkok Post.* Retrieved August 2007, from http://www.wildlifealliance. org/news/in-the-news/turning-villagers-from.html

Vellayan, S. 1981. The Nutritive Value of *Ficus* in the Diet of Lar Gibbon (*Hylobates lar*). *Malaysian Applied Biology* 10: 177–181.

Wallis, J. 1997. From Ancient Expeditions to Modern Exhibitions: The Evolution of Primate Conservation in the Zoo Community. In *Primate Conservation: The Role of Zoological Parks,* ed. J. Wallis, 1–27. American Society of Primatologists.

Waser, P. M., and R. H. Wiley. 1979. Mechanisms and Evolution of Spacing Behavior. In *Handbook of Behavioral Neurobiology,* Vol. 3, ed. P. Marler and J. Vandenberg, 159–223. New York: Plenum Press.

Washburn, S. L. 1951. The New Physical Anthropology. *Transactions of the New York Academy of Science* 13 (2d ser.): 298–304.

Wendeln, M. C., J. R. Runkle, and E. K. V. Kalko. 2000. Nutritional Values of 14 Fig Species and Bat Feeding Preferences in Panama. *Biotropica* 32(3): 489–501.

White, F. J., and W. Wrangham. 1988. Feeding Competition and Patch Size in the Chimpanzee Species *Pan paniscus* and *Pan troglodytes*. *Behaviour* 105(1–2): 148–164.

Whitington, C. L. 1990. Seed Dispersal by White-Handed Gibbons (*Hylobates lar*) in Khao Yai National Park, Thailand. M.Sc. Thesis, Mahidol University, Bangkok.

Whitington, C., and U. Treesucon. 1991. Selection and Treatment of Food Plants by White-Handed Gibbons (*Hylobates lar*) in Khao Yai National Park, Thailand. *Natural History Bulletin of the Siam Society* 39: 111–122.

Whitmore, T. C. 1984. *Tropical Rain Forests of the Far East,* 2nd ed. Oxford: Clarendon Press.

Whitten, A. J. 1982a. Diet and Feeding Behavior of Kloss Gibbons on Siberut Island, Indonesia. *Folia Primatologica* 37(3–4): 177–208.

———. 1982b. *The Gibbons of Siberut*. London: Dent.

Whitten, A. J. 1984 Ecological comparisons between Kloss gibbons and other small gibbons. In Preuschoft, H., Chivers, D.J., Brockelman, W.Y., and Creel, N. (eds.), *The Lesser Apes: Evolutionary and Behavioural Biology*. Edinburgh University Press, pp. 219–227.

Wich, S. A., and C. L. Nunn. 2002. Do Male "Long Distance Calls" Function in Mate Defense? A Comparative Study of Long Distance Calls in Primates. *Behavioral Ecology and Sociobiology* 52(6): 474–484.

Wickler, W. 1980. Vocal Duetting and the Pair Bond. *Zeitschrift für Tierpsychology* 52: 201–209.

Wickler, W., and U. Seibt. 1983. Monogamy: An Ambiguous Concept. In *Mate Choice*, ed. P. Bateson, 33–50. Cambridge: Cambridge University Press.

Wildlife Alliance. 2007. Khao Yai National Park. Retrieved August 2007, from http://www.wildlifealliance.org/where-we-work/thailand/surviving-together/khao-yai/.

Wildlife Conservation Society. 2007. Saving Tigers: Thailand. Retrieved August 2007, from http://savingtigers.com/st-home/st-inthewild/research bycountry/thailandtigers.

Wilson, E. O. 1975. *Sociobiology*. Cambridge MA: Belknap.

Wittenberger, J. F., and R. L. Tilson. 1980. The Evolution of Monogamy: Hypothesis and Evidence. *Annual Review of Ecology and Systematics* 11: 197–232.

Wolda, H. 1978. Fluctuations in Abundance of Tropical Insects. *The American Naturalist* 112(988): 1017–1045.

Wrangham, R. W. 1979. On the Evolution of Ape Social Systems. *Social Science Information* 18: 336–368.

———. 1987. Evolution of Social Structure. In *Primate Societies*, ed. B. B. Smuts, D. L. Cheney, R. M. Seyfarth, R. W. Wrangham and T. T. Struhsaker, 282–296. Chicago: University of Chicago Press.

Wrangham, R. W., N. L. Conklin, G. Etot, J. Obua, K. D. Hunt, M. D. Hauser, and A. P. Clark. 1993. The Value of Figs to Chimpanzees. *International Journal of Primatology* 14(2): 243–256.

Wright, P. C. 1984. Biparental Care in *Aotus trivirgatus* and *Callicebus moloch*. In *Female Primates: Studies by Woman Primatologists*, ed. M. F. Small, 59–75. New York: Liss.

———. 1986. Ecological Correlates of Monogamy in *Aotus* and *Callicebus*. In *Primate Ecology and Conservation*, ed. J. Else and P. C. Lee, 159–168. Cambridge: Cambridge University Press.

Yerkes, R. M., and A. Yerkes. 1929. *The Great Apes: A Study in Anthropoid Life*. New Haven: Yale University Press.

Index

A

Activity budgets:
  age-sex differences in,
    46–47, 56–57
  annual, 43
  definition, 39
  monthly, 45–46
  resource availability and, 45–46,
    53–54
Activity classes, 37 (table), 41–42
Activity period:
  definition, 39
  monthly, 43
  predator pressure and, 54–56
Affiliative encounters, 111–112
Agile gibbons, see *Hylobates*
  agilis
Agonistic encounters, 110
Alarm calls, 107–108
Alouatta palliata, 8, 137
Alphonsea boniana, 70, 76
Anthracoceros albirostris, 29
Aotus trivigatus, 138
Aphananthe cuspidata, 70
Apoblastosis, 9
Appearance, 22–24
Aquilaria crassna, 152–153, 154
Arctictis binturong, 79
Asiatic Primate Expedition
  (A.P.E), 8
Ateles geoffroyi, 8, 140

B

Bearded sakis, see *Chiropotes*
  satanas
Behavioral data collection
  of gibbons:
  data analysis, 36–38
  data collection, 34–36
  study groups, 33–34
Bingham, H. C., 6–7
Binturongs, see *Arctictis binturong*
Black giant squirrels, see *Ratufa*
  bicolor
Black-crested gibbons, see *Nomascus*
  concolor
Brachiation, 2, 3
Brockelman, Warren, 16, 28,
  31, 152
Brown hornbill, see *Ptilolaemus*
  tickelli
Buffon, Comte de, 5

C

Callicebus moloch, 138
Carpenter, C. R., 2, 7–11
Cebus olivaceus, 40, 82, 100
Chiropotes satanas, 138
Chivers, D. J., 13–14, 15
Choerospondias axillaris, 32, 33, 66, 70,
  76, 119
Coolidge, Harold J. Jr., 8, 14

167

Insectivory, 82
Intergroup encounters, 106–107, 109
    affiliative, 111–112
    agonistic, 110
    male and female interaction
        during, 112–113
    monthly variation in rates of,
        113–114
    neutral, 110–111
    vocal, 110
Intragroup agonism, 51–53
Intragroup social interactions, 48–53

J

Juvenile gibbon, 47, 50, 59

K

Khao Yai Conservation Project
    (KYCP), 154
Khao Yai National Park, 2, 16, 26–28
Kloss's gibbon, see *Hylobates klossii*
Kruskal-Wallis test, 42

L

Lagothrix lagotricha, 40, 82
Lekagul, Boonsong, 25

M

Macaca nemestrina, 26, 29
Major feeding visits of gibbons, 65,
    70–71
Male mate guarding model, 131–132
Male parental care model, 132–134
Male resource defense monogamy:
    revised model for evolution of, 140,
        141 (figure)
    small-patch model for evolution of,
        136 (figure)
Male services to females, 134–135
Mann-Whitney *U* test, 92
Mating monogamy, 145–148
Mo Singto study site, 28–30
Monogamous social system, models
        for, 129
    female dispersion, 130–131
    male mate guarding, 131–132

male parental care, 132–134
male services to females, 134–135
Monogamy, definition, 5
Mt. Ailao, 143
Mt. Wuliang, 143
Mueller's Bornean gibbons, see
    Hylobates muelleri
Multiadult gibbon groups, 142
Multimale gibbon groups, 144–145

N

National Parks Act, 25
Natural History, 5
Neutral encounters, 110–111
"The New Physical
    Anthropology", 11
Nissen, H. W., 6
Nomascus concolor, 23, 62,
    142–143, 144

O

Owl monkeys, see *Aotus trivigatus*

P

Palombit, Ryne, 16, 84
Pathfinder, 91, 92
Pig-tailed macaques, see *Macaca
    nemestrina*
Pileated gibbon, see *Hylobates pileatus*
Play behavior, 50, 51, 57, 59
Primates:
    flexible versus stable foraging in,
        127–129
    foraging adaptations in, 18–19
    group size in, 123, 138–139
    patch size preference in, 138–139
Prunus javanica, 67, 70, 76
Ptilolaemus tickelli, 29

Q

Quiatt, D., 18

R

Ratufa bicolor, 78
Reichard, U., 55
Research, 16–17